Gypsy Folktales

Photographs by Diane Tong

Gypsy Folktales

Diane Tong

HARCOURT BRACE JOVANOVICH, PUBLISHERS

San Diego • New York • London

HBJ

Requests for permission to make copies
of any part of the work should be mailed to:
Permissions, Harcourt Brace Jovanovich, Publishers,
Orlando, Florida 32887.

Library of Congress Cataloging-in-Publication Data
Tong, Diane [date]
Gypsy folktales/Diane Tong.—1st ed.
p.   cm.
Bibliography: p.
Includes indexes.
ISBN 0-15-138310-3; ISBN 0-15-637989-9 (pbk.)
1. Tales, Gypsy. I. Title.
DX157.T66 1989
398.2'08991497—dc19   88-21066

Printed in the United States of America

First edition
A B C D E

Permissions acknowledgments appear on pages 245–247, which constitute
a continuation of the copyright page.

To the memory of my colleague and close friend

José Vigo (1950–1988),

whose sensitivity, intelligence, humor,

and gift for friendship are missed by many people

CONTENTS

The photographs of Greek Gypsies following page 126

were taken by Diane Tong in the cities

of Thessaloniki, Athens, and Volos between 1982 and 1988.

ACKNOWLEDGMENTS

Many people were extremely supportive during the writing and publishing of this book. Of all the Gypsy friends and colleagues who offered their insights, warmth, and generosity, I am particularly grateful to Kostas and Anastasia Dimou, Polixeni Apostolaki, Najma Ayashah and Lazaros Harisiadis, and Ian Hancock. Of course, the storytellers get my special thanks.

Many other talented and busy people gave their loyal support. I am deeply indebted to Neal T. Jones of the Syene Press for his invaluable publishing versatility through all the stages of this book; to Douglas Woodyard, a gifted stylist whose commitment to *Gypsy Folktales* went beyond the usual requirements of copyediting; and to Robert Roth, whose original, brilliant, and subtle understanding of political realities both enhanced and sustained my own political thinking about the Gypsies.

My editor at HBJ, John Radziewicz, deserves particular thanks for his consistent backing of this project, and especially for his humor in difficult moments.

My sincere thanks to the following people for their contributions: Alice Acheson, Ann Adelman, Carol Blank, Craig Castleman, Dinos Christianopoulos, Maria Clark, Frank Curtis, Beatrice and Harold Deitchman, Betsy Distler, Pat England, Camilla Filancia, Jamie Gagarin, Rena Gropper, Mozes Heinschink, Beverly Heyward, Chantal Hilaire, Milena Hübschmannová, Mirella Karpati, Chuck Kelton, Donald Kenrick, Phyllis Korper, Kiril Kostov, Judith Kuppersmith, Marianna Lee,

Jean-Pierre Liégeois, Dana McDaniel, Paul Meissner, Carol Miller, Lance Moles, Enid Pearsons, Ann Petracek, Bertha Quintana, Yrjö Qvarnberg, Zita Réger, Phoebe Ruiz-Valera, Rachel Salazar, Maria João Pavão Serra, John Singler, David Sternbach, Johanna Tani, Lolo Vitróvič, and Kirsten Wang.

NOTE
TO THE READER

In the stories that follow, terms from Romani, the language of the Gypsies, are used from time to time. Though many of these terms are defined as they occur, for the reader's convenience the most frequently encountered ones are defined here: *Romni*, adult female Gypsy; *Rom*, adult male Gypsy; *gaje*, non-Gypsies (a male is *gajo*, a female *gaji*; in Spain a non-Gypsy is *payo*, in England *gorgio*); *petulengro*, blacksmith; *drom*, the road.

The ornament used throughout this book is a modified version of the wheel found in the center of the Gypsy flag. The original flag, adopted in 1933, had the form of a rectangle halved horizontally: blue on top for the sky, green below for the earth. At the First World Romani Congress, held in 1971 in London, this design had the red sixteen-spoked wheel, or *čhakra*, added to it in recognition of the Gypsies' Indian origins—a similar wheel appears on the Indian flag. The wheel represents not only movement but also the burst of fire from which all creation emerged at the beginning of time.

Gypsy Folktales

INTRODUCTION

It is September 1987, on the night train from Athens to Thessaloniki. Katina Makri, a forty-year-old Greek Gypsy, is telling one folktale after another to the other passengers in her compartment, all of whom are *gaje*—that is, non-Gypsies. All of them are adults, too. But whenever she stops to try to get some sleep, her engrossed and delighted audience pleads for just one more story. Makri, whose warmth and generosity come through in her stories no less than her sense of drama, does not refuse . . . and so the entire night goes by as the train moves north.

Makri was taking the train home to Thessaloniki to rejoin her husband and daughter after a month in Athens, where she had gone to visit a son in the hospital. She earns her living selling such things as lace tablecloths door to door, mostly to housewives for their daughters' dowries, and often travels around Greece with a group of friends who do the same work. In the evenings they gather for storytelling sessions, and Makri's Gypsy friends are even more enthusiastic about her stories than were her companions on the train. Two of her tales are included here: "The Tailor's Clever Daughter" on pages 35–41 and "Yannakis the Fearless" on pages 145–150.

In Greece and elsewhere, Gypsy culture has a pervasive, thriving oral tradition. Stories are told by females and males, children and adults, on various occasions, whether casual—a lengthy train journey, a long, sociable evening, other informal get-togethers—or formal: baptisms, and especially wakes, which can last several days and nights and where some stories are told not to entertain or edify but to console. Nowadays, however, even among Greek Gypsies, an evening's entertainment at home could just as well be a TV show or a Turkish movie on a VCR. And so, in an effort both to share many different Gypsy voices with a larger audience and to preserve their tradition in a written form, I have collected the stories that make up this volume: a tiny sample of a rich, and still growing, international repertoire.

Precise statistics are not available on the world Gypsy population. What we do know is that there are many large groups of Gypsies, each consisting of many smaller groups. The main groups in Europe and America are the Vlachs, the Romanichals, the Sinti-Manouche, and the Calé. In the Middle East are, among others, the Nawar and the Ghagar, and in India still more groups. Gypsies have settled in every country in Eastern and Western Europe, in the Middle East, the Soviet Union, North Africa, North and South America, Hawaii, Australia, and New Zealand. Sociologist Thomas Acton estimates that there are ten to twelve million Gypsies outside of India and perhaps twenty million on the Indian subcontinent.

The word *Gypsy* derives from *Egypt*, where many people (including Gypsies) mistakenly thought Gypsies originated. But in fact the Gypsies (or *Rom* in their own language, which they call *Romanés*—in English, Romani) started out in northern India. Beginning around the tenth century many of them left, in several waves, moving westward into Europe. No one knows exactly why they left India (though there are countless theories), but the routes as well as the times of their various migrations can be traced through linguistic evidence: the dating of borrowings from Persian, Armenian, and Byzantine Greek into Romani, for example. The earliest known reference to Gypsies in Europe appeared in the fourteenth century; by the early sixteenth, Gypsies could be found in nearly every European country. Their traditional occupations—the ones most likely to appear in their folktales—included blacksmithing, music, basketmaking, woodworking, horse trading, fortune-telling, chair-mending, seasonal agricultural labor, sievemaking, shoemaking, and storytelling.

Being outsiders, Gypsies were persecuted everywhere they went, by massacre (including the sport of "Gypsy hunt"), systematic deportation, and—for more than five centuries in southeastern and central Europe, especially the Rumanian principalities—enslavement. Officially freed in the mid-nineteenth century, the Gypsies have since had to endure programs of forced assimilation in many countries, not to mention less official (though not necessarily more subtle) pressures to abandon their culture. As sociologist Jean-Pierre Liégeois has remarked, "The Gypsies, moving about in their nomadic groups, were seen as physically threatening and ideologically disruptive. Their very existence constituted dissidence."

Centuries of violence against Gypsies culminated in the savagery of the Second World War. Hunted down by the Nazis, who were trying to wipe out the entire Gypsy population of Europe, at least half a million Gypsies perished in the Holocaust. The following story from that time, "The Little Gypsy," has recently become part of the Gypsies' oral tradition. This eyewitness account was set down by Sara Nomberg-Przytyk, a Polish-Jewish survivor of Auschwitz, in her book *Auschwitz: True Tales from a Grotesque Land*:

> The German doctors used to come about twelve o'clock. They would look over the sick who had checked into the hospital that morning, and then sign the so-called *beffkarte*, which amounted to a permit to remain there for a day. Later, we were on our own. We cleaned and prepared dressings for the evening when the *komando* returned from work. At such times we felt a little less tense.
>
> We were sitting in a little room in the infirmary when Marusia yelled, "Achtung!" We jumped up quickly and ran inside. We were standing at attention when Mengele walked in with a little Gypsy boy who may have been about four years old. The little boy was a beauty. He was dressed in a gorgeous white uniform consisting of long pants with an ironed-in crease, a jacket adorned with gold buttons, a man's shirt, and a tie. We stared, as if bewitched, at that beautiful child. It was clear that Mengele was pleased to see us thus enchanted. He placed a chair in the middle of the infirmary and sat down in it, keeping the little Gypsy squeezed between his knees. The little boy understood German.
>
> "Show them how you dance the *kozak*," he said. As Mengele clapped his hands in rhythm, the little one kicked up his heels while maintaining a sitting position. He was astonishing. "Now sing a song." The little one sang a haunting Gypsy melody.
>
> We continued to stand at attention while the little one was showing off in front of Mengele. You could see that Mengele liked him. He hugged him and kissed him. "That was beautiful. Here is something for the performance," he said, taking a box of chocolates out

of his pocket. They left. We looked at each other, not understanding why Mengele brought the boy to us. Why did he want to exhibit the child's talent to us?

"I am sure that Mengele will kill him soon," Marusia said.

We felt a cold chill.

The whole summer Mengele paraded around the camp with the little Gypsy, who was always dressed in white. Even when the selections took place, the beautiful little boy dressed in white stood at his side. There was a family camp for Gypsies in Auschwitz on field "C." There were twenty-five thousand Gypsies in the camp. The children lived together with their families. It is hard for me to say why they opened the family camp in Auschwitz, why they permitted the Gypsies to believe that they would be allowed to live through the war. In the fall of 1944, the end came for the Gypsy camp. I don't remember the exact date, but the liquidation took place one October evening. In the morning all the young Gypsy women were taken. As they were being herded to the transport the women cried bitterly. Evidently they understood that those who were staying in the camp were condemned to death. It was true. The same evening you could hear the murmur of the engines. They were all taken to the gas chambers. In that one night, twenty thousand Gypsies were murdered.

It is peculiar. But throughout that whole slaughter we could think of only one. Was Mengele going to protect the beautiful boy from the gas? The next day he paraded through the camp without the little Gypsy. The men told us that at the last minute Mengele had pushed him into the gas chamber with his own hands.

Today the Gypsies' situation is often grim. In 1986, for example, a shocking scandal was brought to international attention. Between 1926 and 1973 several hundred Gypsy children in Switzerland were taken from their parents and placed in foster homes and institutions by Pro Juventute, a government-backed youth charity, presumably because the Gypsies didn't know how to care for them properly. (There is an ugly irony here, for according to a longtime and widespread stereotype it is the Gypsies who steal children.) The Swiss government apologized publicly to the Romani people in 1986. But despite an investigation into Pro Juventute's program "Operation Children of the Road," the authorities have declined to turn over any documentation on the children to their families.

Bulgaria, Rumania, Czechoslovakia, and possibly other Eastern European countries today have sterilization programs for Gypsies. In parts of Czechoslovakia, Liégeois has reported, the sterilization of Gypsy women "has become a common practice, and the success of officials is measured by the number of women they have convinced to get sterilized."

In Spain there have been many instances of non-Gypsies burning down Gypsy quarters in their neighborhoods and stoning Gypsy children on their way to school. And in 1986 in Examilia, near the Greek city of Corinth, non-Gypsy parents removed their children from elementary-school classrooms because Gypsies were also attending, then proceeded to cut off the Gypsies' water supply, and finally refused to let them bury their dead in the local cemetery.

In the fall of 1987 Roberto Suro reported from Rome in *The New York Times*: "In the suburbs where this city becomes an impoverished and ramshackle metropolis, old women blocked railroad tracks this week and young men set tires aflame at a highway toll station, all because they had heard a rumor that the government was going to build a settlement camp for Gypsies in their neighborhood, or maybe just in a neighborhood nearby." One participant in the anti-Gypsy demonstration said, "We are not racists. We are only against Gypsies."

But the Rom have begun to organize politically to demand their rights and to fight racism and xenophobia. In North America, for example, a Romani anti-defamation league based in Montreal, Los Angeles, Minneapolis, and Austin, Texas, was formed in 1977 to protest racist stereotypes in the media and to counter the almost universal refusal to see Gypsies as people. Since 1979 the International Romani Union, which unites seventy-one national Gypsy associations in twenty-seven countries on a voluntary basis, has had permanent membership in the United Nations. Many European Rom, fearful of losing their culture, have publicized their desire for coexistence without assimilation to the majority. And in 1987, after seven years of intensive lobbying by Gypsy groups, the U.S. Holocaust Memorial Council accepted, with great reluctance, a White House–appointed Gypsy member: William Duna, of the Hungarian-Slovak American Gypsy community. (The Council is a federally appointed group established to foster remembrance of the

Holocaust and to construct the United States Holocaust Memorial Museum in Washington, D.C.)

There is also a language movement among the Gypsies, concentrating on an attempt to develop a standardized Romani, and the International Romani Union is currently standardizing an orthography. Spoken by Gypsies in many countries, Romani is a highly inflected language and, like Hindi, is one of the modern descendants of Sanskrit, as eighteenth-century European linguists discovered. Being a diaspora language, Romani has many dialects, including Angloromani, which is essentially English with Romani words and phrases—a kind of restructured Romani. In Spain some Gypsies speak Caló, or Hispanoromani. On page 223 is an example of one of the many dialects of Greek Romani: "The Old Couple and Their Pig," the edited English version of which can be found on pages 209–210. Definitions of the few Romani terms I've decided to retain throughout the stories can be found in the Note to the Reader on page xv.

When Gypsies appear in the folklore of other people, either as real characters or as symbols, they generally get a bad press. In one Syrian tale a man pretends to be a Gypsy to get out of a marriage obligation, and succeeds: his prospective father-in-law is only too happy to be rid of him. When Rom are depicted more benignly, it is usually in the only positive image universally acceptable to non-Gypsies—as entertainers. The following, from a Hungarian folktale, is typical:

> "I'll make you dance, all right," said Uncle Szabó, and with the piece
> of charcoal he drew a complete Gypsy band on the wall, to the right
> of the doorpost. "Strike up a tune!" he commanded the band, and
> the Gypsies broke into such a lively tune that the windowpanes fell
> out and the doorpost almost popped out of its place. And the band
> went on playing livelier and livelier tunes, and the gentlemen con-
> tinued to dance to it . . .

Gypsies are tolerated, even enjoyed, as a picture on the wall, as in the ubiquitous kitsch paintings of flamenco dancers.

Not surprisingly, in their own folktales the Gypsies portray themselves in a more balanced way—as the narrator concludes the story "Phara-un, God of the Gypsies": "So he remained the god of the Gypsies and is like them, neither all good nor all bad"—and in a greater variety of occupations. The (male) metalsmith is a prominent figure in several tales ("How the Gypsy Went to Heaven," "The Gypsy Smith," "Alifi and Dalifi," "The Bird"). A possible allusion to Gypsies as professional storytellers appears in the Polish Gypsy "Tale of a Foolish Brother and of a Wonderful Bush," where the mother berates her youngest son, "Fool that you are! Your brothers go there to tell tales, while you, you know nothing. What could you tell?" Gypsy fortune-telling as essentially nothing more than common sense is depicted in the Greek Gypsy tale "The Gypsy Woman and the Cave":

> Well, the Gypsies were wandering along from place to place. In one city there was a woman who didn't like her neighbor—the two women were always quarreling, day after day. This woman called a Gypsy woman over to tell her fortune: "Come here. I'll give you whatever you want if you can tell me what's in my heart."
>
> Just at that moment the neighbor came out of her house and made an insulting gesture to the first woman. The Gypsy woman noticed this and said, "You live in a really bad neighborhood and things aren't going well for you in this house. Your neighbors are jealous of you, because you're a good housewife and all that."

One of the most straightforward and pervasive themes in the stories is the contempt in which Gypsies are held by the rest of the world and the forms that this contempt is likely to take. In "The Rom in the Piano" the narrator depicts the hero's humiliation when no one will give him a cigarette. "The Gypsy Woman and the Cave" makes reference to the difficulty Gypsies have in finding campsites: "Now, Gypsies were forbidden to camp for the night near the city, so they had set up their tents some distance away." The horror with which many non-Gypsies view intermarriage is described in "The Bird." The bird's prophecy: "Listen, gentleman! Listen, Gypsy! Tonight both your wives will become pregnant. The Gypsy will have a son and the gentleman a daughter. They will look alike. Their fate is to become man and wife." Although the Gypsy forgets the prophecy, "the gentleman never forgot those words, and day by day the thought that the Gypsy's son would become his son-in-law tormented him more and more." In the American Gypsy story "Alifi and Dalifi"—the longest and one of the most complex in this volume—the young boy has learned that it is generally wise not to reveal his ethnic identity: "The little boy didn't want to tell about himself because he know that he would not be wanted as a Gypsy. When he see the beautiful home and the way the people treated him, he refused to tell about himself—where he come from, who his parents are. He pretended he didn't know nothing."

There are times in the stories when the *gaje* are friendly or empathetic, which comes as a surprise. In "Alifi and Dalifi" the childless Gypsy is invited by the childless king: "And the king says, 'Here you are. I know you for a long time. You are respectable. We both are lonely. Stay with me.' The Gypsy was surprised that a king should ask a Gypsy to stay, and he remained. He was glad to accept, and now they had much talk about no children." The storyteller of "The Enchanted House" portrays a non-Gypsy woman as sensitive to the Gypsies' feelings: "A neighbor woman came up to them and, when she heard what had happened, told them, 'That was a close call!' Then she explained that she had seen them approaching the house and had thought to warn them not to go in, but then decided not to, afraid the Gypsies would think she was just trying to keep them from taking refuge."

Two stories that communicate the Gypsies' anger at their treatment, "The Toad's Revenge" and "How It Is in the Gypsy Paradise," include fantasies of revenge. Inspired by both hunger and feelings of powerlessness, the latter tale reverses life as the Gypsies experience it: "In that Gypsy paradise of ours all our Gypsy sons meet and boast and drink to each other's health. The sons of the *gaje* are outside shivering with cold and hunger, and beg a morsel of food from our children. Our lucky Gypsy sons laugh, really laugh, at them. They mock them, then eat, and then eat more, but they don't give them one bit of food."

Another prominent theme in the stories is pride in being Gypsy. Pride in traditional Gypsy appearance is expressed in "The Creation," where it is the Gypsies' color that is "just right." In "Alifi and Dalifi" we find the following description: "Early in the morning, when he got out of the house, the man saw the little boy sleeping under his steps. The boy was the most beautiful boy that time have ever see. He had dark, curly hair. The most beautiful creature ever to be created . . . When this man saw him, he thought he was some kind of saint under his steps." And in "The Gypsy Woman and the Cave" the storyteller concludes by extolling Gypsy intelligence and resourcefulness: "And that's why since then people, even today, ten million years later, still say that Gypsies know everything. And it's true."

Distinctive storytelling conventions have been noted in various Gypsy communities. Dora Yates, for many years the Honorary Secretary of the Gypsy Lore Society in England, wrote in 1933 about Black Ellen, a member of the Wood family in Wales (see "Frosty," pages 188–191), who was known as the Romani Scheherazade. Black Ellen "used to relate to a company of Gypsy men, women and children tales often long enough to occupy a whole night in the telling. Suddenly, to test the interest and wakefulness of her listeners she would interrupt her narrative to interpolate the meaningless exclamation *Tshiocha* 'Boots!'; and unless the sleepy boys and girls or their fathers and mothers immediately responded *Cholova* 'Stockings!', the tale would be broken off never to be resumed." From Spain, writer and musician Walter Starkie reported that the Coppersmith Gypsies "use music as an adjunct to storytelling. Ask them to tell you a *paramish* [folktale] and they will first of all clear their throats and hum a tune, and then fit the words of the story to the tune. One of the women recited a long poem for me about a ship that had been wrecked and described the adventures of the passengers, repeating over and over again [a] musical phrase, occasionally changing it into the minor key . . ."

For that matter, music has always been central to Gypsy culture, and some forms of Gypsy music have found wide acceptance among non-Gypsies—for example, flamenco, Hungarian Gypsy violin, and the school of jazz inspired by the Gypsy guitarist and composer Django Reinhardt, whose music was so popular that some Gypsies in the concentration camps tried to save themselves by claiming to be him. However, as Gypsies know, *gaje* can love the music and still feel contempt, or worse, for the musicians. (Parallels with the African-American experience come to mind: Lionel Hampton being made to stand behind a curtain when performing years ago in the South to audiences who loved his music.) As slaves in Rumania, Gypsy musicians were forbidden to play music for their own enjoyment.

Even when music is not the subject of the tale or the technique of its telling, Gypsies often incorporate their feelings for music into the plot. "Alifi and Dalifi" contains the unusual images of a guitar with twenty-four strings, each of which plays twenty-four songs, and a crown of roses and a white pigeon that appear above the musician's head when he plays the guitar, as well as a statement of the musician's need to share his music with an audience.

Certain motifs in the stories are thought to be original to the Rom. One depicted here is the somersault that precedes a metamorphosis, as in the eerie Rumanian tale "The Red King and the Witch," where the diabolical little sister first turned a somersault and "then her nails became like an ax and her teeth like a shovel." Another is the practice of either throwing swords or shooting arrows into the air and then waiting for them to fall to determine one's fate, as in the American story "Sam Patra and His Brothers": "Then he took the bow and arrow of his brother Sylvius and shot the arrow straight up into the air. 'I will see if it is to be,' he said. For three days and nights the arrow did not come down and he did not move. On the fourth day he saw it coming, and he gave a kiss to Auska and said, 'Good-bye, wife. And good-bye, wives of my brothers.' The arrow struck him right on top of the head and pinned him to the ground."

Some stories, such as the Swedish "The Silly Man Who Sold His Beard," are entirely original to the Gypsies, while others sound familiar— as well they might, since they belong to a vast Indo-European folklore tradition. In fact, it may have been the Gypsies who, on their travels and in their role of professional storytellers, brought some of the tales to different places. Gypsies are often protagonists in universal folktale types that allude to or treat more fully such considerations as old age and death; forays into the world to explore, learn, and be tested; the predicament of childlessness; and the conquest of fear.

Unconventional heroines turn up as rarely in Gypsy tales as in other groups' folktales, and Ulla in the Finnish "Deceiving Sleep"—a woman whose mind isn't on marriage—is alone in this collection. More typical are the storyteller's observations in "Alifi and Dalifi" on the daughter's required deference to her father's judgment ("The girl cried, but she had no right to tell her father how she feels about the treatment") and the wife's to her husband's: "It doesn't matter how bad the mother feels; she is not to tell the father his business. After the son is out, she talks secretly to the father. The father keeps saying, 'You keep out of this. I want to make a man of him. No matter what I am doing. He is my son as much as he is yours.' The father can't help it even though he feels badly."

Gypsy values are an integral part of their folktales. For example, central to traditional Gypsy culture is the deep dislike of a work-centered life—as expressed in the title of the Spanish tale "You Will Eat, But You Will Not Work." Many of the stories reflect the high value the Gypsies place on freedom and autonomy, for example "St. George and the Gypsies" from Russia and "King Edward and the Gypsy" from England. As Liégeois points out, these values are not exclusive to the Rom: "Certain aspects of Gypsy life, perhaps paradoxically, mirror the aspirations of some members of settled society (more free time, greater self-reliance, more cooperation and 'togetherness,' and so on)." A corollary value, antimilitarism, finds expression in the comic Czech tale "The Rom in the Piano," where the Gypsy hero proposes to a group of kings an easy way to avoid war.

The Gypsies' high regard for hospitality is evident in numerous tales. In "The Enchanted House" from Spain, only the Gypsies treat the old man (the ghost) hospitably, enabling him to find peace at last. The hero of the Greek tale "Yerasimos," visited in the wilderness by Christ and his disciples, is unaware of his guests' identities but "gave them the best of everything he had in his hut. Whatever he had was at their disposal—they ate and drank well and slept soundly by a big fire. He had no bedclothes to give them, but he made a nice fire."

Besides values, Gypsy beliefs and customs appear in the stories. The brideprice, a Gypsy marriage custom, figures in "Alifi and Dalifi," where the childless Gypsy wishes for a daughter because he doesn't have enough money to pay the brideprice if he has a son. (The money is considered compensation for the loss of a daughter's potential earning power.) In "Yannakis the Fearless" from Greece, both the fairies and the mermaid take an oath on their mother's milk that they will stop harming innocent people. According to an essay by Lafcadio Hearn, who was part Gypsy, this was traditionally a strong oath among the Gypsies. And the narrator of the Turkish story "Bread" explains that "Bread is the dignity of life. Our old people say, 'The more you take care of your bread, the more you guard your luck. If you don't take care of your bread, you don't protect your luck. Throw your bread away and you throw your luck away!' "

Quite a few of these tales touch upon how the Gypsies view death. In "Voso Zachari Tells His Tale" from France, the following description of a *gajo* corpse reveals the Gypsies' sense of respect for the dead: "He was a man of about forty years, dressed like a peasant. He appeared to be asleep. His hands, folded on his breast, held a cross. He must have died that very day, but it was strange that no one watched over him. Could he have no relations? Is it possible, then, for the dead to be left alone?"

Thomas Acton's description of Gypsy burial traditions—"The body itself is usually given a religious burial, but a dead Gypsy's possessions are smashed, and his [/her] clothes burnt"—is echoed dramatically in the description of the husband's grief in the Yugoslav story "Vana": "He tore all her clothes to shreds and then burned them. He shattered her guitar and threw the fragments onto the burning rags. Her coffeepot, cup, and plate were smashed and buried. The only thing of hers he kept was her photograph—that he could not bring himself to destroy." Some tales serve to admonish those who do not follow Gypsy customs regarding the dead. In "Jorška Who Came Back from the Dead," the narrator relates, "Jorška said, 'Oh, my dear friends, I have permission to live six weeks more. But had you [mourned me] bare-headed, I would have been allowed to live on for many years.' "

In one widespread type of folktale, the explanatory, or *pourquoi*, tale, the Gypsies imaginatively account for some of the distinctive aspects of their life-style and culture. Some examples in this collection are "Why Gypsies Are Scattered About the Earth," "How the Gypsies Became Musicians," "The Church of Cheese" (why the Gypsies don't have their own church), and "Why the Gypsies Don't Have an Alphabet."

One of the best-known *pourquoi* tales in Gypsy folklore is some variation of the Gypsies' apocryphal role in the crucifixion of Christ— in fact, the Rom reached Palestine some centuries afterwards—whether they were supposed to have fashioned the nails or stolen them (see "The Wooden Horseshoe and the Three Nails," pages 156–158). This cluster of stories helps to explain to non-Gypsies the nomadic life-style characteristic of many Gypsy groups until settlement, forced or voluntary, came about. Liégeois ends his history of the Gypsies with a new version of this tale, which in reflecting the storyteller's cynicism vis-à-vis settlement demonstrates how the Gypsies use storytelling to bridge their past and their present:

One day I read somewhere that one of our ancestors is supposed to have made the nails used to crucify Jesus Christ, the Son of God, and that after this "good deed" the whole world cursed him. Then he was damned and banished from the face of the earth, him and all his family and descendants (namely us). My personal epilogue to the story: God says to His son: "You've been punishing them for nineteen centuries, that's enough already. I, your father, order you to take a rest, my son, because now it's my turn. I condemn them to nineteen centuries of settlement, and after these nineteen centuries of wandering that you gave them, it isn't going to be easy. Good luck to them. Concrete will give them all the psychological disorders they need, imaginary ailments and so on. Don't worry, my son, get some rest, papa's taking over now. Thus your revenge endures."

As for the sources of the tales: Some of them I taped on my travels in Greece, some in New York City, where I live. Others were sent to me by Gypsy and non-Gypsy colleagues. I found still others in books, many of them out of print, and in scholarly journals. Information on sources is given in the Notes, pages 227–237.

There is a perspective to the issue of "country of origin" of these stories that does not apply to most other groups. Because some Gypsies have moved from one country to another, it can be misleading to assign a specific nationality to them. And so I've now and then made some semi-arbitrary decisions. For example, it seems to me that storyteller Lazaros Harisiadis's main cultural identity is Greek (see the stories on pages 65–75), though he has lived in New York City for more than twenty years. On the other hand, prize-winning novelist Matéo Maximoff, though originally from Spain of Russian Gypsy parents, has established himself as a literary figure in France (see "Voso Zachari Tells His Tale," pages 210–216).

Not all Gypsy groups are represented. Some people have become acculturated or are passing as non-Gypsies and no longer tell the old stories, or perhaps simply don't want to share them with outsiders. There are Gypsies in important professional positions in the United States, Greece, and other countries, who over the years have "passed" in order to safeguard their jobs. Like other oppressed minorities, the Gypsies have reasons for choosing to leave certain aspects of their culture behind.

The storytellers presented in this book are diverse in personality, background, age, and profession. There are several musicians, a conductor, a dancer, a factory worker, several political activists (one of whom is also a migrant agricultural worker), a novelist, a shopkeeper, a professor, a plumber, the owner of a health clinic, itinerant vendors, a lacemaker, and a cook. Some tales were originally told in Romani, some in English, some in other languages. The time span represented is just over a century, from the 1870s to the 1980s, the older stories tending, of course, to have a somewhat archaic flavor. The voice is essentially that of the narrator, although at times the translator has apparently imposed a style. Three of the tales originally narrated in English I decided to preserve just as they were told, since they are a valuable record of Gypsy speech. These tales are "The Robber and the Housekeeper," "The Gypsy Smith," and "Alifi and Dalifi." Most of the rest have been edited for the sake of readability. My introductory remarks to each story are meant to underscore the diversity of narrative voices and, when possible, to provide information about the storytellers and their lives as well as about the stories themselves.

At either formal or informal storytelling events among the Gypsies many kinds of tales are told, and I've tried in this collection to reflect that variety. An enormous range exists in style, theme, and genre. The stories can be ironic, poignant, playful, somber, frightening, romantic, or any combination of these. The heroines and heroes are both Gypsies and non-Gypsies; the themes sometimes reflect specifically Gypsy concerns, beliefs, and customs, and sometimes are universal.

Rather than arrange the stories by theme or by country of origin, I've ordered them, with few exceptions, along the lines of a spontaneous storytelling session at someone's home. The book does, however, begin with Najma Ayashah's stories from the Indian subcontinent, since that is where the Gypsies' story began.

Diane Tong
New York City
1988

How the Gypsy Went
to Heaven

Indian subcontinent

This story and the four stories that follow were told by Najma Ayashah, a Banjara from Hyderabad who has been living in New York City since 1963. A musician, dancer, and dance teacher, she performs classical Kathak dance in addition to the Gypsy dances she learned from the age of seven.

The Banjara are a Gypsy group in India and Pakistan which has seventeen subgroups; total population is approximately fifteen million. They are famous in India and Pakistan for valuing friendship very highly. The Banjaras do not participate in the caste system, and they speak their own form of Hindi, which has many words in common with Romani. They are nomadic and have diverse occupations. Even when Banjaras are not entertainers by profession (as Ayashah's subgroup is), dancing and music are part of their daily life.

About the stories, Ayashah had the following to say: "These are traditional stories in Gypsy culture handed down through generations—grandmothers to mothers to children. The stories each put you in touch with a particular feeling. You hear them over and over, in the village, in school, at work, all around you, and this forms the morals in your mind. There are so many of them. I heard them first in Pakistan and India, a lot of times from *hakims*, religious men. Wherever there's a lot of Gypsies, you always hear these stories."

This story is a Banjara version of a folktale type known as The Smith and the Devil. There are many Gypsy as well as non-Gypsy versions of this story, including the African-American "Jack and the Devil," with other tricks for keeping the devil away.

Once God visited a small Gypsy village, and nobody was there except the *petulengro*, or blacksmith, and his wife. And so God slept all night at their house. When morning came, the *petulengro*'s wife said to God, "I want to go to heaven when I die."

And God said to her, "You are such a good wife that you can't end up in hell. There's all that crying and suffering there. And as for your husband, because I had such a nice, peaceful night, I'm going to give him the four things that he wants most in his life." So God asked him what he wanted most in his life.

The blacksmith answered, "The first thing I want is this: whatever man I tell to go up in my apple tree, may he never come down until I say so. This is the first thing I want. And whoever I tell to go sit on my mare's blanket, may they never get up unless I tell them to. These are the two things that I want most in my life."

"And the third thing?" said God.

"Whoever goes into my little iron box, may they never come out till I say so."

And God said, "Okay, that's three things. And the last thing?"

"I want my turban with me all my life, and when I sit on it, may no man be able to make me get up."

The Gypsy blacksmith lived a long time. One day after many years the angel of death came to him and said, "Come with me."

And the Gypsy said, "Just let me say good-bye to my wife and my family first."

The angel said, "Okay."

And the Gypsy told him, "Why don't you go up in my apple tree and wait, and I'll be right along."

The angel of death went up in the apple tree, and he couldn't come down. Then the Gypsy said to him, "You let me live another twenty years and I'll let you come down."

And the angel of death said, "Okay, you'll live another twenty years."

After another twenty years the angel of death came again and said to the Gypsy, "Your time is up. You must come with me."

The Gypsy said, "Let me say good-bye to my children and make things ready for them. You go sit on my mare's blanket."

The angel of death went and sat on the mare's blanket, and he couldn't get up. "What's this?" he said. "I can't get up again."

And the Gypsy said, "Give me another twenty years to live and I'll let you get up."

And he said, "Okay, you can live another twenty years."

After twenty years the Devil came and said, "Now is your time, you come with *me*."

"You're so nice," the Gypsy said to the Devil. Then he added, "Let me see you go into that little iron box."

The Devil said, "Oh, I can go in there. No problem."

The iron box became red-hot and the Devil was trying to get out of it, but the Gypsy put it in the fire and the Devil fought and fought with him until he had no strength left. And the Gypsy said, "If I let you out, you have to leave me alone all my life."

And the Devil said, "Okay. I don't want to see you ever again."

Another twenty years passed, and another angel of death came—the one who judges where you should go—and said to the Gypsy, "Your time has come."

The Gypsy said, "I have some work to do in my house."

"Now your time is come," said the angel. "You can't say no now."

So he took him first to the Devil. And the Devil said, "No, I don't want him here, he's such a bad man, get him out of here, quick!"

And then the angel took the Gypsy to God, who said, "No, I don't want him here, please get him out of here."

And the Gypsy said to God, "Can I see what your big kingdom is like?" The Gypsy opened the door a little bit and looked through the crack, then threw his turban in and sat down, and nobody could get him up off his turban. And that's how the Gypsy went to heaven.

The Mouse's Wedding

Indian subcontinent

Ayashah comments that this is a moralistic story about how you should stay with your own kind. It could also be read as a lesson in letting people make their own choices.

This is a story of a magician and the marriage of a mouse. Along a big river lived a Gypsy magician. Once he was washing his face and taking a bath in the river when a mouse fell out of a big bird's beak and landed right in front of his face. He couldn't believe it, so he washed his face again, but the mouse was still there. He picked the mouse up and with the help of the magic river transformed it into a little girl, who he brought home to his wife. The Gypsy magician and his wife were childless, so when the wife saw the little girl, she said, "Oh, I'll take good care of her and bring her up very well and proper."

The years went by and the girl became twelve years old and the Gypsy magician said, "It's time for your wedding. We should marry you to the Sun God." And he did magic again in the river and called the Sun God to the daughter and said, "Daughter, do you find the Sun God proper for marriage?"

The daughter said, "No, I don't like him. He's too hot and I'd get burned by his rays."

Then the magician said, "Is there someone stronger and more powerful than the Sun God to marry to my daughter?"

And the Sun said, "Yes—the cloud, because the cloud can hide me."

And then the magician brought the cloud down and said, "Would you want to marry my daughter?"

The cloud said, "Yes, but ask your daughter."

"Daughter, would you want to marry the cloud?"

The daughter said, "No, I don't like him because he's too dark and he covers up everything and makes it dark and dirty."

"Is there somebody more powerful than the cloud who would marry my daughter?"

And the cloud said, "Yes. Somebody more powerful than me is the wind."

"Why is that?"

"Because the wind blows me away and I have no stability."

So the magician brought down the wind. "Daughter, do you want to marry the wind?"

The daughter said, "No, because it's too changeable and too cold. I don't want to marry the wind."

And the Gypsy asked again, "Is there somebody more powerful than you?"

"Oh yes, the mountain."

"Why is that?"

"Because I can't move the mountain."

Then the magician brought down the mountain and asked if it wanted to marry his daughter.

"Yes, but ask your daughter."

"Do you want to marry the mountain?"

"No, it's too tough."

And then the Gypsy asked the mountain, "Is there somebody stronger and more powerful than you?"

And the mountain said, "Yes—a mouse."

"Why is that?"

"Because a mouse makes holes in me and makes me crumble."

The magician had the mouse appear. "Daughter, do you want to marry the mouse?"

Then the daughter said, "Yes, but you'll have to change me back into a mouse again."

So the Gypsy changed her back into a mouse and the two mice got married.

Husband or Brother?

Indian subcontinent

The greater affection for a brother than for other members of the family is a very old folktale motif. Here, as told by Najma Ayashah, the whole family is reunited thanks to the maharajah's regard for the Gypsy woman's intelligence. Another story of a Gypsy woman using her wits to get her family back together is the Czech tale "The Romni's Riddle," pages 133–134.

Once upon a time there was a family of Gypsy thieves who lived near a jungle. There was a big *meydan*, a pasture, where everybody could plow and grow things: that's where the Gypsies would ambush and rob anybody who went through. The maharajah of the town was getting very upset and wanted the thieves caught, so he sent the police, but the police couldn't catch them.

Then one day he went himself, disguised as a farmer, and caught the three Gypsy men. After he put them in jail, there was a woman complaining in the streets, "Give me something to cover my body." All the people heard "Give me something to cover my body."

So the maharajah sent her some clothes. But she said, "No. I don't need any clothes."

He asked, "Then what do you want?"

She replied, "A woman's real clothing is her husband. If a woman doesn't have a husband, then she is naked in the world."

The maharajah liked what the Gypsy woman said. "Yes. What is a maharajah without a raj? And what is a river without water?"

So then she said, "You have my husband and my brother and my son in the jail."

"Yes. Which one do you want me to let go?"

"If I live a long time after this, I'll meet another man and get married again, and I'll also have another son. But since my mother and my father are dead, I'll never have another brother. So you must let my brother go."

The maharajah liked the way the Gypsy woman expressed herself—she was very smart. So he let all three of them go.

And that's how they got their family back together.

The Faithful Mongoose

Indian subcontinent

This story has some key elements in common with the story in Rudyard Kipling's *Jungle Book* about Rikki-Tikki-Tavi, another faithful mongoose.

One time there lived in a Gypsy village a husband and a wife and their little baby. This family had a mongoose, which they treated the same as their child—they bathed him, they fed him, just like a child. One day the wife said to her husband, "I'm going to get some water from the well. You keep an eye on the baby."

After she left, the husband remembered that they had no food for the evening, so he went to get some. He thought he would be gone only a short time and that it would be all right to leave the mongoose and the sleeping baby alone in the house.

While the baby was sleeping, from a little hole suddenly appeared a big black snake. It was moving toward the baby when the mongoose pounced and fought with it and finally killed it—but not before it bit the mongoose on one paw. By now there was blood all over the house, and the mongoose went out on the front veranda, where it licked its injured paw and cleaned the blood off its body.

When the woman of the house returned bringing water from the well, she saw the mongoose lick the blood dripping off its body and thought right away that it had killed the baby. (See, the husband trusted the mongoose completely, but the wife had always had her doubts about keeping an animal in the house.) So she threw a big heavy pot at the mongoose, killing it instantly.

Only then did she go inside to find the baby sleeping peacefully with a dead snake lying next to it. So she had jumped to the conclusion that the mongoose had killed the baby. Then she had made the big mistake of killing the mongoose. And the moral of the story is not to jump to conclusions. And that's the end of that story.

The Gypsy Boatman

Indian subcontinent

One traditional point of view—intellectual pursuits seen as an impractical luxury—is expressed in this anti–ivory tower story.

Once upon a time a grammarian wanted to spend some leisure time taking a boat ride on the river. So he rented a boat from a Gypsy whose business this was. During the ride the grammarian asked the Gypsy boatman, "Do you know anything about literature? Do you know how to write? Do you know how to read?"

And the boatman answered, "No, I'm always working, always trying to make ends meet, trying to feed my family, and never had time to learn to read. To me it's just a waste of time—I know my work, all there is to know about boats, and that's all I have to know."

And the grammarian said, "What a shame—you've wasted half your life with boats and know nothing about the more refined things in life."

So they went arguing back and forth about the need to know about reading and literature and the more refined things in life. All of a sudden a big whirlpool came up and things got scary. The boatman asked the grammarian, "Hey, do you know how to swim?"

"No."

"Oh, what a shame—you've spent half your life studying grammar and literature and writing, and you didn't learn how to swim? Well, if you don't learn how to swim now, it's going to be the *end* of your life!"

Vana

Yugoslavia

This ghost story was told at Liebach, Yugoslavia, in 1951 by a Gypsy woman who, the collector states, showed him the grave of Vana and her baby.

The return of the dead in their proper form on friendly missions is discussed by Stith Thompson in *The Folktale*: "Best known of such stories, both in tales and ballads, are those concerning the return of a dead mother . . . either to suckle her neglected baby or otherwise aid her persecuted children."

The storyteller introduced her story by commenting on the power of this theme: "Once, many years ago, when I was still a girl but not yet a woman, a curious happening occurred in our family. I for one will never forget it, for it shows very clearly that great though your love for your husband may be, your child is part of yourself."

My cousin Niglo married a girl from one of the Serbian Gypsy tribes, and for a year they lived the carefree life of two courting butterflies, chasing and catching each other the whole day through. And at night they lay entwined together, sighing and murmuring their love in each other's ears. Soon their love produced a physical form in the depths of her womb, but as she grew heavier she seemed to grow weaker. Niglo, in his love for her, would do anything to ease her life. He fetched water, gathered sticks, and washed clothes: nothing seemed too much trouble for him. Yet Vana, for that was his wife's name, grew increasingly weaker. At last Vana's time came, and soon there were three of them at that campfire. Vana was not able to get up, for her labor had been difficult and she had lost much blood. As the child steadily gained weight, her strength ebbed away. One night, as Niglo slept with his arms around both Vana and the baby, she died.

A devil seemed to possess Niglo the next day. He tore all her clothes to shreds and then burned them. He shattered her guitar and threw the fragments onto the burning rags. Her coffeepot, cup, and plate were smashed and buried. The only thing of hers he kept was her photograph— that he could not bring himself to destroy. The village priest buried her in the churchyard of St. George in Liebach. Vana's family threw many gifts onto her coffin as the sexton covered up the grave. Then they went their way, leaving Niglo alone with his baby, for he could not bear to be near anyone else at that time.

Niglo fed and washed the child well, but he half hated the life that had drawn its strength away from his Vana. He would sit for hours gazing dreamily at the squalling baby, wondering how God could be so stupid as to make a lusty wife die and a whimpering, whining child live.

One night, when a bright moon gave strange shadows and shapes to everything, Niglo suddenly woke up. Crouched by the windblown embers of the fire was a woman holding his baby, who was gurgling happily. A shiver ran down Niglo's spine. It was Vana. She sat there, softly crooning an old country song, pinching her nipple and pressing it into the child's eager mouth. Soon the specter returned the baby to his basket and covered him up. Then, with a long, tender look at the petrified Niglo, she turned and walked away, vanishing into the dark trees. Niglo crept over to the sleeping baby and gazed at him as dawn stole over the mountains.

The next evening Niglo deliberately dressed the baby in his clothes, but inside out and back to front. Then he hung a necklace of garlic around the baby's neck and prepared to wait for the ghost of his Vana.

Soon he saw her, stepping quickly and anxiously, just as a mother returning to her child would do. Niglo then realized that there was no need to be afraid. Suddenly Vana recoiled from the crib. The garlic repelled her, and the clothes confused her. She turned to Niglo and said sadly, "Niglo, dear Niglo, why do you keep a mother from her child? Is your love so shallow that it cannot reach as deep as the grave?"

Niglo looked into her eyes and saw such pain and misery there that his heart swelled with pity. Vana groaned in despair and then looked at the baby whimpering in the basket. He arose and removed the garlic, loosened the clothes, and offered the child to Vana, who quickly snatched up the precious bundle and sat crooning and talking to the baby the whole night through. Niglo's heart ached with a desperate joy.

For nearly a month Vana came every night. But the child seemed to be sickening slowly, as if an odor of death in its nostrils were gradually driving its life away. Niglo became increasingly anxious for the life of his child. Eventually he took the baby to the priest for a blessing and soon had told the priest the whole tale. The priest thought hard and long, and at last told Niglo that he must wait until Vana was about to leave, just before dawn, and then lay hold of her and keep her in the camp until God's sun could shine on her.

That night Niglo watched Vana squatting in her usual place by the embers of the fire. Bit by bit, as the moon moved across the branches of the trees, Niglo gained courage. When the first faint flickerings of light appeared in the east and Vana bent over the crib to replace the child, Niglo leapt at her small black form and locked his arms around her waist. Her desperate struggles were useless, but her pitiful cries wounded Niglo to the heart. His mind was swimming with terror at what he was doing. With agonizing slowness the red sun peeped over the crags, and Vana's struggles grew weaker as yellow sunbeams filled the valley. Quite suddenly she just crumpled up, leaving Niglo holding only a black shroud cloth that disintegrated first into rags and then into dust. When Niglo stumbled over to the crib and saw the baby lying very still, its little face creased into a smile, he knew instinctively that the baby was dead and with its mother. He threw himself across the blanket and sobbed so violently that the priest, who arrived at first light, thought that he must surely die also.

They buried the baby in the coffin with its mother. And when they opened the lid, Niglo knew from the sweet smile on Vana's face, untouched by decay, that at last mother and child were again together.

The Enchanted Frog

Canada

It was in Toronto on a winter night in 1982 when Catherine Philippo told this story at the request of French anthropologist Chantal Hilaire. Drawn by the tale, Philippo's daughter-in-law and grandchildren came and sat around her in a circle. Hilaire, who has collected many of Philippo's tales and translated them from Romani into French, observes that Philippo's Romani vocabulary reflects the adaptations she has made to various groups of Gypsies in her audiences.

Catherine Philippo was born about 1920 and traveled around Europe with her extended family until after World War II, when they settled in Paris. She married a Canadian Gypsy in the 1950s and emigrated. At the conclusion of this story, she blessed her sisters and brothers in Paris.

There was and there wasn't a rich *gajo* couple who had three sons. When their parents told them to get married, they all replied, "No, no, we don't want to, we want to stay home with you."

One year both their father and their mother died, and the sons were left alone. All three of them were rich, and all three remained unmarried for ten years. By then the oldest was about forty years old, the middle one thirty, and the youngest twenty. The oldest son said, "We've been bachelors all this time, and we'll never find wives in this village." And so they left home, saying, "Let's cross the whole world until we find proper wives as our parents wanted."

They walked so far that they wore out their shoes. Then they made themselves iron shoes and continued on foot or on horseback (in those days there were no cars). No matter where they went, they couldn't find wives. According to them, the women were fat, nasty, miserable, and anything but desirable. "Let's continue our search," said the oldest brother.

Now, when their parents were dying they had told their sons, "Each of you take one of these three stones, and when you want a wife throw it behind you." They didn't want to throw the stones yet, but they had traveled the whole world over and worn out even their iron shoes.

When they finally returned to their village, the oldest brother said, "I'm so exhausted and miserable, I'll take whatever comes my way." And so he took his stone and threw it behind him. When he turned around he saw a beautiful woman standing there, so he helped her up on his horse and they went home. Next the middle son said, "Am I any better than my brother?" And he also threw his stone behind him, a woman came for him too, and they went home together. Then the youngest son said, "Am I any better than they?" But when he threw his stone behind him, it landed in a pond. A frog hopped out, looked at him, and said that she would be his wife. The youngest brother told her, "I don't want you." The frog replied, "You have to marry me anyway." (Of course this frog was not really a frog but a young woman whose mother had put a curse on her.)

Well, the young man went right home and closed the door, saying to himself, *I've left the frog behind in the water.*

"No, you haven't—I'm here with you," said the frog.

"Frog, get out. My brothers have real wives and you're just a frog."

"How can I be a frog if I'm talking with you? When you look at me you see a frog only because my mother put a curse on me."

"Get out!"

"No!"

The young man argued with the frog for so long that he finally fell asleep. While he was sleeping, the frog shed her skin and became a beautiful young woman. She heated water, washed, straightened the house, and cooked, but changed back into a frog before the young man woke up and smelled hot food the next morning. He exclaimed, "The house is arranged differently and there's food on the table!" But when he asked who had done these things, the frog didn't answer.

Well, he sat down, he ate, and he drank. Just then his two brothers knocked on the door. "Brother," they said, "open up so we can see your new wife!"

But the youngest brother, without opening the door, called out, "I can't—she's ill."

"Well then, we're going out walking with our wives."

"Go ahead, and as soon as my wife is well, I'll join you."

Every day his brothers came, and every day he told them his wife was ill.

When the emperor heard that the three brothers had gotten married, he wrote to each of them, "I want your new wife to make me a lavish and exceptionally magnificent coverlet."

When the oldest brother received his letter and told his wife what the emperor wanted, she said, "I'll sew it," and asked for thread, pearls, and everything else she needed. At the second brother's, his wife also agreed.

But when the third brother read the letter, he cried. His wife asked why, and he answered, "The emperor wants you to make him a splendid coverlet."

"Don't worry," she said. "Just bring me the most expensive thread and the most luxurious silk and satin." After he brought her these things, she told him to sleep until two and she would take care of everything.

Well, she had the cloth and thread, and he had nothing to do but sleep. She blew three times, and the coverlet was done: Her breath turned the expensive satin, silk, and thread into pearls and diamonds. Then the satin, silk, and thread became a long ribbon, which she put in a large box. When the young man woke up, he asked, "Frog, was it you who did all this?"

"Yes, but don't look at my handiwork. Take this box at once to the emperor and tell him to close all the windows, shut off the lights, and only then unroll the coverlet."

"Fine, frog, whatever you say."

The three brothers went to the palace together. When the two elder brothers asked the youngest, "Where's your wife?" he replied, "She's so ill she couldn't come." "Well, did she make the coverlet?" "She did." And so they went in to see the emperor. The oldest brother showed a lovely coverlet, and so did the middle brother. But the youngest brother said, "Emperor, I'll show you the coverlet as my wife requested—the windows should be shut and the lights turned off."

Then he said to himself, *Oh, God, why on earth did she tell me to cover the windows and extinguish the lights? If the coverlet isn't astonishing, he'll cut my throat.* But when he put out the lights, closed the curtains, and unrolled the coverlet for them to see, the darkness turned to light. The coverlet was so magnificent—it was a beautiful quilt covered with small diamonds—that the emperor fainted. When they pinched his nose and he revived, he said, "Oh, what marvelous woman was able to make this coverlet? What talent! Now go home and tell your wife to make me a golden bridge from your house to mine for people to walk on and a silver bridge for the carriages and the horses to ride over."

At home, the frog already knew what the emperor had said, and even before her husband returned she blew a little puff of air and the golden bridge was built. The young man was just as confused as his brothers, who said, "What kind of wife do you have? We want to see her!"

When the emperor looked outdoors, he saw two little bridges from his window to the young woman's window. "My God! What a woman! I have to bring her to the palace."

He sent a letter to each of the three brothers: "I want you to bring your wife to me." So the two older brothers knocked on the door of the youngest and asked, "Can't we see your wife at last?"

"No, she's still sick."

Well, the two older brothers left, and the youngest wept. "The emperor said that he'll cut my throat if I don't bring you."

The frog answered, "Don't be afraid. At the stroke of midnight I'll become a young woman. But don't look at my feet, because if you do, I'll remain a frog all my life. When I get out of my frogskin, take it and throw it into the stove, don't look at me, and go to sleep immediately. If you even peek, the emperor will cut your throat and I'll remain a frog the rest of my life."

The young man agreed to do as she said.

The clock struck midnight, and the frog became a young woman with blond hair down to the floor, green eyes, a lovely face, and a slim body. The young man didn't look at her, but as soon as he spotted the skin he took it and burned it in the stove. Then he went to sleep. When he woke up some time later and saw that the frog had become a beautiful and naked young woman, he fainted. She revived him and said, "This is no time for fainting but for going to the palace." Since she didn't have any clothes, he asked, "What will you wear?"

"Take the big silk scarf off the piano," she replied. She wrapped herself in it and said, "Go into the garden and pick three flowers for me." He did, she put them on, and they went off to the palace. As soon as they arrived at the entrance and his brothers saw his wife, they were amazed. "Where did you find her?" they asked.

He said, "I found her just the way you found your wives."

When they entered the palace, the emperor saw the very beautiful wife of the oldest brother and embraced her. Next he saw the middle brother's wife and said to them both, "May you live and grow old together." Then he said to the youngest brother, "I guess you weren't able to bring your wife, who made me that superb coverlet and the bridges." But then he saw the wife, and again he fainted. They had to pinch his nose and slap his face before he came to. The emperor danced one dance with the youngest brother's wife, but when he started to dance with her again, she told him, "Don't behave this way—you're embarrassing my brothers-in-law. They are married, they have wives: dance with their wives too."

His Majesty said, "We will do whatever your heart desires."

So he danced with the other two wives and then stopped the musicians and said, "I leave half my kingdom to this young woman and her husband." The young woman was called Anuska and her husband Jolska. They all ate and drank, the young man was happy with his wife, and that's how the story ends.

The Mosquito

Belgium

Jan Yoors (1922–1977) collected and translated this story, which he published in Romani and in English translation in the *Journal of the Gypsy Lore Society* in 1946. At the age of twelve, Yoors left his home in Belgium to join a group of Lowara Gypsies, with whom he traveled many years as an adopted member. Yoors wrote three popular books about his experiences: *The Gypsies, Gypsies of Spain*, and *Crossing: A Journal of Survival and Resistance in World War II*.

The story itself is highly original, not just because of the unusual plot but because of the narrator's ironic commentary on the hero's exploits.

In the golden holiness of a night that will never be seen again and will never return, there lived in a certain country far, far away at the other side of the great waters a little mosquito.

This mosquito, let me tell you, was so conceited that the like of him was never heard of or seen in this world. Everybody hated him for his wickedness. He was constantly boasting about his intelligence. As for beauty, he was unequaled in the whole earth—or so he said.

Everywhere he passed or paused on the roads, the peasant girls and young Gypsy girls were dying for him. So *he* said about himself. Even Gypsy women, married and with children (forgive me if I allude to such things in your presence!), fell in love with him.

In a wild country not very far away there was an ancient ruined castle in the heart of dark woods. And in this old ruin there lived, all by herself, an old candle that burned eternally.

Numerous were the men who, on hearing of the candle's fabulous reputation, set out for this country to match their strength against hers. But whoever tested themselves in a duel with the wretched little candle came back scorched and roasted.

Well! When our mosquito heard all the talk concerning this business, he paused a little in inner speculation. Then he took a big knife, cut two thick slices of bread, and buttered them generously. He roasted two pieces of meat, peeled three onions, helped himself to three big pimentos, and took a pinch of salt.

Then he packed up all these provisions in his mother's big golden kerchief, knotted it, and went on his way in search of the village where the invincible candle lived.

He was choked with anger to think that anyone in the world could be stronger than he was. (And who told you that he was so strong? He was indeed no bigger than a fly.)

He walked for one month, he walked for yet a second month, and in the third month at last he arrived where he wanted to arrive. (May God strike him for his pride!) Truly the mosquito looked upon himself already as a personage of importance. (May God cause the earth to swallow him up!)

He pulled his cap over his eyes, thrust his hands into his pockets, and set out in the direction of the ruined castle where the candle lived.

When he got there, he simply forced his way into the room where he wanted to be.

But when he saw the tiny candle standing upright in front of him he was at first taken by surprise. What was he to do now? First he coughed very loudly to see what the candle would do. She did not stir. He turned up his nose and whistled. Even then the flame did not budge. Now the mosquito, possessed by the devil, grew furiously angry. His blood was boiling, his heart was beating fiercely, and his eyes were shooting sparks.

The candle remained herself: none of this moved her at all. (May the holy God bless her and keep her enemies far away!) She was a church candle, you see, and had come here from a holy place of pilgrimage.

Our mosquito drew close to the candle and looked down upon her mockingly. She did not condescend to say anything at all. Our quarrelsome mosquito got more and more enraged, and began to mock and insult her and her mother as well in a most obscene manner. The candle did not answer.

Then the mosquito even began to curse the poor candle roundly, for no reason whatsoever. But it was impossible for him to make her lose her temper by any means: the candle did not even glance at him.

So now he flew into a rage and shrieked at her in Lowari: "Come outside with me if you are a true man and let us try our strength in duel!" (May shame devour his face! By what right did he desire the poor little candle to try her strength with him, especially since she had never done him any wrong?)

Then he insulted the candle's ancestors, those who are under the earth. He no longer knew what fear was. And the candle did not speak a single word in reply, only this time her light quivered slightly. When he perceived that nothing was of any use, neither scorn nor insults, even against the memory of her ancestors, he took a step backward and, in Gypsy style, gave her a blow under the chin with his fist.

"Oh! oh! oh! I have burned myself! Oh! candle, you have devoured my hand! How is it that you did not understand I was only joking with you? Why are you so cruel to me? I was not trying to take advantage of you. I had not a suspicion in my mind of any bad intention toward you." In fear and pain he stood there weeping tears as big as my fist. "Who," he went on, "would believe that a candle could be so strong in very truth? Let me have news of my father's death if she did not appear to me to be timid!"

The mosquito then abandoned his mother's kerchief with his provisions on the spot—he ran away so fast he also forgot his cap and scattered his shoes on the way. Eventually he arrived in tears at his mother and father's.

"What have you done, my boy?" And his old mother became wild with grief when she saw his burns and that he had no hand. She tied a kerchief around her head, took out the pennies she had hidden inside her mattress, and set out with her son for the big hospital.

"O great doctor," she said, "to you I have come that you may heal my son. God grant you luck and health! The money that is required shall be paid to you. Even thick gold sovereigns we will give you, if you are skillful enough and have the ability to replace the hand of my son. Oh, my God! They have ruined my son, ruined him!"

"Your son, madam, will need a new hand," replied the doctor, "but where shall we get one? We have only the hands of men. We cannot cure him because we have no mosquito hands to graft onto the limb."

"Go and look in all the shops," said she. "You may find something that might do."

They went and searched in the town. They asked and begged, but they found no hand.

When they realized that it was futile to search further, all the Mosquito tribe gathered together and made the feeble suggestion: "Why not graft onto our cousin the foot of a fowl?"

"What, the foot of a fowl?"

"Yes, truly, Gypsies, the foot of a fowl."

They went once again to the hospital. (Let it disappear with the night, and let it not trouble my dreams!) And the cleverest surgeons sewed a huge chicken's foot onto the small mosquito. (Good! let us get on!)

Well, do you think that this brought the mosquito back to his senses? Not at all! As soon as his fist was healed and no longer gave him any pain, he took his big knife and went off again to find the candle.

Nine times more the mosquito did battle with the candle, nine times more he saw himself vanquished, and nine times more he returned to the big hospital before God allowed him to come to his senses and he no longer sought to pick a quarrel with the poor candle.

When people saw him walking along, they stopped in the road to wait for him to pass by and then shout after him: "O miracle of a child, who are you? Are you a male or a female? To what class of animal do you belong?" For by this time the mosquito had six chicken feet, four chicken wings, and also the head and rump of a chicken. And in truth I must tell you he looked like a miracle of God. The stupid country folk went on their knees in his presence and prayed to him as if he really had been God. Every day his pride increased, till his folly again turned his head.

Well! One day he was sauntering by some running water and saw the mayor of a peasant village swimming naked in the stream. A vagrant robber had come upon the mayor's clothes, seized them, and disappeared. The mayor now had nothing left to cover himself with and did not dare to go home, naked as he was. He called out to the mosquito, begging him to help him somehow or other. He promised money, more and more money.

But the mosquito put forward his own views: "O farmer, I can help you, but only on the condition that you believe what my mouth says and that you do what I order."

The mayor answered: "I agree, O master, I agree. Act as you consider best."

Then the malicious mosquito made a barter with the mayor. First of all they exchanged heads, after that their behinds and bellies, and last their hands and feet. And when they had finished, our mosquito looked like a man and the stout mayor was transformed into the miraculous mosquito.

The mosquito who had become a man then went to the mayor's home. Since he was not used to living in the company of human beings, he felt no shame at all at walking naked through the streets and passing in this state near to women. All the village urchins ran after him, singing and dancing. They thought he was drunk.

When he arrived at the mayor's home, he entered the house and dressed himself in the man's most gorgeous clothes. And that is how the foolish mosquito became a wise mayor.

Two weeks later, his marriage to a rich farmer's daughter took place. About the food and drink we will make no further mention . . . but there was music and dancing, and our mosquito enjoyed himself thoroughly.

But now the real mayor arrived to change back with the mosquito, since he wanted to become a man as before. The mosquito, already intoxicated, had fallen in love with the girl, and she was infatuated with him. Why should he observe the pact he had made with the mayor?

Since it had occurred to that fool of a mayor to put so much faith in him, why, it must have been God who duped him!

Wine was flowing freely, and the guests were drinking hard. But the old mayor insisted on talking and talking so much that everyone present grew infuriated with him. Who could believe him when he said that he was the *real* mayor?

The young bride, who had been his own betrothed before, wrung his neck, and they roasted him over the fire and devoured him at the wedding feast.

I was there also, hiding under the table, and I heard and saw everything. As I was famished, I secretly tried to snatch a morsel of the six-legged chicken for myself and my old mother. But the farmers saw me and forced me to flee. That is the only reason why I cannot give you a proof of the truth of my story. All the same I tell it to you, in the hope that it will give you pleasure and help to pass away the time.

Why Gypsies Are Scattered About the Earth

Russia

I found this unusual version of a recurrent explanatory tale—the other accounts usually deal with war—in a collection of Russian Gypsy folktales published in Scotland in 1986. The collectors are Yefim Druts, son of a Moscow rabbi, and poet Alexei Gessler.

This happened long ago.

A Gypsy and his family were traveling along. His horse was skinny and none too steady on his legs, and as the Gypsy's family grew he found it harder to pull the weighty wagon. Soon the wagon was so full of children tumbling over one another that the poor horse could barely stumble along the rutted track.

As the wagon rumbled on, veering first to the left, then rocking to the right, pots and pans would go tumbling out, and now and then a barefoot child was pitched headlong onto the ground.

It was not so bad in daylight—then you could pick up your pots and tiny children—but you could not see them in the dark. In any case, who could keep count of such a tribe? And the horse plodded on its way.

The Gypsy traveled right around the earth, and everywhere he went he left a child behind: more and more and more.

And that, you see, is how Gypsies came to be scattered about the earth.

The Tailor's Clever Daughter

Greece

When I arrived in Thessaloniki for New Year's 1985, I heard about the recent death of a friend's father-in-law. My friend told me about the wake, where Katina Makri, the narrator of this story, had entertained everyone all night with tale after tale. Makri comes from a long line of gifted storytellers, mostly male: her father is also known in this community for his talent, and her grandfather and great-grandfather were storytellers in Turkey.

I finally met Makri on a summer evening later that year, when she told this story to a group of ten or twelve people in the courtyard of another friend's home in the Gypsy quarter in Thessaloniki. Everyone was enchanted with the tale and remarked on how real the story's events seemed when Katina related them. That the protagonist is a dynamic, independent woman is one of the tale's many charms.

This story has much in common with modern Turkish folktales, and in fact the children's names are Turkish: Narinbey and Turujbey are proper names, as is Selvinasalim, from the Turkish "Selvinaz"—implying "someone who is as graceful as a cypress tree swaying in the wind." One innovative feature of the story is what has been

called "modernization of props"—for example, the use of the aluminum chair and the airplane as integral parts of what is largely a
traditional plot.

There once was a tailor who had three daughters, and they were the
most beautiful girls in Greece. The tailor made the most beautiful suits
and clothes—all very beautiful.

The king was jealous because he could not find a tailor like this one
for himself. So he went to the tailor's home and said, "Tailor"—the tailor's
daughters weren't in at the time—"I want a suit. Without measuring,
without cutting, without sewing, without doing *anything*, you have to
make a suit. If you don't do it in three days, I'll cut off your head!"

"But Your Highness," replied the tailor, "how can I make the suit
if I don't take up my scissors, if I don't measure, if I don't take up my
needle to sew?"

"Just do what I told you," said the king. "Do it in three days or I'll
cut off your head."

Now this tailor was so rich that he had two chairs, one of silver and
the other of aluminum. Whenever he was depressed, he would sit on
the aluminum chair; when he was cheerful, he'd sit on the silver one.

As soon as his daughters came home (they were motherless: the
tailor didn't have a wife, and they'd all grown up together) and saw their
father sitting on the aluminum chair, they said, "Papa, what's wrong?"

"Out," he said. "For what's bothering me, there's nothing you can
do to help. Out." From all sides they cried, "Papa, tell us what's wrong."
"Go away," he said. "I've only got three days. Go away." They tried and
tried, but he still wouldn't say anything. But then the youngest daughter,
who was very clever, said, "Come here, Father, tell me what's wrong.
And if I don't help you . . . if I don't solve your problem, you can kill
me and trample me."

"Listen, my child," the tailor began. "The king came and told me I
have to make him a suit without sewing, cutting, or measuring. How can
I do such a thing?" He started to cry.

The girl broke into laughter. "That's all it is, Father? I thought you'd
lost the ring my dead mother left me, since you once told me that is the
only reason you'd ever get depressed. That's all? That's nothing, Papa.
I'll get it straightened out. First you'll get up in the morning and put a
large round table in the sun. You'll climb up on it and you'll take the
cloth for the suit and you'll turn it this way and that way over and over

for about an hour before the king comes to behead you. You'll turn it round and round and the king will show up. He'll say, 'What's going on? Still no suit? Cut off his head!' And you'll say, 'Stop. Take the sun away so I can finish the suit. Take the sun away, it's bothering me. I can't work, I'm just turning the material around.' "

That was the youngest daughter's advice. As soon as she had finished speaking, the tailor embraced her and said, "Yes, my child."

"Don't worry, Father. If he says, 'And *how* am I supposed to take the sun away?' you'll say, 'Well, how am *I* supposed to make a suit without cutting, without sewing, without doing *anything?*' You'll see, Father, how our trick will be successful."

On the morning of the third day the tailor put out a round table, climbed onto it, took out the material, and turned the material around and around. The king ordered him down to be beheaded. "I'm trying to make the suit, only the sun is bothering me. Take the sun away and I'll make the suit."

"Are you *mad?*" the king responded contemptuously. "Can the sun be removed from there? Is it a vase or something that I can remove it just like that?"

"Are *you* mad? How can I make you a suit without sewing, cutting, without even using a needle?" And so the tailor won the round. But the king said, "One more task: and if you win, okay, but if you don't, you'll lose your head." (He wanted to kill the tailor.)

"What must I do?" asked the tailor.

"Bring me three girls who are both pregnant and virgins. If you don't do it, I'll cut off your head."

The tailor went right back to his aluminum chair, and again his daughters asked him what was wrong. "Go away," he said, "you can't do anything. The first time, you managed it. But now—girls who are both virgins and pregnant—where am I supposed to find them?"

"Father, don't be afraid," said his youngest daughter. "If I don't drive this king crazy, you can disinherit me." (In fact, though, she'd taken a liking to the king—fallen in love with him, to tell the truth. The more she saw of him, the more she liked him.)

So she got her two sisters together and said, "Let's each of us stuff some material under our clothes. We're going to become pregnant." One of them four months pregnant, another three, and the third one five. And now the tailor took them to the king.

Knock, knock, knock. What did the king see? He nearly fainted.

Girls both pregnant and virgins! They were examined—they were really virgins! The king went crazy. How could such a thing happen? Then he asked each girl, "Okay, you're both a virgin and pregnant. Who got you pregnant? Who's the father?"

The oldest daughter said, "You have the nerve to ask? The father's your vizier."

"My vizier? Come here, vizier." And the king slapped him hard and said, "Quickly, take this girl to church and marry her." Now, all the girls were beautiful, and their father had nearly as much money as the king, since he was the best tailor in the kingdom. So the vizier said, "I'll marry her gladly." They got married and left.

Then the king said to the second girl, "Who's the father?" "Your servant," she replied. He brought the servant, slapped him too, and said, "Marry the girl immediately." So the servant took the girl away and married her.

Then only the youngest daughter was left. Remember: she was in love with the king. "You—who got you pregnant?" he said, without looking at her.

"Have you forgotten?" she asked. "Look at me carefully."

He looked at her and said, "Who?"

"You. You forgot?"

The king slapped her. "Take her," he ordered, "and throw her in the dungeon. Pregnant by *me*? When? How? What are you talking about?"

They took her, tied her up, and locked her in the dungeon. The king couldn't believe it: "*Me!* I was the one who wanted to kill your father, and now I'm supposed to become his daughter's bridegroom? Out of the question!"

The girl was in the dungeon about a year—her nails got really long, and she became like a cat, transformed. One day water, the next day bread: the king treated her this way because he couldn't stand it that she had accused him of making her pregnant.

The girl found soft earth in the dungeon, and she dug a hole large enough so she could go out at night to see her father. By day she was back in the dungeon again—she would close up the hole and hide it well. This way she went back and forth.

One day the king proclaimed that he would go on a journey to a city called Narinbey—a long journey, and he was going by ship to see all the places on the way. As soon as the girl heard that he was preparing to leave, she went to her father. "Papa, quickly, a new dress." She got dressed up, she fixed her hair: how would the king ever recognize her?

The king went by ship, but *she* went by plane, and got there ahead of him.

The girl had taken a backgammon set and a pair of dice with her. As soon as the king arrived, she approached him. "Come here. Where are you going? If you want to leave here, we'll have to play a game of backgammon."

The king said, "And what do I win?"

"My virginity," said the girl. "If I lose, you'll take my virginity. If I win, you'll take me along on a trip."

"Okay," he said, and he won the game. He took her to the hotel with him and took her virginity. When the king knew she had become pregnant, he said to her, "Narinbey. When you baptize the child, name it Narinbey. And take this sword and sheath for the child to wear. When he grows up, give him this golden sword." Then she took the same airplane back home. She went to her father, kissed him, and returned to the dungeon.

Meanwhile the king feasted, drank, partied, and returned after three or four days. As he passed by the prison he said, "Ah, I eat and drink and you'll rot there in the dungeon." And the girl replied, "Ah, I've tricked you once; I'll manage it twice more, and then you can do whatever you want." How was the king supposed to understand?

Some time passed. When the girl felt labor pains, she went to her father's, gave birth, cleaned herself up, and left the baby for him to raise. Then she returned to the dungeon.

The child, a boy, became a year old. Now the king decided to go to Turujbey. Again the girl sneaked off to her father's. "Papa, make me another beautiful dress." Again with the backgammon set she arrived ahead of the king, who again thought he had never seen her before. She told him, "Look, we'll play, and if you win, you'll have me." (No more virginity.) They played, the girl lost, the king took her to the hotel, ate, drank, slept with her, and again left her pregnant.

The girl again returned home by plane. When the king came back, he passed by her and said, "Ah, I eat and drink and you'll rot in there." The girl replied, "Ah, what a fool you are. I've tricked you twice, one more time remains." For he had given her a second gift, a golden belt, and said, "If it's a girl, sell the belt and use the money for her dowry, and if it's a boy, have him put it on and enjoy it."

The girl gave birth to another boy and named him Turujbey. When the first child was three years old, and the second one two, the king again prepared to go on a journey—this time to Selvinasalim, another city. Again the girl went to her father. "Father, make one last effort, though I've tired you out." He made another dress, and she fixed her hair differently so the king wouldn't recognize her. Again on the plane ahead of the king, and back to the same ploy. She said, "Let's play a game of backgammon. And if you win, we'll celebrate."

He threw the dice. Again they ate, drank, and went to the hotel. She became pregnant again—Narinbey, Turujbey, and this time Selvinasalim. The king said, "Take these golden clogs. If it's a girl, have her wear them; if it's a boy, sell them." (Of course, the king thought he had been with a different woman each time.)

The girl returned by plane. The king stayed in Selvinasalim, eating and drinking, and then returned home also. "Ah," he said, "I eat and drink and you'll rot in this dungeon." And she said, "What a fool you are."

When the king was in Selvinasalim, he had met a woman from there—like him, from a royal family. One day, after a year had passed, her whole family was about to arrive so the king could get to know her and marry her. That day the horses were constantly going back and forth. After all, the king was getting married.

"So you're getting married today," the girl said to the king as he passed by her dungeon. "Let me out of here just for a little while. Put me in the kitchen instead of here—at least I can wash the rice."

"Let her out," the king said. "I'm getting married today."

She was released. She dressed herself in a sari, took the rice, and started washing it. Earlier, she'd gone to instruct her father: "Papa, dress the children. Put the golden clogs on Selvinasalim, on Narinbey the sword, and on Turujbey the belt. Dress them well and have them speak their names loudly at the wedding."

So at the palace the older brother shouted, "Turujbey, go tell your sister Selvinasalim to be careful of the horses."

All the important people, all the kings who were there for the wedding, were listening, and they said, "What strange names! Whose beautiful children are these, dressed like that?" And they took them by the hand and led them to a corner, and hundreds of people gathered around. "What's your name?" "Narinbey." "And yours?" "Turujbey." "And yours?" "Selvinasalim." "The belt?" "A gift from my father." "Who is your father?" "We don't know. Only our mother knows—she's washing the rice."

So many people had gathered that now the king became curious and came over to find out what was going on. All those important people and their horses! "Whose children are they?" the king asked, on his way to the church for his wedding.

Turujbey called out, "Narinbey, take care Selvinasalim doesn't get trampled by the horses." "Yes, Turujbey." And they kept shouting each other's names. And the crowd started saying, "What odd names—names of places where only great kings go to visit."

So the king, their father, went over and said, "What's your name?" "Narinbey." "And yours?" "Turujbey." "And yours?" "Selvinasalim."

"The children . . . the gifts I gave . . . where's your mother? Whose children are you?"

They pointed out the woman with the rice.

"Ah." He fell to his knees. "My children!" He embraced them. He had spat at their mother, but now he embraced his children.

"I beg of you, stop the horses," he said to the crowd, "because I have found my children. These children are my own. And this woman who is washing the rice will be my wife. Wash her hair, clean her up, and dress her in the bride's clothing. I beg your forgiveness, but I can't abandon my own children."

At that moment the woman said, "I did it because I loved you."

Then they washed her, took the bridal clothing and wreath from the other bride, and dressed her in them. And the couple took the three children and ate and drank, and we have told their story.

A Deceiving Sleep

Finland

This unusual story of an independent woman was told to Dr. Yrjö Qvarnberg in 1987 by Hulda Baltzar, a sixty-four-year-old Gypsy woman he met in the hospital in Jyväskylä, where he works. Baltzar, now retired from her job as a lacemaker, says the story is about someone in her family, and she remembers her father, who had his own horse farm, telling this story when she was a young child. Rautalampi is a village of 4,600 in central Finland.

About two hundred years ago an unmarried Gypsy woman named Ulla was living in the village of Rautalampi. All the peasants, landowners, and servants knew her well and thought highly of her. She traveled, like all Finnish Gypsies, from village to village on horseback from one familiar house to another. Whenever she arrived at a house, the people there always unharnessed her horses and treated her respectfully. Because she was so well known, almost like a member of the family, she could stay as long as she wanted.

In the old days it was a tradition that if a Gypsy man fell passionately in love with a Gypsy woman and wanted to marry her, he had to catch her by force—steal her away or kidnap her. In this village the Gypsy men were willful and strong and tall. Among them the major question was who would be accepted by Ulla—all the Gypsy men were rivals in Rautalampi.

One time Ulla happened to stay overnight in a house, and in the early morning, after the people of the house had gone out to work in the hayfields, she was sleeping alone, not imagining that anything evil could happen to her. Then two Gypsy men came to that house. One of them had been in love with Ulla for a long time, and when he saw her asleep he went in and snatched her out of bed and took her away. The other Gypsy harnessed Ulla's horses.

When Ulla awoke she was very angry. Long ago she had decided to live alone and not to marry. She felt very bad about being taken by force while she was sleeping and unable to resist, especially since she herself was strong and tall. In her innermost soul she decided to escape from this situation—she wanted to live alone.

To the men who had kidnapped her she said, "Let's go to the house known as Puhjo and do some cooking. We could even stay over there and take a sauna together." And in this way she lured the men to travel with her to the house called Puhjo, where she was very well known. When the three of them arrived, their horses were unharnessed by their hosts and, once inside, Ulla announced her decision to stay there, and the people of the house came to her aid. In this way Ulla's trip did not last long.

For a long time Ulla was very angry because she had been kidnapped while sleeping, when she wasn't able to defy those men, even though she was very strong and tall. In her anger she wrote a ballad: "Sleep deceived Ulla as Ulla's knife could not sing." She sang her new song many times during her stay in that house because she wanted future generations to know that she had not been taken willingly. Her travels with the Gypsy men had ended abruptly. Many times afterwards Ulla continued to sing her ballad "Ulla's Sleep," and she continued to live in her old way, traveling alone in Rautalampi village.

The Silly Man Who Sold His Beard

Sweden

This and the following two stories are from the large and varied repertoire of the famous Swedish Gypsy storyteller Johan Dimitri Taikon (1879–1950), who is also known by his Romani name, Miloš. Taikon's stories have been translated into several languages, and his narrative skill has been discussed by folklore scholar Max Lüthi. One of the standard works in Romani linguistics, on which Taikon collaborated, is based on Taikon's own dialect. More than five thousand people, many of them non-Gypsies, attended the storyteller's funeral in Stockholm.

This tale is said to be found nowhere outside the Swedish Gypsy community.

Once there were two merchants who were good friends. One was smart, and one was silly; the smart one was clean-shaven, like a young boy, and the other had a long, thick beard. Take my word for it, it was a very handsome beard.

One day they were sitting together, talking of this and that. Said the one who had no beard, "Little brother, would you like to sell me your beard?"

The one with the beard answered, "Why not, if you'll pay me a good price."

"I'll give you whatever you ask for that fine beard of yours."

"I'll let you name the price, good friend. I know you'll be fair," said the one with the beard.

"Fine. I'll give you a good sum, but on one condition. I want the beard to keep on growing on *your* face, but *I* will take care of it—how it is to grow, how it is to be combed, what perfume is to be put on it, and how it should be cut. Everything will have to be done as I like it. You won't have the right to say anything about it. That beard will be all mine. If anyone says to you, 'What a beautiful beard!' you'll have to answer quickly, 'Sorry, my good man, it's not my beard, it belongs to so-and-so.' That's what you'll have to say."

The man with the beard had no objection to that.

"Sure, friend," he said. "You can keep looking after my beard—I mean your beard. It will be cheaper for me!"

So they wrote out a contract, and the merchant who was clean-shaven paid a good sum to the other.

Mishtó! Fine and dandy. From that day on, the clean-shaven man was very particular about taking care of the beard he had bought on his friend's face, and he stopped at nothing to show it. Whenever he felt like it or thought of it, which was many a time during the day, he came to tend to the beard his merchant friend had on his chin. It made no difference to him whether his friend had company or whether he was asleep. And sometimes he wasn't too gentle about the beard, either. He'd pull it and tug it. Sometimes he'd cut it to a point, sometimes in squares or zigzag. One day he'd smear sweet-scented oil over it, and the next he'd pour on it heaven knows what.

If the poor sufferer complained, it was like talking to the wind. His crying and wailing just struck a stone wall.

"Listen, friend; listen, you there! Are you out of your mind? You're acting like a madman. Leave my beard in peace."

"Well, here is something," the one who had bought the beard cried. "Grumbling and kicking! Maybe you'd like to break your contract! You'll get into trouble if you do. The law is on my side. Just keep calm. That beard belongs to me, and I have the right to do with it as I wish."

And then he went at that beard hammer and nails. He tugged it and pulled it until the poor merchant screamed to heaven.

So time went by while the one who had bought the beard kept tearing and teasing the beard of the one who had it on his chin. In the end the poor sufferer couldn't stand it any longer.

"Little brother, good friend, I want to buy back my beard. For the love of our good God, let me have my beard again. You are making my life worse than if I lived with the Devil."

"Don't talk foolishly. I am very happy with my beard on your face. It's a nice beard; it's thick and glossy. Look how strong the roots of the hair are," he said as he began to pull it. "I want to keep it. Maybe later on we'll see what can be done."

And so he kept on taking care of the beard in his own way and as he felt like it. In the end it was too much for the bearded merchant.

"I want to buy my beard back!" he cried. "Little brother, I want my beard, you are driving me crazy. Give it back to me and I'll pay you any price."

"How much do you offer?"

"I'll give you twice as much as you paid me."

"Twice as much for this fine, thick, glossy beard! Just feel it," and he took hold of it. "You'll have to go higher, brother."

"Ow! Let go! Name any price. I'll give you whatever you ask."

"That's talking! Give me four times as much as I gave you, and you'll pay just right for your beard—and your foolishness!"

So the bearded merchant paid the other. And then he quickly went to the barber and had his beard shaved off.

The Gypsies' Fiddle

Sweden

The origin of Gypsy violinists, whose music banishes both unhappiness and strife, is explained in this tale told by Taikon, who said, "Perhaps I should not tell it to you, for part of it is very sad—how little a daughter thought of her parents and brothers and how she was punished for it. But all stories have things that are good and things that are not good. And this one also has something so good that Gypsies all over the world know it and tell it."

See also the stories "How the Gypsies Became Musicians" (pages 102–103) and "The Rom in the Piano" (pages 216–222).

In the days when the Gypsies had no fiddle on which to play, there lived a very beautiful girl who was a little bewitched. She was silly and did all kinds of foolish things.

For that reason, even though she was very beautiful and very rich, no young man would look at her or marry her.

Now, there was a young fellow, the son of a man who lived next to them, with whom she was in love. He was handsome and strong, and he was a good worker. But he would have nothing to do with the girl. He would hardly speak to her, and he never invited her to a dance, and that made her very unhappy.

One day she was walking in the woods, singing and weeping at the same time. She was thinking of her love and how unhappy she was. Suddenly there was a man walking by her side. She didn't know how he came, for she had not seen him or heard his steps. He was dressed all in green, and he had burning black eyes. From the black hair on his head stuck out two little horns, and one of his feet looked like a goat's hoof. You can guess who that was. The Evil One himself.

"I see you are crying," he said to the girl. "You are in love with the son of the man who lives next to you, and he does not love you. But if you are willing to do a little thing for me, and do what I tell you, he will love you more than life and marry you quickly."

"I will do anything in the world for him to love me," the girl said.

"Then just make me a present of your father and mother and your four brothers, and in return I will give you an instrument and teach you how to play it. When he hears you play he will love you with a love that has no end, and he will do everything in the world for you."

And the silly girl said, "You can have my father and mother and brothers, you can have everything, so long as my love will marry me."

Goat's-Foot changed the father of that girl into a fiddle, her mother he changed into a bow, and out of her white hair he made the bowstrings. The four brothers he changed into four fiddle strings. Then he sat down with the girl and taught her how to play the violin. Soon she played so sweetly the insects stopped flying to listen and the boughs of the trees began twisting and dancing. It was music that went into the heart and brought tears to the eyes.

No music like it had ever been played before. When the young man she loved heard it, he forgot home and hearth and work and dance. He married her at once, and they were very happy together for many years. No sadness ever came to their home, because the silvery music of the fiddle worked a spell that drove all unhappiness away, even as it does to this day.

One summer day the two were in the woods. After playing tunes on the fiddle that melted the heart, they went to look for berries, leaving the fiddle behind. When they came back in the twilight to look for it, they could not find it. All the looking in the world was of no use, because Old Nick with the horns had hidden it from their eyes. As the two walked home without the fiddle, he came with a carriage and four black horses and whisked them away, and they were never seen again.

For years and years the fiddle lay in the woods, hidden under moss and leaves. How long it lay there I don't know, so I can't tell you.

One day some Gypsies camped in that forest. One of the Gypsy boys went out to gather sticks for the fire and came to the place where the fiddle lay and by accident hit one of the strings with a piece of wood. There was a sound more beautiful than any he had ever heard, and he was frightened and ran off. But he couldn't forget the magic sound, and so he came back and got the violin and bow out from under the moss and the leaves. As he began moving the bow on the strings, rich and exciting sounds poured forth. He kept on moving that bow, making up music, which Gypsies always do to this day. The birds stopped singing and the wind stopped blowing just to listen to him. He ran back to camp and played the fiddle for his tribe. Never before had they heard such melodies, and it worked a spell on them. When the tune was sad, they were sad; when the music was wild, they felt wild.

Quickly the other Gypsies learned how to play the fiddle, and they made other fiddles and taught other Gypsies how to play. So now nearly all Gypsies can play it, and they play the most heavenly melodies in the world. For only such melodies can come from that instrument.

That is how the Gypsies got their fiddle, and it has been their instrument ever since, the instrument they love most.

Jorška Who Came Back
from the Dead

Sweden

This third tale from Taikon's repertoire is a "true" story about
what can happen when Gypsies don't follow the old ways. For a
similar story, see the Argentinian tale "The Gypsy of Tucumán,"
page 165.

There was a woman called Jerja. She was the mother of Vorja,
Bessik's wife. Her husband was named Jorška, of the Perikoni, I believe.
Now listen!

Jorška died. This happened somewhere in Russia. It must have been
at the end of the last century. But his children were all young; the eldest
boy, Grantja, was only twelve or thirteen years old. Jorška died a sudden
death, without any illness. As is customary, they dressed him in his Gypsy
clothes, bought a coffin, and laid him out in it. According to custom they
held a wake for him, and this they did in the usual manner. They were
poor people, so it wasn't very elaborate.

When death is in a home, no one goes to bed. But they do not always
sit up with the dead person: sometimes they mourn in their own tents.
His wife sat up with him, but the others held a wake in their own homes.
Jorška did not want to die. He had his small children and a young wife,
and it was sad to leave them alone.

"Now they are all grieving and mourning bare-headed," he says—
to those he meets in the next world, you understand.

"Oh! Only your wife sits up and mourns. The others are in their
own homes, they are not sitting up," reply those in the world where the
dead man has gone.

"But no! How can you say such a thing? I know they are mourning:
they are weeping and lamenting."

"Well, if you doubt our words, go back. Go and see for yourself if
what we said is true: only your wife is mourning."

So he returned to life! He said to his wife, "Jerja, give me your
hand."

And although she was afraid, she gave him her hand, calling out loudly, "Jorška is awake! He has come back to life!"

Then they all came running—but had their hats on their heads!

Jorška said, "Oh, my dear friends, I have permission to live six weeks more. But had you come bare-headed, I would have been allowed to live on for many years."

The coffin was then burned: they did not return it.

And now they lived gloriously for six weeks. They gave Jorška the best of everything and entertained him in the finest manner: they all helped. You see, it is uncanny to know when one is going to die. And when other Gypsy clans heard about it, they came to the camp and went along with Jorška's folk to see what would happen.

And exactly six weeks after he had come to life, he died. Since then no one has heard from him.

The Bride and the Egg Yolk

United States

Carol Miller, writer and anthropologist, who was told this story in the 1960s, comments, "Among the American Rom, a wedding is a party, noisy and lively with music and dancing, cakes, whiskey, and tables of food. The star of the wedding is the bride, and, as in the story, she is often too nervous to eat. Arriving in a red ballgown, she is dressed by the new mother-in-law and sisters-in-law, this time in white and twenty-four-karat gold. It is the pride of the groom's family to cover her chest with gold coins, chains, gold jewelry of the best quality, heirloom gold, gold with meaning to the family history . . . So arrayed, she is danced in a line with her male relatives, and then the female relatives, the wedding staff leading the way, tapping out an insistent beat that pays little mind to the music. By tradition, the wedding will last three days, three parties, and nearly every ritual event finds the bride at the center."

Notice the thwarted *gaje* thieves, as it is the Gypsies who are usually cast in this role.

This was in the old days. A young girl was very nervous at her wedding. She didn't eat—there was too much to do. It was a big wedding, lots of people, a big party that lasted into the night. Late that night she peeled an egg, ate the white, and put the yolk in her mouth. She was so nervous she forgot to chew, and the yolk stuck in her throat and she died. So instead of a wedding the people had a funeral.

The next night two *gaje* men who had seen her all dressed up for the wedding with all the gold chains and gold coins came to rob her. They opened her coffin. One of them placed his foot on her chest to yank off the necklaces, and the yolk popped out. Catching her breath, she coughed and said, "What am I doing here?" She frightened the *gaje* away. They didn't get the gold.

Then she walked back to the camp and found her people. They were scared because they knew she had died. She said, "I'm not a ghost, I'm alive." And she lived another forty years.

This is a true story.

The Jealous Husband

Rumania

The popularity of this tale in both oral and literary traditions reflects the eternal status of jealousy as an issue in relationships. (Alfred Adler once opened a jealousy clinic but had to close it because it wasn't effective.) The theme of the wager on the wife's chastity figures in Shakespeare's *Cymbeline* and also in Boccaccio, the probable source for this plot element of Shakespeare's play.

This Gypsy version is one of several folktales and songs published by Dr. Franz Miklosich in 1874 in Romani and Latin. Groome writes in his introduction, "They were collected by Professor Leo Kirilowicz, of Czernowicz, but when, where, or from whom is not told."

Once there was a great and wealthy merchant, and he had a beautiful wife. He never let her go out of the house.

One time he and another merchant each went in a ship on the Danube to buy goods. On their way home they hauled their ships to the bank and moored them there for the night.

They started talking, and the second merchant said, "Does your wife have a lover at home?"

And he answered, "My wife doesn't have a lover."

"Come, what will you wager that I cannot become her lover?"

"If you do, I will give you my estate, and my merchandise too, ship and all."

"How will I prove that I am her lover?"

"If you tell me her birthmark and if you take the gold ring from her finger. But my wife is more likely to thrash you if you but hint of such a thing to her. I left a maid with her to see that she doesn't leave the house."

"I will succeed, though."

"Go to my home and try. I'll bring your ship."

So to the first merchant's home went the second merchant. Knowing that he could not approach the wife, he found an old woman and asked her, "What must I do to get the lady's ring?"

"What will you give me if I contrive that you get it?"

"I will give you a hundred florins."

"Have a big chest made with a window in it and get into it. Make a bolt inside and I will carry you to her."

She carried him in the chest under the wall of the house and went to the lady. "I beg you, lady, to take in my box of clothes, to keep them from being stolen."

"Carry it into the hall."

She called the maid, who helped her to carry the chest into the hall.

"I beg you, lady, to let me take it right into your house. I'll come in the morning to get it."

"Well, put it in a corner." The old woman did, and went home.

At night the lady took a bath. She put her ring on the table while she washed herself. Through the little window in the chest the merchant saw a mole under her right breast.

The lady slept all night in her bed, having forgotten the ring on the table when she put out the candle. The merchant let himself out, took the ring off the table, got back into the chest, and bolted himself in.

The old woman came next morning at daybreak and carried her chest outside. The merchant opened it, came out, and departed with the chest. He went to meet the husband and found him on the way.

"Have you slept with my wife?"

"I have."

"What is her birthmark?"

"She has a mole under her right breast. If you do not believe me, here is the ring as well."

"Then you must take the ship and everything in it. Come home with me, and I will give you the estate as well."

He went home and said never a word to his wife. He made a little boat and put her in it and let it go on the Danube. "Since you have done this, away you go on the Danube."

He gave away his whole estate, and became poor, and carried water for the Jews.

A whole year the wife floated on the Danube—the year went like a day. An old man caught her boat and brought it to shore. He opened the boat and took her out and brought her to his house. She lived with him three years and spun with her spindle and made some money. And she bought herself splendid men's clothes and dressed herself and cut her hair short and set off for her husband's city.

Now, in that city the emperor was blind. On her way the merchant's wife stopped by a lime tree to rest, and fell asleep. Then she had a dream: in the lime tree was a hole filled with water, and if the emperor would anoint himself with that water he would see.

She arose in the morning and searched around and found the hole. With a little bottle she drew some water from it and put it in her pocket, then went into that city to an inn and drank three kreutzers' worth of brandy. And she asked the Jewish innkeeper, "What's the news around here?"

"Our emperor is blind, and he will give his kingdom to him who shall make him see."

"I will do so."

The inkeeper went to the emperor with this news, and the emperor replied, "Ha! Go and bring him to me."

So she was brought, still in disguise, to the emperor. "Will you make me see? Then I will give you my daughter."

She took some water from the bottle and anointed his eyes, and he saw. The emperor set his crown on her head. "You be emperor. I want nothing but to stay beside you." The emperor clad her royally, called his army, beat the drum. "Now there's a new emperor."

And she saw her husband carrying water for the Jews. "Come here. Tell me, have you always been so poor?"

"No, once I was not poor, I was rich. I had an estate and I was a great merchant."

"Then how did you lose your estate?"

"I lost it over a wager. My wife was unfaithful and I gave up the estate and sent her adrift on the Danube."

Straightaway she sent for the other man, and he was brought. "How did you come by this man's estate?"

"Over a wager."

"What was your wager?"

"That I would make love to his wife."

"Then you did so?"

"I did."

"And, pray, what were her birthmarks?"

"Under her right breast she had a mole."

"Would you know the mole again?"

"I would."

Then she drew out her breast. "Did you sleep with me?"

"I did not."

"Then why all those lies? Here, take him, and cut him all to pieces."

And she looked earnestly at her husband. "You, why did you not ask me at the time?"

"I was a fool, and I was angry."

"Here, take him outside and give him five-and-twenty, to teach him wisdom."

Then she took off her robes and put them on him. "You be emperor, and I'll be empress."

The Toad's Revenge

France

This lyrical, anonymous story comes from a contemporary French children's book meant in part to acquaint readers with the Gypsy point of view. The tale ends with a fantasy of Gypsy revenge against the racism of the dominant society, a sad comment on Gypsy/non-Gypsy relations.

This happened before people existed and took control of the earth.

At that time only the trees were immobile. All other living things moved around freely. Even the flowers went visiting their friends: rabbits, squirrels, hedgehogs, birds, insects—everything that walked or crawled or flew. Sometimes the fish would join them, because they could leave the water. They all could speak and understand each other.

One night, in a clearing, there was a big celebration: people told stories, and the birds gave a concert followed by a dance. The squirrel danced with the periwinkle, the rabbits with carnations. Each flower had its partner. Even the spider frisked about with the dragonfly. Joy was everywhere.

The toad, who hadn't been invited because he was too ugly, showed up anyway. He turned to a tulip, but she rejected him.

Everyone began making fun of him and joined together in a circle around the poor toad, who was shaking with rage.

"You're hideous! You're hideous!" hooted an owl. Animals and flowers turned and pointed their fingers, repeating, "You're hideous! You're hideous!"

Then the toad lost his temper. "You awful things!" he shouted. "I'll have my revenge on you!"

He blew himself up more and more, so much that the poison spurted out of his skin and splashed over them all.

The fish took refuge in the water, the birds dispersed among the branches, and when the flowers tried to hide by embedding themselves in the soil, they drooped instead.

And since that night nothing was as before: animals and flowers could no longer speak, and didn't understand. The flowers couldn't move from their places. As for the fish, they died as soon as someone took them out of water.

This story is of the Gypsy who perhaps one day will get revenge for the scorn of the *gajo*.

Tale of a Foolish Brother and of a Wonderful Bush

Poland

This story of a male Cinderella was told to Dr. Isidore Kopernicki by John Čoron sometime between 1875 and 1877 in Cracow. The theme of the triumph of the humble hero and everyone's eventual recognition of her or his worth has always been very satisfying psychologically and politically, which accounts for the universal popularity of this tale type.

There is a hint at the start of the story that the characters are meant to be Gypsies: the mention of the two "wise" brothers' narrative abilities alludes to the Gypsies' tradition of being distinguished storytellers.

There was once a poor peasant who had three sons, two of them wise and one foolish. One day the king gave a feast, to which everybody was invited, rich and poor. These two wise brothers set out for the feast like the rest, leaving the poor fool at home crouching over the stove. He thereupon begged his mother to allow him to go after his brothers. But his mother answered, "Fool that you are! Your brothers go there to tell tales, while you, you know nothing. What could you tell?"

Still the fool continued to beg his mother to let him go, but still she refused. "Very well!" he said. "If you won't let me go there, with the help of God I will know what to do."

Well, one day the king built a tower. He placed his daughter on the second story and issued a proclamation that whoever could kiss his daughter there would have her in marriage. Well, various princes and nobles hastened to the place, but not one of them could reach her.

The king then decreed that the peasants were to come and try. This order reached the house of the peasant who had three sons, two wise and one foolish. The two wise brothers arose and set out. The fool pretended to go in search of water, but instead he went to a bush and struck it three times with a stick. Whereupon a fairy appeared and asked, "What would you have?"

"I wish to have a horse of silver, garments of silver, and a sum of money."

After he had received all these things, he set out on his way. Whom should he happen to overtake on the road but his two wise brothers?

"Where are you going?" he asked them.

"We are going to a king's palace—the one with the tower upon the second story of which he has placed his daughter; and he has proclaimed that whoever kisses her shall become her husband."

The fool got off his horse, cut himself a cudgel, and began to beat his two brothers; finally he gave them each three ducats. The two brothers did not recognize him, and so he went on by himself, unknown.

When he had come to the king's palace, all the great lords looked with admiration at this prince mounted on a silver steed and clad in garments of silver. He leapt up with a great spring toward the princess and almost got near enough to kiss her. He fell back again and then took his departure.

These noblemen then asked one another, "What is the meaning of this? He had scarcely arrived when he all but succeeded in kissing the princess."

The fool then returned home and went to the bush and struck it three times. The fairy again appeared and asked him, "What is your will?"

He commanded her to hide his horse and his clothes. He took his buckets filled with water and went back into the house.

"Where have you been?" asked his mother.

"Mother, I have been outside, and I stripped myself, and—pardon me for saying so—I have been hunting lice in my shirt."

"That is well," said his mother, and she gave him some food.

On the return of the two wise brothers, their mother wanted them to tell her what they had seen.

"Mother, we saw there a prince mounted on a silver steed, and he was himself clad in silver. He had overtaken us on the road, and asked us where we were going. We told him the truth, that we were going to the palace of the king who had built the tower, on the second story of which he had placed his daughter, decreeing that whoever should get near enough to give her a kiss would marry her. The prince dismounted, cut himself a cudgel, gave us a sound beating, and then gave us each three ducats."

The mother was very well pleased to get this money, for she was poor and could now buy herself something to eat.

Next day these two brothers set out again. The mother cried to her foolish son, "Go and fetch me some water." He went out to get the water, laid down his pails beside the well, and went to the bush; he struck it three times, and the fairy appeared. "What is your will?"

"I wish to have a horse of gold and golden garments."

The fairy brought him a horse of gold, golden garments, and a sum of money besides. Off he set, and once more he overtook his brothers on the road. This time he did not dismount, but, cudgel in hand, he charged upon his brothers, beat them severely, and gave them ten ducats apiece. He then took himself to the king.

The nobles gazed admiringly at him seated on his horse of gold and attired in golden garb. With a single bound he reached the second story and gave the princess a kiss. Well, they wished to detain him, but he sprang away and fled like the wind.

He came back to his bush, and the fairy appeared and asked him, "What is your will?"

"Hide my horse and my clothes."

He dressed himself in his wretched clothes and went into the house again.

"Where have you been?" asked his mother.

"I have been sitting in the sun, and—excuse me for saying it—I have been hunting lice in my shirt."

She answered nothing but gave him some food. He went and squatted down behind the stove in idiot fashion. The two wise brothers arrived. Their mother looked at them and asked, "Who has mauled you so terribly?"

"It was that prince, Mother."

"And why have you not laid a complaint against him before the king?"

"But he gave us ten ducats apiece."

"I will not send you anymore to that king," said their mother.

"Mother, they have posted sentinels all over the town to arrest the prince; for he has already kissed the king's daughter, after which he took flight. That's when the sentinels were posted. We are certain to catch this prince."

The fool then said to them, "How will you be able to seize him, since evidently he knows a trick or two?"

"You are a fool," said the two wise brothers to him. "We are bound to capture him."

"Capture away," replied the fool.

Three days later the two wise brothers set out, leaving the fool cowering behind the stove.

"Go and fetch some wood," called his mother.

He roused himself and went. He came to the bush and struck it three times. Out came the fairy and asked, "What do you demand?"

"I demand a horse of diamonds, garments of diamonds, and some money."

He arrayed himself and set out. He overtook his two brothers, but this time he did not beat them. He gave them each twenty ducats. He reached the king's city, and the nobles tried to seize him. He sprang up to the second story, and for the second time he kissed the princess, who gave him her gold ring.

Well, they wished to capture him, but he said to them, "If you had all the wit in the world you could not catch me."

But they were determined to seize him. He fled like the wind. He came to the bush and struck it three times. Out came the fairy, who took his horse and his clothes. He gathered some wood and returned to the house.

His mother was pleased with him and said, "There, now! That is how you should always behave." And she gave him something to eat. He went and crouched behind the stove. His two brothers arrived, and their mother questioned them.

"Mother," they answered, "this prince could not be taken."

"And has he not given you a beating?"

"No, Mother, on the contrary, he gave us each twenty ducats more."

"Tomorrow," said their mother, "you will not go there again."

And the two brothers answered, "We will go there no more."

Aha! So much the better.

This king gave yet another feast, and he decreed: "All the princes, as many as there shall be of them, shall come to my palace so that my daughter may identify her husband-to-be among them." This feast lasted four days, but the intended husband of the princess was not there. What did this king do? He ordained a third feast for beggars and poor country folk, and he decreed: "Everyone come, be he blind or lame, let him not be ashamed, but come."

This feast lasted for a week, but the fiancé of the princess was not there. What did the king do then? He sent his servants with the order to go from house to house and bring back the man upon whom should be found the princess's ring. "Be he blind or lame, let him be brought to me," said the king.

Well, the servants went from house to house for a week, and all who were found in each house they called together, in order to make the search. At last they came to the house in which dwelt the fool. As soon as the fool saw them, he went and lay down upon the stove. In came the king's servants, gathered the people of the house together, and asked the fool, "What are you doing there?"

"What does that matter to you?" asked the fool.

And his mother said to them, "Sirs, he is a fool."

"No matter," said they, "fool or blind, we gather together all whom we see, for so the king has commanded us."

They made the fool come down from the stove; they looked; the gold ring was on his finger.

"So then, it is you who are so clever."

"It is I."

He made ready and set out with them. He had nothing upon him, this fool, but a miserable shirt and a cloak all tattered and torn. He came to the king, to whom the servants said, "Sire, we bring him to you."

"Is this really he?"

"The very man."

They showed the ring.

"Well, this is he."

The king commanded that sumptuous garments be made for him as quickly as possible. In these clothes he presented a very comely appearance. The king was well pleased; the wedding came off; and they were living happily.

Some time after, another king declared war against this one: "Since you have not given your daughter in marriage to my son, I will make war against you." But this king, the fool's father-in-law, had two sons. The fool also made preparations and went to war. His two brothers-in-law went in advance, and the fool set out after them. He took a shortcut and, having placed himself on their line of march, sat down on the edge of a pond and amused himself hunting frogs. These two wise brothers-in-law approached.

"Just look at him, see what he is doing; he is not thinking of the war but only amusing himself hunting frogs."

These two brothers went on, and the fool mounted his horse and went to his bush. He struck it three times, and the fairy appeared before him.

"What do you demand?"

"I demand a magnificent horse and a saber with which I may be able to exterminate the entire army, and some of the most beautiful clothes."

He speedily dressed himself, girded on his saber, mounted his horse, and set forth. Having overtaken his two brothers-in-law on the road, he asked them, "Where are you going?"

"We are going to the war."

"So am I. Let's all go together."

He reached the field of battle, where he cut all his enemies to pieces. Not a single one of them escaped.

The fool returned home. He hid his horse and his saber and all the rest so that nobody would know anything of them. The two brothers arrived after the fool had returned. The king asked them, "Were you at the war, my children?"

"Yes, Father, we were there, but your son-in-law was not there."

"And what was he doing?"

"He! He was amusing himself hunting frogs. But a prince came and cut the whole army to pieces. Not a soul of them has escaped."

Then the king reproached his daughter thus: "What, then, have you done to marry a husband who amuses himself catching frogs?"

"Is the fault mine, Father? Even as God has given him to me, so will I keep him."

The next day the king's two sons did not go to battle, but the king himself was to go, along with his son-in-law. The fool mounted his horse quicker, however, and set out first, so the king came after, not knowing where his son-in-law had gone. Arriving at the battlefield, the king found the whole of the enemy's army already cut to pieces, but the one who had done this he did not recognize as his son-in-law. The other king said to this one that he would never again wage war against him. They shook hands with each other, these two kings.

The fool had been wounded in his big toe. His father-in-law noticed it and dressed the wound with his own handkerchief, which was marked with the king's name.

The fool got home before his father-in-law. He pulled off his boots and lay down to sleep, for his foot pained him. When the king came home, his sons asked him, "Father, was our brother-in-law at the war?"

"No, I saw nothing of him there, but a prince was there who has exterminated the whole army. Then this king and I shook hands in token that never more should there be war between us."

Then his daughter said, "My husband has my father's handkerchief around his foot."

The king bounded forth. He looked at the handkerchief: it was his! It bore his name.

"So, then, it is you who are so clever."

"Yes, Father, it is I."

The king was very joyful. So were his sons and the queen and the wife of the fool—all were filled with joy. Well, they held the wedding all over again, and they lived together with the help of the good, golden God.

The Dream

Italy

This entertaining story of the Gypsy outwitting his opponent by employing a dream is an Italian version of a tale also found in collections of Czechoslovakian Gypsy folktales. The storyteller here is Bruno Levak, also known by his Gypsy name, Zlato. Mirella Karpati, editor of the Italian journal of Gypsy studies, *Lacio Drom*, collaborated with Levak on the book in which this story and "The

Gypsy Lawyer" (pages 142–143) are found. Zlato and his son Mile and his family spent the winter of 1975–1976 in an old convent near Rome made over into a meeting place for Gypsies. Sitting in front of the fireplace in the evenings and telling folktales to his extended family, Zlato first had the idea of publishing his stories.

Once there was a Gypsy hammering away at a pot behind a hedge, where he was taking shelter from the wind. A rabbit passed by, and the Gypsy threw his hammer at it. Exactly at that moment a hunter shot at the rabbit. The rabbit fell dead, and the two quarreled over whose it was.

"Okay," said the Gypsy. "If you invite me for dinner at your house, we can think about what to do."

They went home, and the hunter's wife prepared a fine dinner for them. Finally the Gypsy said, "Listen, I know what we'll do. At this point the rabbit is neither yours nor mine. We'll go to sleep, and the rabbit will belong to whoever has the more beautiful dream. And don't worry about me: just give me an old blanket and I can sleep on the floor here in the kitchen near the stove."

And that's what they did. The hunter went upstairs with his wife, and the Gypsy stretched out on the kitchen floor.

Morning came. The hunter came downstairs and said, "Okay, let's get started. Tell me your dream."

"No, no, tell me yours first. You're more important than I am."

"Then I'll tell mine. Last night in my dream I saw a long, long staircase. I kept climbing up and up . . . At a certain moment the heavens opened and I entered paradise: flowers, light, music. I couldn't possibly tell you how beautiful it was. Well, it was so beautiful that I didn't want to return. A splendid dream. And you, what was your dream?"

"Oddly enough, I had the same dream. I saw you climbing that long staircase into heaven. And I figured you wouldn't want to come back, so I ate the rabbit."

The Golden Girl

Hungary

This story, a folktale/lullaby, was told in 1985 by twenty-nine-year-old Mihály Jakab to his six-month-old son, David Jakab (nicknamed Dénesh). They live in Gyöngyös, a city forty miles from Budapest in northeast Hungary, where Jakab is a factory worker.

The story was collected by Judit Szegő as part of a research project designed and headed by Zita Réger on the linguistic socialization of Hungarian Gypsy children. The researchers discovered that a rich oral tradition surrounds the Gypsy child from birth onward. Besides folktales such as this one, the tradition includes long, improvised monologues in which the child's mother tells of events and conflicts in the child's future life in a folktale-like way.

Now my Dénesh will fall asleep at once—for I will tell him a beautiful tale. Once upon a time, if this evening had not been, even this tale would not have been. Well, there was a small boy and a little girl whose mother and father had died. They had nothing, and they had to wander and wander from one village to another just to get a piece of bread for themselves. One time the brother said, "Oh, my sister, how thirsty I am! But look, here's a little puddle, I'll take a drink from it."

"My dear brother," she said, "for God's sake don't drink from it. Something bad could happen to you."

Well, the boy drank from the puddle anyway, and he turned into a fawn. His sister cried over him, "What have we done? My little brother drank from the puddle, and now he's a fawn."

They kept walking along and it happened that whenever the girl laughed gold coins dropped from her mouth, and when she cried diamonds fell from her eyes.

Now it happened that the boy changed back to his original form and left the girl alone while he went to serve the king as a coachman. And it struck everyone there that though this coachman never lit a lamp, the stable was always lit as if a hundred lamps were burning. Well, my son, one day the king called him in and said, "Listen, if you don't tell me immediately where you get that light from, I'll cut off your head."

And the boy answered, "Listen, my great king, I'll tell you. The light comes from my sister's hair."

"Well then, tell me where she is."

Then the boy answered that he had left his sister in the forest in a little hut, and he added, "My sister laughs gold coins and cries diamond tears, and when she combs her hair golden hairs fall from her head."

Then he set out after his sister. But meanwhile, you know, an old witch and her daughter, who were traveling through the forest, found the golden-haired girl and put her in their cart. When the cart jerked, the witch said that she would take out one of the girl's eyes—and indeed she did. And then, there you are, the cart jerked again, and this time the witch took the girl's other eye. When the cart jerked for the third time, what did the witch and her daughter do? They told the girl they'd throw her in a puddle—and so they did.

Soon they arrived at the king's palace, where everyone had been waiting, and they mistook the witch's daughter for the golden girl. First they made her laugh, and frogs came out of her mouth. Then they made her cry, and lizards fell out of her eyes. Last, they combed her hair, and out fell frogs and snakes. Well, they could do nothing but take the boy and throw him into prison.

The boy said, "Dear Lord, what's happened to my sister? Where can she be?"

Well, my Dénesh, there was an old woman walking along with brushwood on her back. She heard a voice calling from the woods: "Oh, what have they done to me? They've taken away my life! Where can my brother be?"

The old woman said, "Oh, my dear child, who are you, crying there? Where three can grow up, you can too." And she took her home, where she bathed her and combed her hair. As she was combing the girl's hair, golden hairs fell all around, and when the other three children made her laugh, gold coins fell from her mouth. Then the old woman said, "My daughter, tell us your story." And she told them everything.

Then the old woman brought the girl all sorts of things—beautiful presents, small chestnuts, pears, apples—and she covered them all with gold, and took them to the market.

At once a girl asked the price, but the old woman wouldn't sell anything—she would only exchange her goods for eyes. Then the girl—who was the witch's daughter—said, "At home my mother's got two eyes up on the rafters." And she ran home to get the eyes and trade them for two golden pears.

Then the old woman went home, washed the eyes, and put them

back in the girl's face. The girl said, "Oh, my dear mother, now I can see again! Thank you for doing this for me. But where can my brother be?"

This was a great problem—do you understand, my son? Now the old woman searched and searched until she found the boy in prison. When she found him, my little Dénesh, she brought him home and he said, "This is really my sister. Look, she is just as I said."

Just then the witch showed up and tried to cut the girl's throat with a big knife, but the boy wouldn't let her. He said, "Wasn't it enough that you put me in prison? And that first you took my sister's eyes out and then threw her into a puddle? Now you want to kill her?"

Now the boy took his sister to the king. When the king first saw her he almost died—that's how beautiful she was. As you are! The girl burst into laughter and laughed gold coins all around. When they combed her hair, gold hairs fell. And diamonds dropped from her eyes when the girl started to cry because of the old woman: "My Lord, where can she be? She who protected me and did not let me get lost and gave me back my eyes."

So they went off and found the old woman. Then they had a very very big feast where everyone ate and drank. We were there too, and I told them to put a piece of bone into your hand, my son, because your mother wasn't with you and you were crying. But in the meantime, you know, the old witch was cut into four parts and they threw her ashes to the wind. Now, this was so, my Dénesh, and here you are, and this is the tale.

The Gypsy Woman and the Cave

Greece

This and the next two stories were told by Lazaros Harisiadis, a Greek Gypsy musician who has been living in New York City for more than twenty years. He comes from a family of musicians in

northern Greece and performs there during the summer festivals.
About storytelling traditions in his family, Harisiadis had the following to say: "My mother and father went around to all the villages
and knew a lot of people. Whenever we would all meet up, the
women would leave and the men would sit alone. In those days
there weren't any radios, TV, phonographs, and so on, but everyone
knew one or two hours' worth of folktales, and so the time went
by until dawn. We didn't have blankets and we were cold, but we
warmed ourselves telling the folktales that I'm telling you now and
other old stories. The old men told them so we, the younger ones,
could learn them, and this is the wealth that stays with us today.
And so our riches are in these stories, not in our pockets."

Once upon a time, in the old days, Gypsy caravans traveled from
village to village, from city to city, and the Gypsies would beg and tell
fortunes for a piece of bread.

Well, the Gypsies were wandering along from place to place. In one
city there was a woman who didn't like her neighbor—the two women
were always quarreling, day after day. This woman called a Gypsy woman
over to tell her fortune: "Come here. I'll give you whatever you want if
you can tell me what's in my heart."

Just at that moment the neighbor came out of her house and made
an insulting gesture to the first woman. The Gypsy woman noticed this
and said, "You live in a really bad neighborhood and things aren't going
well for you in this house. Your neighbors are jealous of you, because
you're a good housewife and all that."

"Bravo! You found out everything! What do you want me to give
you? I'd even give you my heart." So she gave her bread, cheese, and
money, and as the Gypsy was leaving for the camp the woman said,
"Come tomorrow, I have something for you to do." And the Gypsy
promised to come back.

Now, Gypsies were forbidden to camp for the night near the city,
so they had set up their tents some distance away. The next day, as the
Gypsy woman was walking back to the city, all of a sudden it started to
rain very hard. It was the month of March. The Gypsy woman searched
everywhere for shelter and finally found an entrance to a cave. She went
inside and looked around carefully in the depths, where she saw a small
light. As she got closer, she saw it was a large fire. "Ah, I'll warm up
nicely here."

She looked around and saw twelve young men in nice clothes and good shoes, and they said to her in unison, "Welcome. Tell us, grandmother, where are you going?"

"I'm on my way back to the city, my children, but I got caught in the downpour, and what could I do? I found this cave and came in through the entrance and found you, my golden children."

"Do you know why it's raining? It's the month of March—and in March the cold is awful and the snow . . . what a terrible month it is!"

"Don't say that, my children. The month of March is the best."

"Why?"

"Because it brings us April, when spring comes. Without the month of March, we wouldn't have any spring. And if there were no February, there would be no March."

And so for each of the months she had something good to say.

"And now where are you going?" they asked her.

"I want to return to my tent to feed my hungry children."

"Bring your sack over here," they said, and filled it and sewed it up. "Take it, but don't open it until you get home."

The old woman returned to her tent and said to her children, "Well, today I didn't go to any homes. But I found golden children, little angels, twelve handsome young men. And they gave me this—what it has inside I don't know. Let's see what's inside."

They opened it, and what did they find? All golden coins. The twelve golden young men were really the Twelve Months, and the Gypsy woman, because she hadn't insulted any of the months, got the treasure.

The next day the weather was perfectly clear. The Gypsy woman ran to the woman she'd promised to see. As much gold as she'd gotten, she still wanted to beg—that's the Gypsy way, and that's why people say Gypsies are never satisfied.

On the way she met the quarrelsome neighbor, who recognized her and said, "Whatever she gives you, I'll give you more. Now tell me what you want."

"What can I say? I don't want you to give me anything, for God has provided."

"What did God give you?"

She told her how she'd found the cave and gone in to get out of the rain.

"Where's the entrance to this cave? I'll go see."

And so she went on her way to the Twelve Months, but without knowing who they were. She found the entrance just where the Gypsy had told her, and went into the cave, pretending to be cold.

"What month is it, old woman, that it's so cold outside?"

"It's March—the cruelest, worst month in the year."

"What do you have to say about February?"

"That stupid February?" And she went on to curse all the months, without a good word to say about any of them.

"Give us your sack." They filled it and sewed it up and told her to open it only when she got home. She hoped to find gold inside—it was heavy! She thought it would be the same as the Gypsy's. But when she got back to the city and opened it, what was inside? Lots of snakes that came out and ate everything, including her.

Her neighbor said, "The Gypsy knew everything. My neighbor was truly a bad woman. So the Gypsy did her magic."

And that's why since then people, even today, ten million years later, still say that Gypsies know everything. And it's true.

They lived well in those days, and we live even better.

Forty Scatterbrained Gypsies

Greece

In this tale Lazaros Harisiadis gives an account of how Gypsies came by the intelligence they are famous for. The antics of the Gypsies bring to mind two of their folkloric counterparts: the citizenry of the Finnish town of Holmola and the Wise Men of the Jewish town of Helm.

Once upon a time, in the old days, in the days of our great-great-grandfathers, seven hundred, eight hundred, maybe nine hundred years ago, there lived the forty Gypsies who will never be forgotten.

A mayor decided to send forty Gypsies to cut down one tree to build the belfry of the city's church. He said to one of the Gypsies, "I'll make you leader and you have to find thirty-nine other Gypsies like you. And I'll give all of you money, axes, heavy ropes, and you can have whatever else you ask for if you just bring that wood from the distant forest."

"Of course, Mayor."

(I heard this, naturally, from my grandfather, he from his own grandfather, and so on, back many hundreds of years. That means this tale is very old. But it won't disappear, because I offer it to my children, and my children will tell it to their children, and so on. And it won't be forgotten, because it's unforgettable.)

The forty Gypsies arose and went on the road into the forest. Each one had forty *groschia*—that was the money then, not drachmas. And each had one heavy rope and one ax. And bread, cheese, halvah, and olives in their sacks. And so they went on their way.

In the forest they kept searching and searching for just the right tree to cut down. By sunset they still hadn't found an appropriate tree. Then they saw a shepherd coming down with his sheep, around seven hundred of them, so they whistled to him and called for him to join them.

"What do you want, young men?" the shepherd asked.

"We want you to slaughter some sheep so we can cook and eat them."

"Bravo. Why not? The sheep have to pass over a stream; any that fall in, we'll keep for slaughter."

All the hardy sheep were able to jump over the stream. Only five old ones fell into the water. When the Gypsies asked the shepherd how much he wanted for the five sheep, he asked for forty *groschia*. There were forty Gypsies, but the leader hesitated: none of them could read or figure at all.

"How come forty? Oh, you mean we *each* give forty." So they ended up buying the whole flock, and they ate the five old sheep.

Night fell. As the forty Gypsies got ready to sleep, anyone who found himself at one end or the other was scared. Three hours went by and they still couldn't figure out how to get to sleep so that nobody would be the first or the last—so that everyone would be in the middle. This was a problem they couldn't solve themselves, so they called over the shepherd, who was sleeping nearby.

"What is it you want?"

"We will pay you to figure out how we can sleep without anyone being at one end or the other."

The shepherd thought and thought. "Come with me."

He took them to a large, thick tree and tied them one by one with their heavy ropes round and round the tree. And so, in a circle, no one was either first or last.

But on one side of the tree it was a little wet. Whoever got wet got wet—they had no mattresses or blankets. When they got up in the morning they were tired and hoarse, but they called the shepherd again.

"What is it you want now?"

"For you to untie us."

"Okay. But since you have no money left, I'll take your heavy ropes and your axes."

The Gypsies were now empty-handed. They went on their way to find the tree for the church belfry, but even if they were to find it, what could they do with it? They might have used their ropes and axes, but the shepherd had them too.

But as they were walking around they saw a tree that looked just right for the belfry. The tree stood at the edge of a cliff. Their leader climbed up first, and each held on to the next one's legs until thirty-eight of them were hanging there trying to break the tree with their weight so that they could take the timber and leave.

The top Gypsy said, "Hold on tight, everyone. I just want to spit on my hands." As soon as he did, all thirty-eight of them fell off the cliff.

And so only two Gypsies remained. These two walked and walked until they were dying of hunger. Then they saw a bird.

"You see that bird?" asked the first.

"Yes."

"You see that village?"

"Yes."

"Go to that village and get fire—a torch—and bring it back so we can cook the bird."

The second Gypsy ran to get a torch while the other one took off his shoes and climbed high into the tree to catch the bird. But every time he would reach out to grab the bird, it would fly away. "Well, so you know how to fly!" he yelled. "And I don't? Here I go!" And down he fell. After he landed, he lay there dead, with his mouth open.

Now the other Gypsy returned with the torch. He had run all the way, shielding the flame so that it wouldn't go out. When he saw the dead Gypsy, he assumed he'd eaten the bird without cooking it. "Since you decided to eat the bird, now you can eat the torch as well."

And so now only one Gypsy was left out of the forty. He went on his way, passed over a bridge, and sat down to think. He started looking at the river below, clear as glass and deep.

He said, "I've lived so many years, and I've never really seen my private parts." So he leaned and leaned over the edge of the bridge in order to see better, until he fell into the river and drowned.

Now not one of the forty Gypsies was left. Truly it's because of these forty that we, the other Gypsies who are alive today, are very lucky and proud. And I'll tell you why: those forty were the scatterbrained Gypsies. All the others who remained in the cities and villages were the intelligent ones, and that's why generation after generation we are smart—those forty were the foolish ones, and all forty of them were lost.

And we're living well and they went to their reward.

Yerasimos

Greece

This tale is one of many exceptions to a standard cliché of Gypsy folklore scholarship: that Gypsy folktales never contain moralizing. Here the moralizing is combined with shrewdness. (Another story where a Gypsy tricks his way into heaven is the first tale in this volume, "How the Gypsy Went to Heaven.")

The belief that Gypsies originally came from Egypt is common to Gypsies as well as to non-Gypsies, and in fact the part of northern Greece where Lazaros Harisiadis, the storyteller, comes from was once called Little Egypt.

Once upon a time there was a Gypsy leader named Yerasimos. He had a lot of money and property left to him by his grandfather. (His grandfather's roots were in Egypt. From *Egyptian* we get *Gypsy*—that's how the name came about. We're not Gypsies, we're really Egyptians.)

One day Yerasimos woke up and said, "Where is the big casino where everyone goes to play cards?"

Some people showed him where all the rich men of that place went to play cards.

When Yerasimos went in, the people there said to him, "Hey, where do you think you're going?"

"To play cards."

"Do you have any money?"

"Of course I do."

"Let's count it then. To climb those stairs you have to show us how much you have."

It was customary for everyone admitted to the casino to have about ten thousand dollars. When Yerasimos took out a hundred thousand dollars, everyone was stunned into admiration and said to him, "After you, Mr. Yerasimos."

Yerasimos, of course, climbed the stairs proudly. In the casino, where they were playing cards, Yerasimos lost, but not a lot. In a week he returned, and the week after . . . Eventually he ruined his family by his mania for playing cards. First he argued with his family, then he sold all his property and gambled away all the money.

When at last he ended up hungry on the street, he decided to go far away from that place—to live in the desert. He actually went five hundred miles away to the desert.

There he started doing whatever an old-time farmer would do—he planted a little wheat, a little corn, so he could have something to eat. Beans, tomatoes, everything in its season. He planted some nice gardens and built a beautiful hut of grass and wood.

And that's where Yerasimos stayed. Of course, this was long ago. Jesus Christ was still alive then. One day Christ passed by with his twelve disciples. He didn't show himself as Christ, just as a simple man with twelve other men. And Christ made thirteen. They knocked on Yerasimos's door.

"Who's there?" asked Yerasimos.

"We're passersby. Night has fallen and we have nowhere to go. If we could spend the night in your hut . . . ?"

"Why not? With great pleasure." Yerasimos opened the door, and they all went in. Then he said, "Welcome. Good evening," and they all sat down. He gave them the best of everything he had in his hut. Whatever he had was at their disposal—they ate and drank well and slept soundly by a big fire. He had no bedclothes to give them, but he made a nice fire. The disciples and Jesus noted Yerasimos's kindness.

In the morning, as soon as it was light and they had drunk their coffee and started to get ready to leave, Christ said, "Yerasimos, I'd like to ask you a question."

"Why not, my son? Ask away."

"How did you end up living here in the desert where there are no other people around?"

"Ha! I needed someone like you to ask so I could tell my tale. Because if I die, no one will know my story."

"Then tell me."

Yerasimos said, "I was a Gypsy with a caravan, with brothers and sisters, cousins, and relatives. After I got married, my grandfather died, my grandmother died, my father died, my mother died, and only I remained—married with a family. Whenever I inherited money, I put it in my pocket—I didn't earn that money, so I had no respect for it. My grandfathers and father had worked for that money, but I squandered it all playing cards.

"One day I found myself on the street without a family, without a house, without property, and with no money in my pocket. And I was forced to take the road to this desert where I am today. But I'm doing fine. I'm happy—I have everything I need, including music."

"What would you wish for from God, Yerasimos? What would satisfy your heart?"

Yerasimos answered, "Oh, my son, what I want couldn't happen."

"Say it anyway—it happens sometimes. Perhaps God is listening."

"The first thing would be to return to my hometown, to see my friends and relatives. And second, to have money in my pocket—not necessarily a lot. And last, that I could always win at cards. That's what I would want."

Christ said—Yerasimos still didn't know who he was—"You have your wish, Yerasimos. Good-bye. Start on your way tonight. Leave here and go back to your hometown. And you'll always win at cards. Look in your pocket and see if you have money."

"I do!"

Christ and his disciples disappeared into thin air and left Yerasimos standing there searching through his pockets for more money. He immediately understood that a higher power was at work.

So he went back to the city he had abandoned more than ten years before. His friends saw him again, well dressed with his new cap, tie, shirt. He asked his friends, "Is that club where I used to play cards still here?"

"Of course it's here. And so are the same people who took your money, all still playing cards."

"Thank you. I'll treat them all to a drink, and you too."

"We should be the ones to treat you," they replied.

"No. Thanks to God, I have everything I need. My pockets are never empty—there's always money inside, and a lot!"

It was God's power. Whenever Yerasimos would take out one bill, ten would still be left—like the three fishes that fed five thousand people.

Yerasimos was on his way into the club when the doorman—who was new since the last time—asked him, "Where are you going, sir?"

"Don't you know me, my son?"

"No, I don't."

"Who's in charge here?"

"So-and-so."

"Tell him it's Yerasimos."

The doorman picked up the phone and called his boss. "A gentleman is asking for you."

"What's his name?"

"Yerasimos."

"Yerasimos? Send him up immediately." After all, he was well known—he'd lost millions there.

As soon as Yerasimos got upstairs, everyone who knew him stood up, and soon all the people who didn't know him found out who he was.

Yerasimos said, "We'll play as friends, calmly, since I'm no longer young. My nerves can't take it—the years have gone by. But I can still manage to play cards."

"What about money, Yerasimos?"

Yerasimos took some pennies out of his pocket, and they turned into gold coins. Of course: God's blessing. He put the coins down.

They played, and Yerasimos kept winning. Everyone was amazed at his perseverance. He won back the property he had lost, and then he started to win the property of the very people he had originally lost his own property to.

He kept winning all kinds of things until he finally said, "That's enough. Of course, I'll give my property to my family, whom I so deprived that they ended up on the street. And I'll give some of my winnings to my other relatives and to other poor people here in the city." He had won houses, farms, plots of land, and he gave them all away to poor girls for their dowries, and so on.

Now he was very old, and as the time was approaching for him to die, he wrote a note: "When I die, friends and relatives, remember to put playing cards with me in my coffin." At last the day came when Yerasimos died, and his note wasn't forgotten—they did put cards in his coffin with him.

For forty days his spirit wandered everywhere, like a young man's. On the fortieth day he came to the door where you go either to heaven or to hell.

Archangel Michael, who along with St. Peter had the keys, asked Yerasimos, "Which way are you going, Mr. Yerasimos?"

Yerasimos answered, "Why should I tell you? Do I need to tell you? *You're* the ones who took me—I just have to keep on going. But open the door."

They opened the door, and he went in. Then they said, "We'll go first and you afterwards. You won't stay here in hell. You'll go straight to heaven."

All the people who were watching him—his old acquaintances who had died before him—ran to welcome him. "We want to go where you're headed—it's no good down here in hell."

One, two, three, four, five . . . they became nine, all friends, and Yerasimos was the tenth. As soon as he opened the door to go to heaven, the others tried to follow him but couldn't.

Yerasimos said, "The man who came to my hut said I would always win at cards. Let's play, and if I win, I can take them with me to heaven. If not, I won't."

The archangel thought, *Could a simple man like this win a game of cards with* me? "Okay," he said. "Let's play. Sit down."

Christ suddenly appeared at the door, just as he had appeared at Yerasimos's hut. "Welcome, Yerasimos," he said. He was alone this time.

Yerasimos said, "So it was you who did me all those favors. Then you had twelve men with you and you made thirteen. Now I have nine and I make ten."

"Okay," Christ said. "Come on into heaven with your friends."

And so they all lived well, and we live even better. And this is a true Egyptian story, because the Gypsies come from the Egyptians.

Phara-un,
God of the Gypsies

United States

This tale was told in English by Diana Mafa, an American Gypsy of
Russian descent, to Frances R. Vandercook, who published it in the
Journal of the Gypsy Lore Society in 1939. (Vandercook had followed
some Gypsies to their temporary home on a Wisconsin fairgrounds
and spent an evening with them.)

This story expresses an idea central to the Gypsy world view: that
neither the good nor the bad exists in isolation.

Yes! We Gypsies have a god; his name is Phara-un. He is part god,
or good, and part human, or not so good. Understand me! He can do
bad things too—like Gypsies do—but he is clean.

Once a Gypsy woman had a baby, and she left him in the woods—
he was little, you know, she still nursed him at the breast. The baby
became hungry, and an angel, a god-being, came by and gave him her
breast, so he grew up part god and part man.

The angel told him that on all days but Friday he must be very good,
but on Friday he could feast and do as he pleased. He could get married
and live as a mortal—not a god.

One Friday he set a table and had a big feast, and there was everything
on the table you could think of but one thing—and that was fish. He
was wrong to forget fish.

Now an unclean person, a man without a soul, came to the feast.
He was jealous of Phara-un, the god of the Gypsies. So he looked over
the table and said, "This is a wonderful feast, but there is one thing
missing," and Phara-un replied, "What can that be?"

And the unclean one said, "Where is the fish?"—thinking Phara-un
could not get any at that late hour.

Phara-un said, "Wait, I'll get fish," and he went out and came back
with some. This made the unclean person jealous, so he said he would
fight Phara-un.

The man was very, very strong because he was evil. Every time he
hit Phara-un he drove him into the ground up to his knees. Phara-un

was getting beaten, so he called on his angel foster-mother to help him.

The angel knew Phara-un had done wrong to forget fish, yet she wanted to help him, so she whispered in his ear, "There is a knife in your pocket: use it."

Phara-un pulled out the knife, and the next time the unclean man drove him into the ground, he ripped his guts open. Out dropped two big snakes. The snakes said to Phara-un, "Open your mouth and let us go inside you; and you will be twice as strong as you are now."

Phara-un said, "That I will not do—I am clean and I will keep clean. You are evil and unclean." All he had to do was to touch the snakes then, and they died.

So he remained the god of the Gypsies and is like them, neither all good nor all bad—but he has kept himself clean inside.

The Sixty-One Skills

Portugal

This story was told around the fire by a Gypsy named Mena to writer and photographer Maria João Pavão Serra. The storyteller and her large family are very poor and live in Lisbon in a little house made of cardboard.

Once upon a time there lived a king and a queen and their daughter, the princess. The princess wanted to study, but one fine day the king said to her, "Daughter, you must learn the sixty-one skills."

She began to cry and went out to the garden, where she sat down and continued crying. Just then a very old man appeared before her and asked why she was crying. She told him what had happened.

The old man said, "Tell your father to build a castle here in your garden. This castle should be made entirely of glass so that whatever happens inside can be seen from the outside and whatever happens outside can be seen from the inside. In that way I will teach you the sixty-one skills."

Feeling very happy, she went to tell her father that she had already found someone to teach her the sixty-one skills. And his royal highness built the castle entirely of glass.

The old man gradually taught her the skills, until one day there was only one skill left: proving whether or not she could keep a secret. That day the princess came to the glass castle and saw the old man cut up a baby and gobble it up. She let out a scream, and the old man came over to reassure her, saying, "Maria, tell me what you saw."

"Nothing, my good old man."

"Tell me what you saw or else I will take you away from here to another country far away and give you a great beating."

"I did not see anything, my good old man."

The old man grabbed her and took her to another country. She was horrified and felt very lonely. She walked and walked and then saw a man near some water. She was so pretty and so lonely that the man took her home. He dressed her as a man so that no one would bother her, and treated her as though she were his daughter.

He was a jewelrysmith, but he was very poor. One day a king showed up with a queen's earring to see if the smith could make another one just like it. The boy (who was the girl) said that she could. She melted down all the materials she had—there was no gold—and made an earring exactly like the other. However, now there was nothing left in the showcase.

When the king came to get the earring, he asked how much it would cost. "Nothing, your royal highness," said the boy (who was the girl). But the king liked the work so much that he went to his palace and returned with a large bar of gold. In this way the boy began to make earrings, bracelets, rings, whatever was needed. And he turned that jewelry business into the most prominent one in the world and in Europe. In the midst of all this, the old man appeared.

"Maria, tell me what you saw."

"Nothing, my good old man."

He grabbed her and took her to another country, one where there was an unmarried prince. The old man left her in the middle of the palace garden. She was very disheartened and began to write on the ground things that she remembered, things that were very important. After writing a great deal, she grew drowsy and fell asleep under a tree. At this point the king's son, the prince, who was out for a walk, saw those writings on the ground. He called for his counselors, saying that there were strangers around the palace.

"Whoever wrote this is a refined person," said one of the counselors to his royal highness.

They found her sleeping under a tree. When they woke her, she said simply, "Yes? Good old man?"

"Who was it that brought you here?" asked the prince, thinking that she was a young man.

She said that she did not know. The prince suspected something because she had a female face, and he questioned her further.

"Yes, I am a woman."

And the prince asked for her hand in marriage. They were married! Some time later she had a son. When she was in the midst of suckling her little boy, the old man appeared. "Maria, tell me what you saw."

"I did not see anything, my good old man."

"Tell me what you saw or else I will eat your son and then tell them it was you who did it."

"I did not see anything, my good old man."

The old man devoured the child and vanished. She screamed, "My son has disappeared!"

Everyone in the palace was horrified, suspecting that she had eaten the child.

"My son," said the king, "your wife eats human flesh. We must kill her."

The prince would not agree to this.

"Make your next child soon. If she eats it as well, then she dies."

Some time passed, and she gave birth to a little girl. Just then the old man reappeared.

"Maria, tell me what you saw."

"Nothing, my good old man."

"Tell me what you saw or else I will eat your daughter."

"I did not see anything, my good old man."

He devoured the little girl and immediately wiped his bloodied hands on the princess's mouth. The princess screamed, and the old man disappeared. This time she did not escape. Everyone came into the room, and the king said, "Do you see, my son, that it is your wife who eats your children?"

And the princess never said anything.

"I will have a castle built and put her within the walls so that she can neither eat nor drink nor move," said the prince. "I don't want her to die right away—she has to suffer."

And so it was done. She was imprisoned there between the walls, unable to do anything.

After a few months his royal highness the king went to the terrace on the roof of the castle where his daughter-in-law was entombed, and he saw his grandchildren playing. When he saw this he began to run back into the palace.

"My son, my son, I must be going crazy."

His son came running.

"I must be going crazy," repeated the king. "Just look at this."

The prince saw his children.

"If you are crazy, then I too am crazy. I see my own children."

They both ran over to the children and embraced them.

"Father, I feel very sad about my wife, who has died although she was innocent."

Just then the old man appeared within the walls of the tomb.

"Maria, your trials with the skills will soon end. Your last skill was to be a woman who could keep secrets. And that you have proved to be. Now you will be saved, you can tell the whole story, and at the end if they ask you who taught you everything, point to the wall, because there I am on a cross." It was God!

And so it happened. The people tore down the walls of the castle, removing the stones with great care so as not to bruise the corpse, because they wanted a lavish burial. There were many cheers when they found that she was alive and more grand than ever.

How the Devil Helped God
Create the World

Hungary

A creation story told in several places in Hungary to collector Vladislav Kornel in the late 1800s.

When there was nothing on earth or in the universe but an immense
quantity of water, God decided to create the world but did not know
how to go about it. Annoyed at his awkwardness, especially since he had
neither a brother nor a friend who could give him good advice, he threw
into the water the stick he leaned on while promenading the clouds.

When the stick fell into the water, a gigantic tree immediately grew
out of it, the roots of which settled in the deep. On one of the branches
of this tree sat the Devil, who was then still white, like humankind,
afterwards created by God.

"Dear little God! My dear brother!" said the Devil, smiling. "I am
sorry for you indeed! You have neither brother nor friend. Well, then,
I will be your brother and friend."

"Oh, nothing of the sort!" replied God. "You can't be a brother to
me—nobody can be my brother. But be my friend!"

Nine days after this conversation, when the Lord had not yet created
the world, as he did not know how to proceed, he perceived during one
of his walks that the Devil was not friendly toward him. The Devil, who
was not stupid, observed that God distrusted him, and he therefore said
to him, "My dear brother, are you aware that we two do not suit each
other? Please have the kindness to create one more so that there may
be three of us."

"It is easy to say create another," replied God, very sorrowfully.
"*You* create him, if you are so wise."

"But I am not able to do it!" cried the Devil. "Long before this I
would have created a beautiful large world, but of what use is my will
when I do not know how to go about it, my dear brother?"

"Well," said God thoughtfully, scratching his head, as if trying to
remember something, "I will create the world, and you are going to assist

me. Quick, then, without loss of time, dive under the water and bring out of the deep a handful of sand, to form out of it the earth."

"Indeed?" said the Devil, seemingly surprised. "And how will you do this? It is incomprehensible to me!"

"When I utter my name, the sand will shape itself into the globe," replied God. "But now, quick, bring the sand!"

The Devil dove under, saying to himself, *Oh, I am not so stupid that I would allow the world to be created by another. I will do it myself, by calling out my name.*

When the Devil arrived at the bottom of the sea, he took hold of the sand with both hands, but when he called out his name he was obliged to drop the sand because it burned his hands.

When the Devil returned, he told God that he could not find any sand.

"Go and search for it, and bring what I have commanded."

For nine days the Devil insisted that he could find no sand, which was a lie, as he tried continually to create the world out of the sand of the sea, but as often as he took the sand in his hands and called out his name, he burned himself. The sand grew hotter and burned him so terribly that one day he turned black as coal.

When God perceived the Devil, he said to him, "You have turned black, I see, and have been a bad friend. Hurry now, and bring sand out of the deep, but do not utter your name, or the sand will consume you."

The Devil dove under and carried out the command. God took the sand, called his own name, and the world was made, which greatly pleased the Devil.

"Here," said he, sitting down in the shade of a large tree, "under this tree I will live, and you, dear brother, can look for other quarters."

This impudence angered God so much that he called out, "Ah! you rogue, only wait—I will teach you sense. Be off at once!"

At that moment an immense ox rushed out of the copse, took the Devil on his horns, and ran with him into the wide world. Fear and pain made the Devil shriek so loud that the leaves fell from the tree and changed into human beings.

Thus did the Lord create the world and the people in it, with the assistance of the Devil.

A Dish of Laban

Syria

This Nawari tale and the following one were collected by R. A. Stewart Macalister in the early 1900s from people he employed to do excavation work for the Palestine Exploration Fund. They were retold by John Hampden in *The Gypsy Fiddle*, a collection of Gypsy folktales for children.

The Nawar, a group of Muslim Gypsies, live in Syria, Jordan, Iraq, Egypt, the Old City of Jerusalem, France, and North Africa.

A young prince went riding. He rode on and on until he came to a city he had never seen before. He went to the king's palace in that city. The king had a daughter, and when she saw the prince she wished to marry him.

The princess said to him, "Go, ask the king, my father, if you may marry me."

The prince went and asked the king for her. The king said, "How can I know that you are truly a prince, the son of a king?"

The prince said, "Try me in any way you wish."

So the king sent for a dish of laban, which is a kind of sour milk, and said to the prince, "Here is a dish of laban. Balance it on your head. Climb that palm tree outside this palace and throw down two bunches of dates. You must not spill one drop of the laban. Do this and the princess shall be your wife."

The prince told the princess. She pulled a hair from her head and put it into the dish. The laban became solid, and the dish became fixed to the prince's head.

The prince climbed the tree and threw down two bunches of dates. He climbed down again and took the hair from the dish. The laban and the dish became as before. So he went to the king.

The king had watched from a window of the palace. The king said, "Truly this lad is the son of a king or he could not have done this thing without spilling one drop of the laban."

The prince and the princess were married. The king gave them two hundred slaves and loaded ten mules with gold for them.

They went to the prince's city. He found that his father was dead, and he became king in his father's place.

A Wicked Fox

Syria

This tale of mischief and abrupt repentance is one of the few animal tales in the Gypsy repertoire. Abu Hassan (meaning "Father of the Little Fortress") is the traditional nickname for the fox in Arab folktales.

A peasant was plowing with two oxen. One of them broke away, and the peasant said, "O wicked ox, if I catch you I will kill you with my knife!"

The ox was afraid, and he fled until he came to a place of long, rich grass. The ox stayed there and ate the grass. Abu Hassan, the fox, saw him there and said, "O ox, why do you stay here? This place belongs to a panther. When she finds you here she will strike you dead and eat you."

But the ox only grunted and went on eating the long, rich grass.

So Abu Hassan went to the panther and said, "There is an ox eating your grass."

The panther came to the ox and said, "Why are you here?"

Said the ox, "I am tired of pulling the plow, and I am hungry. I found this place and I wish to eat in it."

The panther said no more and went away. The ox ate the grass for ten days and grew as large as a camel. Then Abu Hassan came to him and said, "The panther has left you in this place to get fat. Soon she will come to eat you. When she comes, look fierce, redden your eyes, and kill her with your horns."

Abu Hassan went to the panther and said, "You have left the ox in your grass, and he has grown fat and fierce. If he sees you, he will want to kill you."

The panther growled and went to the grass. The ox looked fierce and reddened his eyes. He thrust with his horns and killed the panther just as she struck with her paw and killed the ox.

Abu Hassan called his wife and children and all his people. They ate the ox and the panther, even the bones, so there was nothing left.

Then Abu Hassan wandered about, looking for more mischief to do. In a place where Arabs had camped he found a sheepskin cloak and spread it over his shoulders. Then he went into a cave where a panther lived, the brother of the panther the ox had killed. The panther said to him, "Abu Hassan, why have you killed my sister?"

Abu Hassan answered, "I am not the ox."

The panther said, "It was you who led them to fight." Then the panther took notice of the sheepskin cloak on Abu Hassan's shoulders. He said, "Will you make me a cloak like that?"

"O panther, I will," said Abu Hassan, "if you will kill four sheep and bring them to me."

The panther brought the sheep. Abu Hassan and his family ate them all and threw the skins into a pit.

The panther came to him and said, "Abu Hassan, where is the cloak you were going to make for me?"

"O panther, I need another sheep," he answered.

When the panther brought him another sheep, he made a good meal of it and threw the skin into a pit.

Presently the panther came and said, "Where is the cloak, Abu Hassan?"

He ran away, and the panther ran after him. Abu Hassan escaped into a small hole, but not before the panther caught his tail and bit it off. "I shall know you again, Abu Hassan," the panther called out. "You are the fox that has no tail."

Something must be done about this, said Abu Hassan to himself. He looked about until he found a vineyard full of ripe grapes. Then he went to the other foxes and said, "Tie your tails under your bellies and I will show you where to get ripe grapes."

When they had done this, they appeared to have no tails. Then he led them to the vineyard, where they ate many grapes.

After this Abu Hassan went to the panther. The panther said, "I will kill you, Abu Hassan. You ate the sheep which I gave you but you did not make my cloak."

Abu Hassan answered, "O panther, it was not I. It must have been another fox."

"It was you. I know you because you have no tail."

"But all my people are without tails," answered Abu Hassan.

"Show me then," said the panther.

So Abu Hassan called his people together. The panther could not see their tails, which were tied under their bellies, so he could not tell which fox had eaten the sheep. He did not know what to do.

Then Abu Hassan invited the panther to dinner. He spread a beautiful carpet over a deep pit, and when the panther came he said, "O panther, here is a place of honor for you."

The panther sat on the carpet, and as he fell into the pit he snapped at Abu Hassan and dragged him along. Abu Hassan fell on top of the panther and was not hurt, but the panther was killed. Abu Hassan ate him but could not get out of the pit, for it was too deep.

Nearby there were women going to market with a large basket full of chickens to sell. At nightfall they came to the pit, and they said, "We will lower the basket into this pit, to keep the chickens safe from the foxes, and we will sleep here." This they did.

In the morning they hauled up the basket. Abu Hassan had eaten all the chickens and was asleep in the basket. He sprang out at them, looking very fierce.

The women were frightened and ran away, weeping and wringing their hands because they had lost all their chickens. When Abu Hassan saw this he was very sorry for them. He said, "I have done wrong to steal all their chickens. I will sin no more. I will go to a monastery and become a holy fox."

And this he did.

Alifi and Dalifi

United States

Rena C. Gropper, anthropologist and author of *Gypsies in the City*, wrote:

"This story was given to me only a month after I began visiting the Bimbo family on New York's Lower East Side in 1947. We had just begun to work together, and Mrs. Steve [Persa (Bess) Bimbo] had made herself responsible for teaching me. She had started to explain weddings and marriage customs, but she stopped to reprimand me for not writing the information down (I had been advised by my professors not to take notes in front of informants). Mrs. Steve was adamant that I be as accurate as possible inasmuch as she was exerting great effort to explain everything in English. Therefore, I began to write down everything she said. About fifteen minutes into the presentation, Mrs. Steve stopped and ordered, 'Read what you been writing so far so's I can see you got it right.' She had not realized I was using shorthand, and beamed at the exact duplication of her words.

"We had talked about non-Gypsy ignorance of Gypsy ways, and I had been given a diatribe against Hollywood when we first met, *Golden Earrings* having been shown in the New York movie theaters just a few months earlier. One morning, Mrs. Steve returned to the subject of *Golden Earrings*, and then she continued by saying that Hollywood was not only a pack of liars but also a den of thieves. 'Yes,' she said emphatically. 'They stole our stories. You know that Sinbad the Sailor? That was ours. They got no right to use our stories like that. Every family got its own stories; nobody can tell a story that ain't theirs. Our stories is *beautiful*, but you gotta have permission. Now, I'm gonna give you one in my family for generations. Write it down.'

"And so I did, and here it is."

Once upon a time was a king in his palace, centuries back, many years ago. At that time there was a Gypsy with his horse and wagons. Every winter he would come to that village near the kingdom where he used to do repairing for the palace—he was a coppersmith—every six months. Of course, the Gypsy was not wealthy; he had no children.

For many years there was two lonely couples. The king had no children neither. At one time the king was much worried because he had no son to succeed him. The Gypsy wished for a daughter to get the brideprice. They both had no luck; they had no children for many years.

So one night, after the Gypsy got to know the king very well and he was a good friend to the king, after the work he did, the king offered to stay for tea and have a talk because he was lonely. The Gypsy fellow was surprised that the king invited him to the table, and they both started to tell the hard-luck story. The king wanted a son to succeed him and he had no children. The Gypsy wanted a girl and he had no children. And the king says, "Here you are. I know you for a long time. You are respectable. We both are lonely. Stay with me." The Gypsy was surprised that a king should ask a Gypsy to stay, and he remained. He was glad to accept, and now they had much talk about no children.

The Gypsy went home and the king remained in the palace. The king and the Gypsy dreamed the same dream. The king dreamed that he should keep on going far away in the woods, so far that he is lost and cannot find his way back, and then he will have a family. The Gypsy also dreamed the same thing. Then they got up, but the men told their wives nothing.

The king got up at daybreak and went away into the woods with his beautiful white horse. The Gypsy man had a red horse and went on, too. They went on and on and on until they thought they were lost. They met at the mountain, the Gypsy and the king. When the king saw the Gypsy, he was surprised.

"Well," the king says. "What are you doing here?" The Gypsy's name was Molin. "What are you doing here, if I may ask."

"Well, Your Highness, I was going to ask you—what are you doing here?—but you asked me first. Seems foolish to tell you. You will laugh." So the Gypsy said. "Well, you asked me first. Even if it is funny. Remember the talk I had last night with you? I had a dream about it."

The king said, "I dreamed about it too. What did you dream?"

And the Gypsy told how he dreamed that he went far into the woods, so far that he thought he was lost, and then he would have a family.

The king said, "My God, it is the same dream! But here we is; what we going to do here?"

All of a sudden appears an old man with a beautiful long beard, looking like Christ. I don't say he *was* Christ; I only say he looked like

Christ, and they thought he was Christ. All they could see was the shadow speaking to them in the woods.

"Well done, both of you," said the old man. "You came to the right place. Now I will tell you what to do." They were surprised. The old man pushed the trees aside. They couldn't get over what the old man is doing in the woods. There is no one within much many miles. They think to themselves, "He must be Christ," but they don't say nothing. No human had ever been there, hundreds of miles from nowhere.

"Well," he tells the king. "First, you go a little ways here on the right side. You will find a leaf all alone growing on that bush. It is very white for a leaf, but you take it and take it home and cook it. Drink it first and then your wife do the same, and you will have within nine or ten months from now a daughter."

The king didn't feel good about it because he wanted a boy. (You know how often the thing you want most you don't get. God knows best.) He was brokenhearted, so he looked at the old man. But the old man shook his head and told the king, "You were praying to have anything as long as you had a family. So take whatever good I want you to have. It is going to be a girl, and don't take it hard. Something is better than nothing."

Then he tells the Gypsy to turn to the left, and he will also find a very narrow leaf, and he will have a son. The Gypsy wanted a daughter. He said, "Go, and get going."

It is not always what the person wants that he gets. It is always what God wants. So he said to the Gypsy, "When the children are both born, I wish to be the godfather. Bring them into the same place, and I will christen them and give them names."

They got their dreams, so finally they came home. The king cooked the leaf and drank first and gave his wife after. The Gypsy did the same with his narrow leaf. So months later the king had a daughter, and the Gypsy had a son. They both were not pleased. They both were still upset because they didn't get what they wanted.

When they were a year old, the time came for the children to be baptized. They were both born, and they were both christened, on the same day—by the same old man who directed the parents to the leaves. He christened the boy first. He gave the boy the name Alifi, and the girl, Dalifi, because they were both born and christened on the same day.

When the girl was eight to ten years old, the father kept her in her room where she could never see menfolks. It was a very large room with forty-eight windows, so no one could see her. So she couldn't make a disgrace. If she wanted a drink of water, she had forty-eight maids, and one would pass it to the next. She couldn't get out of the room. The king kept her there in a place to remain until she is old enough. He gave her embroidery to pass the time, so her mind will be occupied. I think the mother died.

The Gypsy's son is grow up old enough to talk. He always wanted a musical instrument . . . not a violin, it is plucked—a guitar. Naturally, the father doesn't like the boy, and he must spend money to get a wife. So this man tells him, "Shut up. Don't ask me for nothing. You should be glad to have a place to eat and sleep. How do you win money to buy the music?" The father always argued with the son because he doesn't want him to have it. So the little boy keeps on asking over and over till his father gets disgusted and beat him up.

It doesn't matter how bad the mother feels; she is not to tell the father his business. After the son is out, she talks secretly to the father. The father keeps saying, "You keep out of this. I want to make a man of him. No matter what I am doing. He is my son as much as he is yours." The father can't help it even though he feels badly. Naturally, the little boy, when he sees the father abuse him, he went away from home. He went away from home into a different village. (This was in the same time that his father was traveling around.)

So that summer the boy took and left his father and went away. He was a little fellow; the boy was about ten years old. Finally night reached the boy, and the boy sneaked into somebody's stairway in a little village. In this village where he stopped was a rich man's house where he parked under the steps inside. He slept there all night under this rich man's steps. Also, this man had been married for a long time and he had no luck, no family whatsoever.

Early in the morning, when he got out of the house, the man saw the little boy sleeping under his steps. The boy was the most beautiful boy that time have ever see. He had dark, curly hair. The most beautiful creature ever to be created, especially of Gypsies. He was very, very charming and good-looking. When this man saw him, he thought he was some kind of saint under his steps. This is how good-looking the boy was. Then he saw that he had raggy clothes—he wasn't well dressed—

but this little boy was shining like a beautiful star. So this man was tickled to death that he saw the boy.

He brought him in his rooms and bought him clothes, fed him well, and called his wife and said, "Look what God rewarded us with. We have a son grown up. God knows where he came from."

The little boy didn't want to tell about himself because he know that he would not be wanted as a Gypsy. When he see the beautiful home and the way the people treated him, he refused to tell about himself— where he come from, who his parents are. He pretended he didn't know nothing. This wealthy man and his wife asked if he was willing to be their son and stay with them. The boy said yes, he would be willing to stay with them if they would buy him a guitar.

"Well," the man said, "I won't buy you one; I will buy you a dozen. But you are sure you will stay with me?" The boy said yes.

So this man was more than glad and went and bought him the best guitar in town—the price didn't matter. He bought all kinds of clothes and shoes and stuff and kept him like his own son. He was proud of the boy when the boy remained with him.

(Of course, the Gypsy never went to look for his son. He was poor and had no money to buy a wife for him.)

This man bought a guitar with twenty-four strings and brought it home. The little boy took the guitar and stood up on a chair so he could play it. He played the most beautiful tunes that anyone ever heard. Each string of the twenty-four had twenty-four voices. All the time he was playing this, suddenly from nowhere used to come a crown of roses over his head and a white pigeon over it. But when he put the guitar down, everything used to disappear. When this man saw this, then he thought the boy was *really* a saint.

When the boy got to be, I should say, fifteen or sixteen years old, the same king who was his father's friend, he put an advertisement that, if anybody could sing or play tunes to make him forget his troubles, whoever could sing to please him, he will give him half his kingdom. But who doesn't please him, he will kill. Doesn't matter if they are blind, smallpocked, crippled, as long as they have an instrument they should come over. Whoever is going to please him with singing, he will get half the kingdom.

Finally the little boy got this and read it. The boy insisted on going with his guitar to sing for the king. The old man who brought him up like his own son refused the boy. "Well, my son, you can't go to the king. Did you read everything? He will kill those who fail."

And he couldn't make the boy listen to him. The boy still insisted to go to the king. But the king doesn't know him.

"No," the father says, "I won't let you go because I know that, if you go there, no one will stop him. He is a king, and he has no sons; and, if he sees you, he will keep you as a son. You have everything—properties, home, money, clothes. Why do you want half of his kingdom? You don't need it. I will sign everything over to you. I want you. When I found you I thought it was the happiest day of my life. I am living for you, and now you want to leave me. I care as if you was my own son. What haven't you got that you want to go to the king for half the kingdom? You have more than half a kingdom with me. Please stay; do not go." For a long time he tried to keep the boy.

For the first time the boy called him father. "Well, my father, my real father didn't buy me what I wanted. What good will it do me to play in this house and no one to hear? You did the favor my father would not do. If you want me to be your son, please let me go. Don't do like my own father did. That's why I left home. I will promise you I will come back. He can't keep me if I don't want to stay."

His father says, "I know what you mean. I know you don't want to stay. But what will you do? His orders means everything. Don't you understand? No one can stop him."

"Well," the boy says. "Well, my father, are you nuts? You can say I'm your son and he has no right to keep me if you refuse." (Also, this man's wife died; he is alone with the boy. This man got old.)

"Well, son, if you insist on going, you go, but I know you will never come back to me. What proof I got that you are my son? I am not a young man; everyone knows me and everyone knows when I got married and that I had no children. But being you want to go, go ahead. I wish you luck in the world." But he knew the king would not let him come back.

"Aren't you going to come with me? The king will like my singing."

"No, my son; I won't go because I know I will come back without you. It would break my heart. As you said, I haven't far to go, and I was the only one to listen to your playing. But you want your freedom. Take good care of yourself, my son," he tells him, and kisses him good-bye. He kisses the boy good-bye, and the boy went on.

Everyone was ready to play for the king when he arrived. The boy arrived in time. He tried to get beyond the crowd. Finally the guards would not let the little boy get through; he was too young. The boy started to argue, and the guards pushed him away. There is a big fuss going on. The king was there to listen.

The boy shouted out loud, "The king advertised it is cripple, blind, deaf, smallpocked, as long as they knew how to play. Why do you push me away?"

"Little boy, you will only get your throat cut. Everybody is afraid they can't please the king."

"I will try," says the little boy. "Let me go."

Finally the king saw the argument going on. "What's going on there?" said the king. The guards tell him all about it. Then the little boy speaks to the king himself. "Didn't you advertise it doesn't matter who he is or what kind of instrument, if he is blind, crippled, deaf, smallpocked, as long as they know how to play, they should come over? You don't have to give me half the kingdom. I have a father nearly as wealthy as you. I only want to play for the public, not for half the kingdom, God forbid. I have everything. I have everything."

Naturally, the king heard that and did not let anyone else play, and he kept the boy by the hand and put him on the stand. The little boy pulled out the guitar and stood on the chair to play for the king.

"Let's see what you will do. But remember, if no one pleases me I will cut the throat off."

"Yes, I read. You can kill me."

"Well, go right ahead."

He takes his guitar—twenty-four strings, each string made twenty-four different kinds of tunes—and the crown came over the boy with roses and white pigeons.

When the king saw that, he couldn't get over it. Well, everybody should go home, and the king made a speech that he will take the boy in the palace to sing for him because he found what he wants. Not only that, not half the kingdom but everything. He will be the son.

He took him home as a son. Now the king was so happy that he got on his horse and went for a long ride. The boy, when he got to the palace, pulled out the guitar and sang again when the king wasn't there. The girl must have been sixteen years old, and the boy, too.

The maids she had asked for a cold drink of water for her. She was embroidering ever since she had been there for her father. She doesn't finish yet. Forty-eight maids came out to get her a drink of water to reach her. The half, twenty-four, when they saw the boy playing and heard him and saw the flowers, they all got like statues and forgot about everything else. The door was open. The girl heard, too, and came out. When she saw the boy playing and the boy saw her, he put his guitar down, and they kept staring at each other, and the forty-eight maids were still remained like a statue.

She was the most beautiful thing on earth—beautiful blue eyes, hair like gold, the prettiest thing you ever saw, and the boy too.

When she saw the boy, she offered him her father's handkerchief as a present which she was embroidering for nine years, and the thing wasn't finished yet. When she gave him that handkerchief, she asked his name. Then she knew who it was because her father told her about the boy born at the same time and baptized on the same day.

So he asked her name, and she told him. Then he know it was the girl born the same day. They both fell in love with each other on sight as soon as they saw each other. She went back with her maids.

(At that time, in that century, they didn't use to wear the handkerchief in the pocket but in the belt.)

After, the king came inside. He says to the boy, but he didn't know the name yet, "Son, can you get up and get me a cold drink of water?" He was so proud of having a son. When he went to get him the water, his hand brushed across his belt, and the handkerchief dropped to the floor. When he dropped the handkerchief, the king picked it up. "It isn't yours, Your Majesty. It is mine."

"Never mind; it was mine until you came along. Now my daughter gave it to you. You can have it; it is yours now."

He says, not calling him son, he asked his name. He answers his name was Alifi. Then he knew it was the Gypsy's son. Then that was more of a disgrace. He brought a no-good Gypsy to the home and the disgrace.

"Now," he said, "I have a little business to finish with you, you no-good Gypsy."

Then the boy was surprised that the king thought of the Gypsy past. "Well," he says, "I am leaving your kingdom. I have a good place to go."

When he heard that the king took his son home, the old man died, but the boy didn't know that, so the king told him, "You only think you have a good place to go. I found out all about you." The man had asked the king to return the boy, so the king didn't learn he was a Gypsy from him.

So he called one of the guards, the man he trusted. This guard had a beautiful puppy, his pet that he raised as a child. He was the right-hand man to the king. He called him to take the Gypsy out in the woods and kill him. But, to be sure, he asked for the both eyes back and his blood in a handkerchief.

The daughter knows all this.

After the king give his orders, he was so disgusted what happened to him with his son being a Gypsy who saw his daughter.

After he give orders to take the man and have him killed, he went to his daughter and spoke to her for the first time since he put her there. "I knew something like this would happen. I wish I had never had that dream. I wish you never were born. I knew disgrace would come if I had a daughter. Now, I was going to keep you here until you was eighteen. But now with the disgrace and you give my handkerchief to a no-good Gypsy who come from nowhere, I am going to punish you and keep you until twenty-one."

The girl cried, but she had no right to tell her father how she feels about the treatment. Her father scolded her and was disgusted and went out for a long ride with a white horse and left orders to kill the Gypsy and bring back the both eyes, heart, and blood, and the handkerchief she gave him.

She watched her father drive on from the windows and she opened up forty-eight windows and ran from one to the other to see which way this guard was going to pass on the way to having the boy killed. She saw the guard carry him out to be killed. She cried and shouted, "Please don't kill him. If you kill him, you might as well kill me too."

"Well," the guard says to her, "well, your father gave me the orders. It's either his life or mine. What do you want me to do about it?"

"Please don't. Have a heart. Don't kill him, for my sake. You can lie to my father and say you killed him, and you can turn him loose far away in the woods and not kill him. Even if I won't have him, as long as he is alive. I will meet him again some day."

"Yes, but I can't do that because your father asked for his both eyes and his heart and his blood back on the handkerchief you gave him."

"Well," she said, "I am going to ask for a big favor that can be done easily if you want to for my sake. You can kill your puppy and take your puppy's eyes and take his heart and smear that handkerchief in your puppy's blood, and show that to my father. As long as he sees this, he will be convinced he is killed."

"Yes," he said, "you asked me for too much. I love my puppy as much as you love the boy."

The girl said, "Yes, he is a puppy you had for years. How long will he live yet? Dogs will not live forever. A dog's life doesn't matter as much as a human's life. It will be two human lives. Yes," she said. "Please do kill your puppy, and I will kiss you for that and I will never forget you as long as I live. Show pity and do it for my sake."

When he heard of her kissing him, he couldn't refuse to kill his puppy. She was so beautiful. "Well," he said, "as long as I have someone like you to think of for as long as you live, with the kiss, I will kill my puppy. One kiss will kill a life."

Then he went into the woods, where no one could see him, and he turned the boy loose in the woods and told him never to show up in the kingdom as long as he will live. Then he killed his puppy. He brought back his eyes and his heart and his blood in the handkerchief. He brought it back to the king and showed him that he killed him.

When he returned to the princess, she refused to kiss him. She told him, "I am sorry, but that kiss I am saving for him. He's the first one I see, and I ain't kissed him at that time."

So this man couldn't tell her father because he would get killed. So he must keep quiet.

Easter Sunday is coming after this happened. The boy became the best painter and made his living that way. He become one of the best painters known, this Gypsy fellow. The music was left to the kingdom. In those days, each house must be painted for Easter Sunday, each house in the village, like we paint eggs here. But first of all the king's house must be painted first. The king was home at that time.

So he had forty-seven friends with him to help paint the palace. So he said while they were painting, "See that guitar hanging there? That belongs to me."

The others shouted and laughed at him. "How can a painter get into the king's house and leave a guitar there?" They couldn't believe it. So he felt embarrassed because they were making fun. To prove it, he got it off the nail and played it. The roses grew in a crown, and a white pigeon flew around. Of twenty-four strings, each one made twenty-four different tunes.

Then the girl knew he was back in the house, and she was crying and praying to take him away lest he be killed. No such luck. The king came and hear the tune and know the boy was back in the house. He asked how big was the best well to drown him. Forty feet was one; forty-five was the second, and forty-eight was the biggest. He ordered him to be drowned in the deepest one.

Now he is after the guard who turned him loose. He got hold of him, the best guard, and killed him.

Then, when the painters went back for supper, the forty-seven of them, one chair was empty. "What happened to Alifi? He is not here." "Well, the last we saw of him was when he played his guitar at the king's palace."

Naturally, they got the news that he had been drowned in the well. So the forty-seven of them went and threw ropes, and he was pulled out and they saved his life. But for them to help him, on the safe side they told he must not stay close to the kingdom where the king would see him.

So he went out some place where he was not near the kingdom. He became a rich man and bought a house. "I will open up my own business some place in the woods where no one is around." He open up a store and a bar but where he is there is no one to get there. But he went and worked a long time to cut up the roads. He connected each road, you would come to the store.

The girl reached the age of twenty-one and got out of the room. She asked her father, "Nothing you can do for me but give me your promise to put in the front of the palace two silver bowls and a ladle and let me pour water from one to the other."

In the meantime, she asks everyone about Alifi who came to have water. Well, nobody heard of him, no trace at all for three or four years, but she still kept on waiting. All this time she stayed and asked all people. No one gave her information of Alifi. She saw one man, he passed on his horse, but he was very ugly, and she said, "He must know. He comes from far away." He passed by on his horse, and she gave him a drink. In the meantime she asked him if he ever heard of the name Alifi or ever saw. After having his drink, he said, "Yes, I had a talk to him." But he lied.

"Well," she said, "please tell me. How can I find him? This means a lot to me. This is the happiest day of my life. I been here for a long time taking water from one cask, putting into the other. I will give you anything. Just tell me where he is."

Naturally, there is no two ways about it, she must kiss him to get the information even if she was upset. After she kisses him, he said, "I only lied. I never saw him."

"But why did you make me kiss you?"

"If I took money, you would take it back. Now try and take the kiss back."

She was tricked the same way she had tricked the guard. So the girl for the first time in her life smiled and cried at the same time. "Well," she said, "anyways, you have the kiss. Can't you do me a favor?" He promised. "You are a traveling man. You go all over. Take the note for him, and if you meet up with him give him the note."

In the note she said, "Alifi—Dalifi. Ever since you went away I can't keep you off my mind. You remain there day and night. I can't forget you, awake and sleeping. Please, wherever you are, I have my freedom now. I am in front of my father's palace. I built up two silver casks and put water from one into the other, and I am giving everyone a drink and asking about you. I am calling on you. Please, Alifi, do answer Dalifi wherever you are. Please come. I am waiting, and I will always wait, no matter how long."

She wrote this note and give it to the traveler. After this all happened, he went away and finally passed the store where Alifi is located. Well, many customers is in the store, and he bought drinks on the house. Everybody is drinking to Alifi and call his name. And this fellow says, "This is the man she is looking for. I have found him at last."

Everybody went away at closing time that night. But the man stayed there. Alifi asked him what he wanted, that he stayed there.

"Nothing much except it's night and let me stay overnight."

"Gladly," answered Alifi. "I am all alone. I can use company. Do stay." He gave him his bed to sleep in. Late at night the traveler went under the bed with the note to Alifi. Alifi smokes in bed and crawls up and down when all of a sudden he closed his eyes and fell asleep. Then Alifi heard everything: "Alifi, ever since you went away I can't get you out of my mind. I can't eat, sleep. I always think of you." And tells about the casks and pouring water, trying to keep her mind occupied. When this Alifi hears this, he thinks he is dreaming all that. He got up like an old man and turned on the light to see where the voice is coming. He forget about the other fellow. He rubbed his eyes and kept on thinking it was a dream. He heard it over again for the third time. He looked under the bed and grabbed the man. He grabbed the note and read it himself.

"Well," he says, "you are welcome to everything here—the store, money, everything. I waited for this for a long time."

He went back to the kingdom. She didn't see him for a long time. He went up his horse and says, "Princess, please give me a drink of water."

"Why don't you get off your horse and get a drink? If you want a drink of water, get off your horse and get it."

"No," he insists, "you give me a drink."

She refuses. After he went away, she says to herself, *My, what a man! No one ever did that to me. It must have been him.* She ran and got a horse and ran after him. Then she knew he was the one. They got together and went away from the palace together. They got married.

The night is coming. At one place there was a fire and at one place a dog barking. He asked her, "Where do you want to go, where is the fire or the dog barking?"

They went where the fire was—a group of forty gangsters. She refuses the dog and wanted to get warmed up at the fire. She indicated he was a Gypsy. "You are a Gypsy. You should like the fire yourself."

He took her where the fire was. The time she run away, not to be recognized she had changed from woman's clothes to men's clothes. So she put boots, men's shirt, and man's hat. The leader of the gangsters recognized she was a woman when they sat down to eat. The next man, the right-hand man, said, "This is a woman, I may bet." The leader says no.

"She's too beautiful for a man."

"We will ask and find out," said the leader.

"We must take your hats off." The girl refused, and they insisted and took off the hat, and her hair fell over her lap.

"Many men wear long hair. Let's remove your trousers."

They did that too. No hair on the leg. Still not convinced. Remove the coats. Breasts—knew it was a woman.

He ordered the Gypsy to be hanged by the neck and the leader took the girl. She seemed to agree. They took him to be hanged. Dalifi went with the leader. There were two Gypsy servants, a couple serving the thugs. This Gypsy, when the gangsters were coming out, he pretends to hang him but he lets him down. They keep on doing that for a long time.

The leader had guns and swords and tried to make love.

"Why with the gun? Put down your arms. Then I can make love."

The minute he puts his gun down, she grabbed it and killed the leader, cutting off his head, and the others couldn't do nothing because she had the guns. The two Gypsies was released and they went away all together.

Naturally, they would live the Gypsy life. They had met up with the other Gypsies. Then they would travel together. Alifi said, "Well, we can't go riding on our horse. Let's buy a little wagon."

For the love, she gave up her princess title and her palace to live his life. Then he bought the wagon and horse and tent, traveling with the Gypsies. The head of the tribe says one day, "Listen, I have met a lot of Gypsies in all my life. I never met a Gypsy before as him. I want to be their godfather." He made a big party to the Gypsy camp.

When the party is over the next morning, the other tribe of Gypsies met together. The leader says, "We are traveling with you all our lives. I don't meet like Dalifi and give to her bread to be her godfather. Alifi is not a rich man, but our Gypsies is rich. I don't care about your people. I like him and his wife, the best Gypsies I have ever met."

Then Alifi comes while they were talking. "You got a lot of presents. What will you give the godfather?"

Then Alifi is covered with shame and goes back to his wife. "Well, Dalifi, every one of the Gypsies was talking to our godfather. Why can't we give something ourselves?"

She said, "Here, take these two walnuts. Give one to him and one to the godmother, and it's a good present for him."

Alifi went back and gave the walnuts to them as a present. Everyone started laughing. It's good to eat. They both broke it up. Many sweaters and shirts and blankets are flowing from the walnuts, and Alifi guards it. Everybody is surprised when all this came from the walnuts. It must be magic.

There were two young fellows. "Maybe Dalifi is magic because she is the greatest woman I have ever seen. Let's have a party tonight and bring Alifi and Dalifi to the party so we can take his wife."

Next night they make the party and go in the back tent. They call him down and put them close to the table. They give Alifi many drinks and make him drunk and paralyzed, and he went to sleep. The two youngsters grabbed his wife and killed Dalifi. Morning comes, other Gypsies breaks camp because Dalifi was murdered. Alifi is still sleeping and is all alone. About eight o'clock Alifi wakes up and looks closely to his wife. He is in a bed, and he thinks she sleeps. He says, calls the name of Dalifi, "Wake up, the camp has broken. Let's catch up." Blanket is grabbed and sees the wound. Then Alifi starts crying. "Why did they do that to her, my own blood?" Well, he prays to the God.

Then God comes down from the heaven, the same old man who baptized them. What happened? Comes like a pale skin. Alifi tells he was accompanied by his own Gypsies. "I saw Dalifi was stabbed too." Then the God says to Alifi, "Maybe you were drunk. She's not stabbed. She's sleeping."

He goes to the bed and says, "Dalifi, wake up." And she woke up. "You see—you was sleeping."

Alifi says, "It's my imagination. I drank too much last night." Then they go where the others went. Going east. "Let's follow them."

They get them. And call from the leader. The leader goes in front of the God. "Are you the leader of the Gypsy crowd?" "Yes." "Well, there was a murder last night." "Yes, that was the boys over there." He called them over, and ask them about the party. Each fellow blames the other. "She didn't want to be kissed." "With what hand did you kill the woman?" "Right hand." "You don't have no more arm." "What eye saw you wink?" "Left eye." Made him blind. Both punished right there.

"Alifi, you are nice man and good-looking, but you in trouble with the Gypsies. Go back to the kingdom. You don't belong traveling."

He doesn't want to disturb the king. They pitch tent in the back, in the back of the yard. "Tomorrow we will go to the palace." That night they fixed a nice big tent all decorated, and they went to sleep. The Gypsy custom—they all sleep together, head to toe, so the feet are not together.

Early in the morning, at seven, the maid get up and looked around in the garden and see the tent. She went up and opened the first door at the right and saw two men sleeping. They tell the king, "Wake up. You got a giant with two heads. He maybe will kill you." King woke up all excited and took a knife and went in the garden and opened the right door of the tent, and saw there was two heads sleeping. He got the sword. Killed Alifi. Then his daughter woke up. "Father, you have killed him. He's my husband."

Then the king went back to the palace and called the maid and said he would kill her. "I missed them and now I must kill you." The maid was killed. The daughter thought he killed Alifi on purpose. "All my life you never left me alone."

The king said, "I realize now I was wrong. I was left all alone. I was more than glad to have you back." To prove it to the daughter, he killed the maid too.

The girl said, "What good will it do me?" She took the scissors, turned it to the heart, and killed herself. The king turned away to be alone, and they quick buried them in the same place where the tent was pitched. He put the girl in one grave and the son-in-law in the other, and the maid was put in the middle. Every time two roses grow and one thorn in between and pushed them so they couldn't kiss.

How the Gypsies Became Musicians

Yugoslavia

There have always been many extraordinarily talented Gypsy musicians, many of them violinists, and this fact has inspired several folktales. This short Yugoslavian story is one example; the Swedish story "The Gypsies' Fiddle," pages 45–47, and the Czech story "The Rom in the Piano," pages 216–222, are two others.

Once upon a time God placed a fiddle on St. Peter's shoulders.

Not knowing that there was a fiddle on his shoulders, St. Peter went into an inn where there were many jolly people.

When they saw St. Peter with the fiddle, they called out, "Play! Play!" But he was frightened at their shouting and began to run away.

At the door the fiddle fell from his shoulders. He picked it up and went straight to God and asked him, "What does this mean, God?"

"I made it for you," answered God, "so that you might play to people when they were lively and keep them in a good humor and prevent them from picking quarrels."

"If that is so, let there be more musicians."

"But who could there be?" asked God.

"Let there be the Gypsies," answered St. Peter. "Let them amuse people so that they may not shed blood when they drink and make merry."

"Let it be so," said God.

And so it was.

The Church of Cheese

Yugoslavia

The church of cheese is a recurrent motif in Gypsy folklore, though a rationale for begging is not always incorporated. This story was told to Tihomir Djordjević by a Gypsy nailmaker in Aleksinac and translated into English by Fanny Foster in 1936. In an Argentinian version the reason given for eating their church is that the Gypsies were hungry, as they hadn't eaten in several days.

Once upon a time the Gypsies built a church of stone and the Serbs built a church of cheese.

When both churches were ready, they agreed to exchange them—the Gypsies were to give the Serbs the stone church and the Serbs to give the Gypsies the cheese church and fivepence as a makeweight. The Serbs had no money, so they owed the Gypsies the five pennies.

The Gypsies immediately began to eat their church, until little by little they had eaten it all up; and that is why they have no church now.

The Serbs still owe the five pennies, and the Gypsies are still asking for them, and that is why the Serbs have to give them alms.

The Robber and the Housekeeper

England

This tale was collected by T. W. Thompson in the early 1900s from "Noah Lock and Others." The language is the vernacular of the English Gypsies, also known as Romanichals. Nevertheless, readers should have little trouble following the text, though the substitution of initial *r*'s for *d*'s (and vice versa) should be noted: *destroy* becomes *restroy; relations, delations; disguise, reguise.*

The hero of this tale is the housekeeper—the storyteller is most emphatically not in sympathy with the robber. The European counterparts of this story type are known generally as The Clever Maiden Alone at Home Kills the Robbers, in which a companion of the robbers then takes revenge by appearing as a suitor for the girl, and she manages to escape. Naturally, this version has stylistic and plot elements that are original to the English Gypsies.

The' was wonst a big high gentleman what lived in a fine mansion, a very grand place it was an' no mistake, standing back in its own grounds, an' the' was a carriage drive leading up to it from the road, an' trees growing all about it. I can't tell you exac'ly who he was, but he was some very high notified gentleman. Now it so come about at the time I'm a-speaking on as this gentleman, an' the lady his wife, an' their son— they only had but one son—an' their two da'ghters, they all went away for a week's holiday. An' they had a little baby, this gentleman an' lady had, but they didn't take it wid 'em; they left it at home wid the housekeeper. An' they left one 'n the sarvant gals as well for comp'ny like for the housekeeper, but the tother sarvant gals they took wid 'em.

They'd be gone away now some two or three days, when the' comes knocking at the door 'n the house an owld woman—or so sh'd 'pear to

be, a rale comital [real comical] owld woman. An' this owld woman got
a-gate telling tales an' things, an' sich funny tales she towld that she kept
the housekeeper an' the tother sarvant in fits o' laughing. She got on an'
got on, one tale a'ter another, an' all the time they was standing at the
back door, all the three 'n they. Whatsumever, a'ter a bit, the one sarvant
says to the tother: "Shall we ax her to come in an' sit down a bit?" "Well,
aye," says the tother, "she'll be a bit o' good comp'ny for we." So they
axes her in, an' sets vittles afore her—plenty to eat an' drink—an' a'ter
when she'd had a bellyful, they all sits talking an' telling tales an' laughing
till nigh upon night time.

So whatever to you, the owld woman now begins to ax 'em for one
bit o' thing an' another, an' they gi'es her these, for they wa'n't o' no
value not to speak on. Getting bowld-like she axes 'em for summat else,
an' this thing it was o' some value, though what it was exac'ly I couldn't
rightly say—not now. Whatsumever, it was kept upstairs, this thing was
what she'd axed for, so the sarvant an' the housekeeper as well they both
goes upstairs, an' they leaves the little baby downstairs in the kitchen
wid the owld woman.

Whether it was they couldn't find it, or whether it was they was
talking it over a bit as to how they should get rid 'n this owld woman,
or what, I couldn't say, but they was a t'emendous long while upstairs,
an' the owld woman gets out o' patience wid waiting. "If you don't come
down at wonst," she hollers out, "an' bring me that thing what I axed
you for, then I shall restroy this baby." Whatsumever, they 'pears to take
no notice on her, so she makes for the baby, an' is just going to knock
its brains out when out jumps a big, black 'triever dog, as had been
sleeping in the corner wid one eye open all the time, an' which she'd
never as much as noticed afore. It has her by the throat afore she could
stir hand or limb to keep it off, an' shakes the life out'n her—aye, kills
her stone dead on the spot it does.

As soon as they hears the baby scream, the housekeeper an' the
tother sarvant they comes rushing downstairs, an' they finds the owld
woman lying dead on the floor an' the big 'triever dog standing over her.
Now being as she is dead, they begins to sarch her, an' what should they
find out but that the owld woman isn't a woman at all, but a man dressed
up in woman's things. There's something suspicious about this, they
thinks, an' they goes through all his pockets, an' there they finds a
'volver—a six-chamber 'volver—a dagger, and a horn.

Whatsumever to you, the housekeeper now takes and blows this horn, three times she blows it, an' no sooner has she done this but what three robbers comes running up the drive as fast as ever they can. She doesn't lose not a minute. She snatches up the 'volver and shoots two'n they dead on the spot, an' the third she'd have sarved the same, only but he run away agen afore she had the time.

Now when the master an' mistress come home agen, it was only nat'ral-like 'at the first thing they should ax was, how had their little baby been this long time. "Oh! quite well," says the housekeeper, for she didn't like to say nothink about the robbers. But the tother sarvant she wasn't agen telling, so she up an' towld the whole story. When the master heeard this, he was very pleased at the way the housekeeper had done to the robbers. He should make her comfor'able for the rest 'n her life, he said, an' she should have a house 'n her own near by to his, an' no more work to do, that was not unless she had a mind to, an' she shouldn't want for nothink, he said, as long as he had money to buy it wid. So soon a'ter he had a very tidy sort 'n a house builded in his own grounds, an' this he gi'ed to the housekeeper for her very own, to do as she liked wid.

Whatever to you, the robber as had run away an' missed getting killed, he put a 'vartisement into the papers saying as how he'd like to find a job as coachman wid some gentleman; he was very used to horses, he said, and a good stidy driver. Now it just so happened as the gentleman what lived in the mansion next to the one where the housekeeper was, stood in want 'n a coachman, so when he seen the 'vartisement into the papers he sent for the robber, an gi'ed him a month's trial, an' when the month was up he took him on for good.

Afore long this robber gets on wid the housekeeper, and goes courting her very strong. An' she gets rale sweet on him, her not knowing like who he is, for he was a very good-looking man, an' pleasant spoken enough when it suited his parpose. A'ter a bit he axes her, will she marry him. She doesn't say yes, nor yet she doesn't say no, but she goes straight to her master an' tells him all, an' axes him, "What shall I do?"

"Oh, that's soon answered," he says. "If you're fond 'n him," he says, "then marry him. But if you don't like him," he says, "then don't marry him."

"Oh! I love him," she says.

"Well, then," he says, "that being the state o' 'fairs, you go an' tell him you'll have him."

So she did, and afore long they got married, an' went to live in the house what the gentleman 'd had builded for her.

At first they was very happy, of course, like everybody is. About six months passed, an' then one day the robber tells his wife as he's going to take her to see his delations. "You know, my dear," he says, "we now been married this long time, an' I ha'n't as much as set eyes on one 'n my own people from that day to this. They must think it strange 'n we not going over to see 'em."

"Yes, dear," she says, "we ought to go, and I'm sure it'll be a great pleasure to me."

"It will," he says, and away he goes to harness the pony an' yoke it. She gets into the trap besides him, and off they sets.

He drives on and on over mountains and all manner o' wild lonesome places all that day, and all the next day, and all the day a'ter that agen. About the fourth day she begins to be a bit anazy [uneasy] in her mind, an' wonders, poor thing, wherever they can be going to, an' whenever will they get there. She works herself up into sich a state till at last she bursts out crying—she couldn't keep it in no longer. "Oh, my dear husband," she says, "where are we going to, an' however much farther is it?"

"Be quiet, woman," he says, "you'll find out just now, an' plenty soon enough that'll be, for if you only knew what was to happen to you when we get to my brothers' house, you wouldn't be fretting your heart out to get there."

"Oh, my dear," she says, "whatever is up with you talking so strange-like?"

"Well, if you will know," he says, "it was you murdered my two brothers, and now we're a-going to take us vengeance on you."

At that she begun crying agen, an' begging him on her bended knees to take her back home. But he didn't take not a bit o' notice on her, only towld her to stop her hollering or it would be the worse for her.

In about another day they comes to the robbers' house, an' the robbers they takes an' shuts up the housekeeper in a room, an' strips her stark mother naked, an' ties her up to the ceiling by the hairs 'n her head, an' leaves her there whils' they go an' talk over what kind o' death they shall put her to. Whatsumever, they hadn't tied her hands, so as soon as they're gone out 'n the room she gets to work breaking her hairs, two or three at a time, bit by bit, till at last she works herself loose. She opens the window as quiet as ever she can, an' Lord! she was a-frightened for fear they should hear her, but they didn't, so she gets out. She takes a good look round to make sartain as nobody is watching her, an' then away she runs as fast as her legs can take her, away back on the road they'd come.

Whatever to you, she might be gone from the robbers' house p'r'aps three or four hours, an' she was fair fit to drop an' all of a faint, when she comes up wid an owld man driving a cartfull o' nothink but apples. An' she towld this owld man 'bout the state she was in—which there wa'n't no need for, as he'd got eyes an' could see for hisself—an' how she was running away from some robbers as was going to take her life, an' where it was she was wanting to get to. "Oh!" she says, "if only you could find it in your heart to do a kindness to a poor woman in trouble, an' help her on her way a bit!"

The owld man was very sorry for her, an' so, being as he was going her road, he towld her to jump up besides him, which she did pretty quick as you can guess. An' he shifts the apples away from one side 'n the cart, an' tells her to lay herself down there, an' she does, an' he covers her all over wid the apples.

He drives on now, an' for about two days they goes on and on over the mountains an' places, an' never sets eyes on a soul. Then a fine gentleman on horseback comes up wid they. It was the robber, this was, an' the owld man knowed it well enough, for he was a cunning owld fellow. He'd heeard the horse coming along behind him all the while, but he hadn't as much as turned round.

"My good man," says the robber, "have you seen annythink on a woman going stark mother naked?"

"N—o," the owld man answers him, an' goes on driving on.

"But she's come this road," says the robber, "an' she must ha' passed you somewheres, for she isn't behind you."

The owld man pulls up. "Well," he says, "now I come to think 'n it, I seen somethink yesterday what looked very funny. I couldn't make nothink on it. Something white it was, 'way back on the owld road right over yonder, miles an' miles back. What it was though I couldn't say, I'm sure."

"Ah!" says the robber, "that must ha' been her," and wi' that he puts spurs to his horse an' gallops off to look for her down the owld side road, what was many an' many a mile back.

The owld man laughs to hisself an' goes on agen, an' he gets a long way afore the robber comes up wid him a second time. "Stop, you owld white-headed rascal," he shouts—the robber does—cussing an' swearing somethink awful. "You been telling me lies for a parpose."

"No," says the owld man, "that I ha'n't, for I ha'n't never towld you no lies at all."

"Well, anyhow," says the robber, "the woman ha'n't gone that road what you towld me."

"Well, I never said as she had," says the owld man, very quiet-like. "All I said was I seen some funny white thing along the owld road. It was you yourself," he says, "as said it must be her."

"Ah," says the robber, "I can see you got more knowledge on her nor what you lets on, you owld varmint. I shouldn't wonder if you ha'n't got her in your cart all the time."

"No, I ha'n't," says the owld man. "But if you don't put no trust in my words, p'r'aps you'll believe your own eyes. Look," he says—an' he pulls off the cover 'n his cart, an' shows the robber his cart full of apples—"she's not here, is she now?"

"No," says the robber, "I can't see nothink but only apples." Then a'ter this the robber leaves him, an' the owld man drives on now till he comes to the place where the housekeeper lives.

Whatever to you, the first thing the housekeeper does is to go an' tell her owld master everythink what has happened to her, an' she begs him to save her from the robber. "My dear," he says very kind-like, "don't you think no more about it. You must stay here," he says, "in my house, an' you shall have everythink what you wants—plenty to eat an' to drink, an' plenty o' grand clothes to wear, an' a lady companion to be wid you always. And as for the robber," he says, "just leave him to me. I'll see to it as he don't do you no harm. I got a plan for catching him," he says. "It's just now come into my head."

An' wid that he goes off, an' orders bills to be put out everywheres, on every barn door, and every tree, and every gatepost for miles an' miles round, saying as on sich-an'-sich a day he'll give a big feast, and as everybody is axed to it, rich an' poor, they'll all be made welcome. Now it gets on an' gets on till it's only but two days afore the feast is to be gi'ed, when the robber he comes back agen into them parts, an' of course it's not long till he sees the bills. He goes to his wife's house, but it's empty. Well, he thinks to hisself, as the best he can do is to reguise hisself an' go to this feast. She is sure to be there, he thinks, an' he can watch her where she goes a'ter when it's over.

On the night 'n the feast there is the housekeeper, all dressed in silks and satins, an' her lady companion at her side, walking up an' down, up an' down, in the grand hall where the supper is laid. An' the master he is standing at the door shaking hands wid everybody as they comes in. Of course, they're both 'n looking out for the robber. Now it's a curious thing that though they seen everybody as come in, they didn't see the robber among 'em, neither the one nor yet the tother didn't. And agen when all the guests is sat down to the tables, they both walks back'ards an' far'ards, an' back'ards an' far'ards, an' they has a good look at everybody, an' yet they can't find him, though they know as he must be in the room somewheres. "Well, this is uncommon strange," says the master. "But I'll find him yet afore the night is out, just you see."

Now a'ter when they'd all eaten till they couldn't eat no more, an' drunk most all the wine, the master he gets up from his place, an' he begins to make a bit 'n a speech. "I been greatly pleased," he says, "afore you go—and I shall be very sorry to have to part from you—the's just the one thing. I'm now going to call for a toast," he says, "which I wants *all'n* you here present, *every one'n you*, to drink standing up, *wid your left hands flat open above your heads*, so."

It was a cunning trick this was, for the robber you see had the two first fingers 'n his left hand cut off by the middle joints, so that when they all stood up an' raised their hands to drink the toast he was f'un' out. The master tells his sarvants to seize him, an' he sends to fatch a rigiment o' soldiers, an' they comes an' they shoots him. An' that was the end 'n the robber.

Why the Sea Is Salty

Greece

This explanatory tale was sent to me in 1987 in Greek typescript
by Yannis Vrisakis, the president of the Pan-Hellenic Cultural Association of Greek Roma. Born in Athens in 1930, he is now a
political leader in the predominantly Gypsy neighborhood of Ayia
Varvara in Athens.

   St. George's Day is a major festive holiday for Gypsies in the
Balkans, where Turkish Muslim Rom call it the Day of the
Cauldrons.

Once upon a time there were two brothers. One was a wealthy mayor,
and the other was an extremely poor man with six children. The rich
brother didn't help his poor brother, except that once a year, for St.
George's Day, he gave him a lamb.

Well, the day before the holiday the poor brother went to his rich
brother for the lamb and said, "Good morning, brother. St. George's
Day has arrived—give me the lamb so I can go to my children and let
them enjoy this holy day. And if you can manage it, brother, please give
me some other food besides."

The rich brother became enraged as soon as he heard food mentioned, and he said without hesitation: "Get out of my sight! Take your
lamb and give it to Satan, the arch-devil, as a gift."

What was the poor miserable brother supposed to do? He took the
lamb and went home. As soon as his children saw him, they started
shouting, "Papa, when can we cook the lamb?"

"Your uncle the mayor told me to give this lamb to the arch-devil.
And so I'll take the lamb and go to find the arch-devil."

His wife started weeping. "Husband, are you telling me that on this
day you'll leave your family and go to find the arch-devil?"

"I have to find him and give him the lamb."

To carry out his mission, he packed some bread, olives, and cheese
and went to the mountains. After a while he sat down under a plane tree
to rest and eat a little bread.

Just as he finished his snack, a small devil appeared and told him, "I
know you're going to the arch-devil to give him the lamb."

"Yes, but I don't know where to find him."

"It's easy: go into the root of the plane tree. There you'll find a hole. Go into the hole and you'll find the devils all together there. Just be careful that you don't take anything they offer you. And ask for the small brown apple."

And he went where the little devil had said, into the trunk of the tree. Right away the arch-devil saw him and welcomed him cordially: "How is it you come to be in my kingdom, friend?"

"I came to give you this lamb as a present."

"Oh, thank you, my friend. Since you came all this way to visit me and brought a gift as well, sit down and eat before you leave."

In fact he fell asleep there. In the morning he got up to go, and the arch-devil said to him, "My friend, I've loaded forty horses with gold. They're all yours."

"I can't accept the gold—I don't want anything."

The arch-devil answered him, "This is the first time a man has ever come to my home. That's why you can ask of me anything you want."

That's when the poor man thought of the apple. "Then give me the little brown apple."

"Oh, no, my friend, I can't do that."

"Well then, I'll be on my way, arch-devil."

Then the arch-devil's wife butted in and said, "Husband, why is he leaving empty-handed? I won't hear of it! You'll give him the thing that he asked for."

What was the arch-devil to do? He gave the man a little brown apple, which had a cap screwed on to one end.

"Take it, my friend, and be on your way."

And so the man went along the road to his village. When he got tired, he sat down to rest and eat what he had. During his meal he said, "Was I a fool! They were going to give me forty horses laden with gold, and instead I took this little apple." Just then he shook it. A little devil appeared and said to him, "At your service, master."

"Bring me some good food." Well, in no time at all a dinner fit for a king appeared.

Then he understood the power of the little apple. He ordered a horse with wings, which came at once, and he said to it, "Take me to my home, and by the time we reach it, may it be a crystal tower." And it truly did happen.

From the balcony of his crystal tower he saw his wife looking for her home. He called to her and kissed her warmly and said, "Wife, call our children." Their children arrived and rejoiced because of their father's good luck.

As the sun rose the next morning and shone on the mayor's hall where the rich brother lived, the man ordered three officers to take him there. When the mayor saw his brother with an escort and, beyond, a crystal tower standing in the place of the man's home, he understood immediately that some higher power was at work. He said, "Tell me what your power is, or I'll kill you on the spot. Show me what you have that built that tower."

"Brother, come to my tower and I'll show you."

They went to his home that had become a crystal tower and sat in the living room. The man took the apple, turned it, and said, "Gold." Golden coins immediately covered the table. Then the rich brother got out his pistol and said, "Give it to me so that I can disappear from this land."

He took the apple and got into a boat that sailed to the middle of the Atlantic. There was food on board, but it was unsalted. The sailors had forgotten to bring salt, so the captain of the sailboat beat them. The miserly brother went down to the hold, uncapped the apple, and asked for salt. Salt, of course, came out, but he forgot to put the cap back on the apple.

By the time he returned to the hold to close the cap, the boat was sinking because the apple had kept on producing salt—as it does to this very day. And that's why the sea is salty. Think of how many billions of tons of rain, snow, and water from rivers flow into the sea, and it continues to be salty. So that apple must still be producing salt.

Death and the Old Gypsy Woman

Czechoslovakia

This short tale of a wise old woman appears in a volume on Romani published in Germany in 1886.

Once upon a time an old Gypsy woman was going to the forest for wood. She picked up a lot of small branches, made a large bundle of them, and put it in a bag. When she had gone a long way, she sat down at the side of the road and said to herself, *Hmm. It's so heavy, this bag! The end of my life is approaching, and I want Death to take me away. I've lived a long time in this world, and I've gotten very little from it. Where are you, Death? Why aren't you coming for me?*

Death heard her words and came quickly to her. "What do you want from me, you poor Gypsy woman? What can I do for you?"

"Oh, my Lord," she said, "hand me that bag to put on my back. Help me."

"Right away."

"I don't want to die, and I want to take this heavy bag farther along. We only want to die when Death is far away from us."

Napolina

Germany

The following "true" story from southern Germany was recorded by Engelbert Wittich, a non-Romani Traveler married to a Gypsy woman, and published in the *Journal of the Gypsy Lore Society* in 1930. Though the central idea involves the devil and his mysterious ways, the storyteller also conveys a lot about Gypsy baptism customs.

Wittich wrote of Moadel's apprehension on hearing the name "Napolina": "The reason for her alarm is not clear to the recorder, who can only suggest that she connected the name with Napoleon."

Listen, then, dear friends. It was in Würtemberg in the Black Forest, and there were a lot of vans of us Gypsies together. There were the five vans of the Rikelengeri, the two vans of the Schnurmichels, Lerli, Hani of Dornstadt, and the Moadlengeri. The reason why so many Gypsies had met together was that Moadel had had a child. It was two days old and had to be baptized soon. Our vans were standing on the outskirts of the village in the middle of the forest, on a fine large patch. The Moadlengeri had caught with their dog, Godlo, several hedgehogs, and we had just begun to roast them. It was midday, twelve o'clock, dear friends. Who do you suppose came all of a sudden out of the forest and stood among us in the camping place? A fine tall gentleman with a fine black beard, black hair and eyes. He was dressed like a forester in fine green clothes, a fine green hat with a fine big feather in it. Nobody had seen him coming, not even the man on guard, until he came out of the forest and stood there. He went straight to the van where Moadel was sitting and asked her whether her child was baptized yet and whether it was a boy or a girl. When he heard it was a girl, he said to Moadel, "If you will do what I tell you and give your child the name I wish, I will pay for all that you eat and drink, all of you who are here: and you shall all have a good time."

Then Moadel asked him what the child was to be called, and the gentleman said only, "Napolina."

Moadel had already been alarmed at the mysterious appearance of the gentleman, but now she was much more so and really believed it was the devil in the shape of a forester. In fear she called her husband and told him what the gentleman wanted, all in Romani. He said to her, "You must not think so. He is not the devil; and all you have to say is—yes."

Moadel wanted Lerli to act as godmother, and the child to have a second name, Rosina. The gentleman agreed to that.

Now they went quickly into the village to the parson and to church, and Moadel's child was baptized and received those two names, "Rosina Napolina."

After the baptism some of our women and girls had to go with the gentleman to all the bakers in the village—I believe there were two or perhaps even three. There the gentleman bought all the white bread and cakes that the bakers had, and they carried the lot in their aprons and their arms too, as best they could.

Then they went back to the inn where we had been waiting, dear friends, such a long time. And you may imagine what a noise our women made. And, good Lord, how we men opened our eyes when the gentleman ordered straight off from the innkeeper, who was a butcher too, four big barrels of beer and half a pig as well. It made all our mouths water when we saw such a lot of meat. But the best and finest of all was yet to come. The innkeeper was to bring ten bottles of brandy too, and one of our girls was to fetch a whole cheese and a dish full of herrings. You may suppose how overjoyed we were at all these good things, and we thanked the gentleman, praying that the great God in heaven might reward him for it all. But that annoyed him, and he said, "I don't want to listen to such thanks as that. Make a good day of it."

So we said no more, for fear that he would be annoyed and take the whole lot back. So they were all merry, and he told them to take themselves to the vans out at the camping place. They were dancing and singing, and he wanted to hear them play. Soon everything was brought to the camping place. Some of our men brought the beer (those barrels) and that half pig out on a cart; and some of them had to run back again with pots and jugs, which the gentleman had filled with wine. Now, dear friends, there was eating and drinking, cooking and roasting: but the best came first—brandy and herrings. Two barrels of beer were soon disposed of, and the children ate cakes and drank coffee. Now they brought their violins out of the vans and fiddled, sang, and danced. We lived like God in France. Here, there, and everywhere, there was the gentleman. From afar we could distinguish him from the rest by his fine green clothes, his fine green hat with the feather in it. He laughed, and all that he said was, "Eat, drink, play, and dance." Everybody was enjoying themselves immensely.

Only Moadel remained alone in her van with her child and would not let it out of her arms day or night, for fear that it would be stolen from her. Not a thing from the feast did she eat or drink. Her fear kept on increasing, and every time she saw the gentleman from afar she thought he was showing his goat's feet under his green clothes: and when he looked at her with his big black eyes that burned like fire, she believed he was the devil. Everybody told her there was nothing to be afraid of, and the men, whose heads were already half-fuddled, laughed at her.

But it was all of no use; her fear would not leave her. So passed the day and half the night, with dancing and playing, drinking and eating, and midnight drew near. Many of us were lying, muddle-headed, on the ground, when all of a sudden the gentleman was nowhere to be seen or heard. All our searching and shouting for him were in vain. But Moadel said he had been with her just now, by the van, and had given his godchild Napolina, as he called her, some gold pieces, which she showed us. Thereafter she had not seen him again. She thought he had gone from her back to us.

From that time on we never saw him again. In the village too, and in the inn, where we inquired in the morning, and had sent earlier in the night, nobody had seen him. He disappeared as mysteriously as he had appeared. At twelve o'clock he came, and at twelve o'clock again he went. There was something not right about it.

Now we were all assailed by fear and soon came to the conclusion there was witchcraft in it. We laughed no more at Moadel. And when in addition all of a sudden a flock of ravens passed over us and our vans with loud discordant croaking and Moadel said there was ill luck to come, we all shook our heads in fear, and now we too believed it was the devil. And, dear friends, it was the devil. Only listen.

Moadel's child had always been good and so quiet. It was so healthy that its cheeks were like milk and blood, and it had a good appetite. But from the hour when the gentleman disappeared, it roared day and night and would not eat at all. It fell desperately ill, shriveled up entirely, and was soon only skin and bone. After three days it died.

Moadel kept on weeping and tore her hair from grief and fear for her stricken child; but still she too was glad it was dead and no longer in such pain. And we were glad that we no longer had to hear the loud crying and weeping of our women and the child's bereaved mother.

At that unlucky camping place we have never stopped again. Now you too know why we elderly Gypsies never used to stop at that place, though it is a fine one, and always passed on from it. What Moadel said was indeed only too true—it was the devil. And even her husband said to her: "You were right, Moadel. That fine gentleman in the forester's dress was the devil."

The Magic Whistle

Mexico

One of many folktales reflecting the Gypsies' pride in their resourcefulness and flexibility, this story was published in the *Journal of the Gypsy Lore Society* in 1961 by anthropologists David Pickett and George A. Agogino. The storyteller belonged to a group of Mexican Gypsies who had recently arrived in New York State.

According to Stith Thompson in *The Folktale*, the play on the word *no* is most popular in the folklore of the Baltic region, though it is known throughout Europe and is found in the Western Hemisphere as well, having been imported from both Africa and France.

In the old days when the Gypsies lived a nomadic life, before they became city dwellers, there was a Gypsy tramp who, becoming discouraged, lay down beneath a tree and began to cry. God in heaven heard his cries and appeared before him, saying, "Gypsy tramp, why are you crying?"

The Gypsy looked up sorrowfully and said, "I cry because I have no food, and when the sun goes down there is no light, and I am cold, and there is no music to make my heart happy. All I think of is pain and sorrow and loneliness. That is why I am crying."

God was touched by the tramp's story and told him to get up, saying, "Take this handkerchief. Whenever you are hungry, spread it out flat, and the most delicious and savory of foods will appear on it.

"If coldness and darkness surround you, take this ring and rub it gently, and warmth and light will issue from it."

God then gave the Gypsy a whistle, saying, "The gifts I give you are great, but the greatest of these is the whistle, for no man who has it can ever be lonely. Whenever you are sad, blow into the magic whistle and you will hear music that will be a blend of Gypsy violins and heavenly harps. No sweeter or clearer melody exists on earth or in heaven."

The grateful Gypsy prostrated himself in humble thanks before the Lord and wept once again, but this time for joy. When he looked up, the Lord was gone.

Now the Gypsy was eager to try out his magical gifts, but before he was able to investigate his new powers he was arrested for vagrancy and thrown with other delinquents into a dark, cold dungeon. Hoping for success but fearful of failure, he took out his handkerchief and spread it over the dark, damp floor of the prison. Immediately the room was filled with the pleasant aroma of rare and exotic foods. Excitedly the Gypsy rubbed his magic ring: the whole jail glittered and shone like a million stars, and the damp floor became comfortably warm. After all the surprised prisoners had eaten, the Gypsy blew his whistle, and the soft strains of fine music filled the air.

The jailer's daughter was attracted by the music and soon learned about the magic properties of the handkerchief, ring, and whistle. She was a spoiled child, and very demanding, and whenever she was denied something she would have tantrums and grow sick until her poor father thought she would die. So when she asked for the magic objects, the jailer went to the prison and tried to buy them from the Gypsy.

"Please let me buy your magic handkerchief, ring, and whistle," pleaded the jailer, "or else my daughter will get sick and perhaps die."

The Gypsy replied, "One cannot buy such treasures, but if you bring your daughter to the prison, perhaps we can arrange something."

In a short time both the jailer and his daughter stood outside the Gypsy's cell waiting to hear the conditions of the bargain. The Gypsy said he would give the magical objects to the jailer's daughter if her father would agree to say no to four requests that the Gypsy would make.

He is a fool, thought the jailer. "Daughter, quick! Bring pen and paper to draw up a formal contract." In a few moments the contract was written out and signed and the treasured possessions given to the selfish girl. As they turned to leave the prison, the Gypsy asked permission to put his four requests to the jailer, who gave it without hesitation, so joyful was he to have obtained the magic objects.

The Gypsy then asked his first question: "Would you refuse to set me and my fellow prisoners free?"

The jailer hated to do this, since he received a fee for every prisoner in his jail, but he had no choice but to answer no.

The Gypsy then asked the second question: "Would you refuse to give me your house and land?"

Again the answer had to be a reluctant no.

The Gypsy then asked the third question: "Would you refuse to give me back my magic treasures?"

"Alas, I cannot refuse," cried the unhappy jailer, "for I have signed the contract. You have tricked me and I am ruined. What more can you take from me? Ask the final question."

The Gypsy smiled as only Gypsies can smile when they have tricked and defeated someone. "Would you refuse to give your daughter to me in marriage?"

The defeated father replied, "If you are as good a husband as you are a magician and businessman, then I shall be only too happy not to refuse you permission to marry my daughter. Perhaps you can teach her not to be so greedy and spoiled. Her selfish desires certainly have ruined me, but if anyone can handle her, it will be someone with the resourcefulness of a Gypsy."

Bread

Turkey

This tale dealing with the traditional Gypsy concern with luck and life's vicissitudes was told by Fatma Zanbakli Heinschink, born in 1948 in Izmir into the Basketweaver group. Her parents came to Izmir in 1922 from the area around Thessaloniki, Greece, and were nomadic until shortly before her birth. Since 1983 she has been living in Vienna.

Heinschink had this to say about "Bread": "I was seven or eight years old when my father told me this story. Actually, he told it often because he would get mad whenever my sisters would throw bread away. He told us that bread must be granted its due respect. In my group it is a sin to step on bread. I entirely agree with my father on this matter, and whenever I see bread lying in the road, I put it aside so that no one will step on it. We even swear on bread sometimes instead of the Koran: we take a piece of bread in our hand and say, 'Look, if I'm lying to you, may this bread make me blind and crippled!' God gave us a soul, and bread nourishes us."

Bread is the dignity of life. Our old people say, "The more you take care of your bread, the more you guard your luck. If you don't take care of your bread, you don't protect your luck. Throw your bread away and you throw your luck away!"

There was or there was not a Gypsy, and he was so rich that he had no idea what to do with all his treasures. Land, cattle, horses, donkeys, sheep—whatever you could think of, he had. Where should he put his money? "God," he said, "what can I do with so much money? Take some away from me!" But God gave him even more.

Once the Gypsy dreamed that he saw an old man talking to him. The old man said, "Look, when you eat bread, don't eat at the table. Eat standing up. Then," he explained, "God won't give you so much wealth."

When the rich man awoke, he wondered what the dream meant. So when his wife set the table, he didn't sit down. What did he do instead? He tied a napkin around his neck and ate standing up. But the bread-crumbs didn't drop to the floor, because he caught them in the napkin. Afterwards he gathered them and ate them too. He held his bread in great esteem.

And look—God again gave him wealth! Prosperity was his fate. "Oh God," he said, "in my dream someone told me to eat while standing up. So I did, but I was given even more wealth. What can I do to lose some of my luck and to get less?"

He dreamed of the old man again. "I told you," the old man said, "to eat while standing. But you took a napkin and didn't drop one crumb. It's important to let them fall to the floor. Eat that way and God won't keep up your luck anymore."

Again the rich man awoke. *Let's see*, he thought, *what happens if I do as I've been told*. He took some bread, eating it the way he had been told, and look—that day it started raining! It rained and rained, and three hundred, five hundred sheep died. There was a big flood, and all his sheep drowned.

"Now," he said, "I've lost all my luck with this bread." The next day he ate his bread the same way, and look—there arose a storm so strong that his house collapsed. And day by day he continued to lose cattle and riches until he finally became quite poor. What to do now?

"Oh God," he said, "what now? I complained and I got this storm. I complained about my wealth, my money. Now let's see if I can get a little luck back."

So, you know, again he caught the crumbs when eating his bread. And God gave him back all he wanted: cattle, horses, donkeys, pigs. And he grew rich again.

I was there and now I am here.

The Enchanted House

Spain

This ghost story was told in Spanish to Antonio Gómez Alfaro by María Jiménez Salazar, a Gypsy who lives in Madrid and occasionally does migrant labor in other parts of Spain. She is vice-president of Presencia Gitana, a Madrid-based group that helps the Gypsies help themselves in their struggle for equality.

The story is one of many that Jiménez Salazar heard from her father as a child. Besides the emphasis on the Gypsies' characteristic hospitality, I find interesting the *payo* neighbor's reason for not warning the Gypsies about the haunted house—not all non-Gypsies are so aware of Gypsies' feelings of rejection.

In Old Castile a summer storm surprised three Gypsy families who were traveling together to seek a living. They saw a small, scattered group of houses, one of which looked uninhabited, and they decided to take refuge there. Happy to have a shelter, they prepared their sleeping mats and went to sleep.

In the middle of the night they woke up unexpectedly with an unusual anguished feeling of hunger.

"Cook some soup, please, I'm fainting," said the Gypsy man to his wife.

"What a long night!" wailed one of the children with a faltering voice.

The Gypsy woman started cooking a meager soup, for she had only a little bread, some oil, garlic, tomato, parsley, a bay leaf, and salt. Looking up from the fire, she saw a very old man, with a blindingly white beard, coming down the stairs.

"Poor old *payo*, he is as poor as ourselves!" said the Gypsy woman compassionately, thinking he was a burglar who had taken refuge in the house as they had. Suspicious because they had not seen him before, the Gypsies asked the old man where he had been.

"I live upstairs," the unknown man answered, and then he asked for some salt.

Once he had taken the salt shaker, the old man went up the stairs back to the loft where he had come from. As he disappeared, before the Gypsies could make any comment, a flash of lightning suddenly lit up the room, and thunder crashed. Scared, they ran to the door, and on opening they saw that, outside the house, the storm was over. Thunderbolts were now occurring inside the house, while outside it was perfectly calm and the summer sun shone.

A neighbor woman came up to them and, when she heard what had happened, told them, "That was a close call!" Then she explained that she had seen them approaching the house and had thought to warn them not to go in, but then decided not to, afraid the Gypsies would think she was just trying to keep them from taking refuge. The house was haunted, and the soul of a *payo* was dwelling in it: the *payo* they had seen. Doubtless the salt he had asked for he needed for an exorcism to break the spell, and the thunderbolts meant that he had finally recovered his peace forever. Before the Gypsies came, some other people were known to have entered the house but nobody saw them go out again. Possibly they couldn't or didn't want to satisfy the old man's demand, which the Gypsies had so hospitably complied with.

Jack and His Golden Snuffbox

Wales

Welsh Gypsy harpist John Roberts (1815–1894) told this story, of the Aladdin type, to Francis Hindes Groome.

Three motifs prominent in the folktales of many other cultures appear here: the character (usually a boy) who sets out to see the world; the prospective bride's father who assigns difficult tasks to suitors; and animals that help the hero in various ways. Bruno Bettelheim, whose psychoanalytic approach to folktales is set forth in *The Uses of Enchantment*, has suggested that helpful animals such as these represent inner resources without which the main character would be unable to lead an effective life.

One element of this story that reveals its origins is the narrator's proud and affectionate attitude toward the Gypsy woman, who earns everyone's high regard.

Once in a great forest there lived an old man and an old woman who had only one son, Jack. And although Jack had never seen any other people in his life, he knew that there were others in the world besides his own father and mother, because he had lots of books.

One day, when his father was out cutting wood, Jack told his mother that he wished to make his living in some other country and to meet some other people. He said, "I see nothing here but great trees all around me. If I stay, I might go mad before I see *anything*!"

The old woman began by saying, "Well, my boy, if you want to go, it's better for you to go, and God be with you." (The old woman thought this was for the best.) "But stop a bit first: which would you rather I made for you—a little cake with a blessing, or a big cake with a curse?"

"Make me a big cake," said Jack. "I might get hungry on the road."

So the old woman made the big cake, went up on top of the house, and cursed him as far as she could see him.

Then Jack met his father, who asked him, "Where are you going, my boy?" When Jack told his father the same tale he had told his mother, his father said, "Well, I'm sorry to see you leave, but if you've made up your mind, it's better for you to go."

Jack had not gone far at all before his father called him back and drew a golden snuffbox out of his pocket. "Here, take this little box, and put it in your pocket. But be sure not to open it till you are near your death."

Away went Jack down the road, and he walked till he was tired and hungry, for by that time he had eaten all his cake. Now night was closing in on him, and he could hardly see. At last he saw some light a long way ahead.

He went towards it, found the back door of a house, and knocked until one of the maidservants came and asked him what he wanted. When Jack said he needed a place to sleep, the maidservant called him into the kitchen and gave him plenty to eat—good meat and bread and beer. As Jack was eating his refreshments by the fire, the young lady of the house came in to have a look at him. And she loved him right away, and he loved her.

The young lady ran to tell her father that there was a handsome young man in the back kitchen. Immediately the gentleman came in and asked him what work he could do. Jack, the silly fellow, said that he could do *anything* (meaning that he could do any odd jobs that might be needed about the house).

"Well," the gentleman said to him, "at eight o'clock in the morning I must have a great lake and some of the largest man-of-war vessels sailing before my mansion. One of the largest vessels must fire a royal salute, and the last round must break the leg of the bed where my young daughter is sleeping. And if you can't do that, you will have to forfeit your life."

"All right," said Jack. And away he went to his bed, and said his prayers quietly. But he slept till almost eight o'clock and had hardly any time to think what he was going to do, when all of a sudden he remembered the little golden box his father had given him. He said to himself, *Well, I never was so near my death as I am now,* felt in his pocket, and drew the little box out.

And when Jack opened it, out hopped three little red men, who asked him, "What do you want us to do?"

"Well," said Jack, "I want a great lake and some of the largest man-of-war vessels in the world before this mansion, and one of the largest vessels to fire a royal salute, and the last round to break one of the legs of the bed where the young lady of the house is sleeping."

"All right," said the little men. "Go back to sleep."

But Jack had barely told the little men what to do when eight o'clock came, and bang! bang! went one of the largest man-of-war vessels. The noise made Jack jump out of bed and look out the window. And I can assure you it was a wonderful sight for him to see, after living so long with only his father and mother in the woods.

Now Jack dressed himself, said his morning prayers, and came down laughing, proud that the thing had been done so well.

The gentleman came up to him and said, "Well, my young man, I must say that you are very clever indeed. Come and have some breakfast." And he continued, "Now there are two more things you will have to do before you shall have my daughter in marriage . . ." And while Jack was eating his breakfast, he had a good squint at the young lady, and she at him.

The next thing the gentleman told him to do was to cut down all the great trees for miles around by eight o'clock the following morning. And, to make my long story shorter, it was done.

The gentleman then said to him, "The other thing you have to do" (and it was the last thing), "you must get me a great castle standing on twelve golden pillars, and it must be guarded by regiments of soldiers who will go through their drill. At eight o'clock tomorrow morning the commanding officer must say, 'Shoulder up.' "

"All right," replied Jack—and when the third morning came, the last of the three great feats was accomplished, and Jack took the young daughter in marriage.

But, oh dear! There is worse to come.

The gentleman now got together a large hunting party. He invited all the other gentlemen around the country to it—and to see his new castle as well. By this time Jack had a beautiful horse and a scarlet uniform so he could go hunting with them.

On that morning his valet, when putting Jack's regular clothes away, put his hand in one of the waistcoat pockets and pulled out the little golden snuffbox, which poor Jack had left behind by mistake. And when the valet opened the little box, out hopped the three little red men, asking him what he wanted with them.

"Well," replied the valet, "I'd like this castle to be moved from this place far across the sea."

"All right," said the little red men. "Do you wish to come with it?"

"Yes."

"Well, get up," they said, and far away over the great sea they went.

Now the grand hunting party came back, and the castle upon the twelve golden pillars was nowhere to be seen—to the great disappointment of those gentlemen who had not seen it before. And poor silly Jack was threatened with losing his beautiful young wife. But the gentleman finally came to an agreement with him: Jack had a year and a day to find the castle. So off he went with a good horse and money in his pocket.

In search of his missing castle poor Jack traveled over hills, dales, valleys, and mountains, through woolly woods and sheepwalks, farther than I can tell you tonight or ever intend to tell you. Until at last he came to the place of the king of all the little mice in the world.

One of the mice was on sentry at the front gate of the palace, and he tried to stop Jack from going in. But when Jack asked the mouse, "Where does the king live? I wish to see him," the sentry sent another mouse with him to show him around.

When the Mouse King saw Jack, he called him in and asked where he was going. Well, Jack told him the truth: that he had lost the great castle and was going to look for it, and he had but a year and a day to find it. And when Jack asked whether he knew anything about it, the Mouse King replied, "No, but I am the king of all the little mice in the world, and I will call them all in the morning. Maybe they have seen something of it."

Then Jack got a good meal and a bed, and in the morning he and the Mouse King went out to the fields. Then the Mouse King called all the mice together and asked if they had seen the great beautiful castle standing on golden pillars. And all the little mice said no, that none of them had seen it.

The Mouse King then told Jack that he had two brothers: "One is the king of all the frogs, and my other brother, who is the oldest, is the king of all the birds in the world. If you go to them, maybe they will know something about your missing castle." And the Mouse King continued, "Leave your horse here with me till you come back. Take one of my best horses with you, and give this cake to my brother. He will know who you got it from. Remember to tell him that I am well and would dearly like to see him."

Then the Mouse King and Jack shook hands. When Jack was at the gate, the little sentry mouse asked whether he should accompany him. Jack replied, "No, I'll get myself in trouble with your king."

But the little mouse told him, "It will be better for you to have me with you. Maybe I'll do you some good sometime without your knowing it."

"Jump up, then."

So the little sentry ran up the horse's leg and made it dance, and Jack put the mouse in his pocket. And Jack rode on his way. But he had a very long way to go, and this was only his first day.

Finally he found the place he was looking for. There was a frog on sentry, a gun on his shoulder, and he tried to detain Jack. But when Jack told him that he wanted to see the king of the frogs, he allowed him to pass, and Jack went up to the door.

The Frog King came out and asked him his business, and Jack told him everything from beginning to end.

"Well, well, come in."

Jack was well entertained that night, and in the morning the King made a curious sound and collected all the frogs in the world. He asked them if they knew anything of a castle that stood upon twelve golden pillars. And they all made a curious sound, *kro-kro, kro-kro*, and said no.

Jack then had to take another horse, and another cake, to the brother who was king of all the birds of the air. And as Jack was going through the gate, the little frog on sentry asked Jack if he should come with him. At first Jack refused him, but then told him to jump up, and he put him in his other waistcoat pocket.

And away he went again on his great long journey—this part of it three times longer than all the rest before it. However, at last he found the place. There was a fine bird on sentry, and Jack passed right by him without saying a word. Then Jack talked with the king of the birds, and told him all about the missing castle.

"Well," the Bird King said to him, "you shall find out in the morning from my birds whether they know anything or not."

Jack put his horse in the stable and, after having something to eat, went to bed. In the morning he went out to the fields with the Bird King, who made some funny noise and summoned together all the birds in the world. He asked them if they had seen the fine castle, and all the birds answered no.

"Well," said the Bird King, "where is the great bird?"

Two little birds were sent high up in the sky to whistle to the eagle to make all possible haste. Then they had to wait a long time until at last the eagle came, all in a sweat. The King asked the great bird if he had seen the great castle. And the eagle said, "Yes, I've come from where it now stands."

"Well," said the Bird King, "this young gentleman has lost it, and you must take him back to it. But stop and have a bit of something to eat first."

So they killed a thief and gave the best parts to feed the eagle on his journey over the seas, and the great bird had to carry Jack on his back.

Now, when they finally came in sight of the castle, they did not know how to get the little golden box back. The mouse said to them, "Let me down, and *I* will get the little box for you." So the mouse stole into the castle and got hold of the box. But when he was coming down the stairs, he fell and was nearly caught. Eventually he came running out, laughing.

"Have you got it?" Jack asked him.

The little mouse said yes, and back they went, leaving the castle behind. As they were all of them (Jack, the mouse, the frog, and the eagle) passing over the great sea, they began quarreling about just who it was that had retrieved the little box, and it dropped into the water.

"Well, well," said the frog, "I knew I would have to do something useful. You had better let me go down in the sea."

And they let him go, and he was underwater for a day and a night before he showed his little nose and mouth above the surface. All of them asked, "Did you get it?" but he had to tell them no.

"Well, what were you doing down there, then?"

"Nothing at all," the poor little frog said. "I just came up for a full breath." Then he went down for the second time. And he was underwater for three days and three nights before he brought the golden box up.

Then away they went, and after a long haul over seas and mountains they arrived at the palace of the king of all the birds in the world.

The Bird King was very glad to see them, and they had a hearty welcome and a long conversation. Jack opened the box and told the three little red men to go bring back the castle: "And all of you make as much haste as you possibly can."

The three little men went off, but when they came up to the castle, they were afraid to go in until the gentleman and the lady and the servants had all gone out to a dance. Then there was no one left behind except the cook and one maid. It also happened that a poor Gypsy woman, knowing that the family was going out, was there at the time. She had made her way to the castle to offer to tell the cook's fortune for a bit of food. And the three little red men asked her which would she rather do: go or stay behind?

She said, "I'll go with you."

So they told her to run upstairs quickly. She was no sooner up in one of the drawing rooms than the gentleman, the lady, and all their servants came into sight, back from the dance. But it was too late for them—off went the castle at full speed. The Gypsy woman laughed through the window at the gentleman and the lady, who were motioning for the castle to stop, but all to no purpose.

The journey took nine days, during which those in the castle tried to keep the Sunday holy, for one of the little red men turned out to be a priest, another a choirmaster, and the third presided at the organ, while the three women (the cook, the housemaid, and the Gypsy woman) formed the choir, and they had a grand chapel in the castle already. At one point there was discord in the music. When one of the little men ran up an organ pipe to see where the bad sound was coming from, he found out that it was the three women laughing at the little red organist stretched full length across the bass pipes. On his head was his little red nightcap, which he never forgot to wear on Sundays but which they had never witnessed before.

At length, after quite a merry journey, they arrived again at the palace of the king of all the birds. The King was quite struck with the sight of the castle, and as he was going up the golden stairs to see the rooms inside, the first thing that attracted his attention was the poor Gypsy woman. He said, "How are you, sister?"

She said to him, "I am very well. How are you?"

"Quite well," he replied. "Come into my palace. I'd like to have a talk with you, and see who you are, and who your people are."

The old Gypsy woman told him that some of her people were from the Lovells, the Stanleys, the Lees, and I don't know all their names. The Bird King and Jack were very much pleased with the Gypsy woman's conversation, but poor Jack's time of a year and a day was drawing to a close. Wishing to go home to his young wife, he gave the three little men orders that by eight o'clock the next morning they should be ready to go off to the next brother, the Frog King, and to stop there for one night. They were then to proceed to the youngest brother, the Mouse King, in whose care the castle would be left until sent for.

Jack said farewell to the Bird King, thanked him very much for his hospitality, and told him not to be surprised should they meet again in some other country.

Away went Jack and his castle to stop one night with the Frog King, then away again to the Mouse King to leave the castle in his care. Jack then mounted his own horse, which he had left behind on first starting his journey. The Mouse King also liked the Gypsy woman very much, and he told her he'd be glad if she would stay with him, so the Gypsy woman remained with him until Jack sent for her.

Now poor Jack left his castle behind once again and turned toward home. After so much merriment with the three royal brothers each night, Jack became sleepy on horseback and would have lost the road but for the three little red men guiding him. When at last he arrived, weary and tired, he was received with no kindness whatsoever, because apparently he had not found the stolen castle. To make it worse, he was disappointed in not seeing his young and beautiful wife, whose parents kept her from coming to meet him.

But this state of affairs did not last long. First Jack and the three little men set off to retrieve the castle. They soon got to the Mouse King, and the first person they saw was the poor Gypsy woman outside gathering sticks for the fire. And when they whistled* to her, she turned around smartly and said to them, "*Dordi, dordi*!** how are you, comrades? Where do you come from, and where are you going now?"

"Well, to tell you the truth, we're here to take this castle away. Do you wish to stay here or to come with us?" asked the three little red men.

"I'd prefer to go with you," she replied.

"Well, come on then, my poor sister," said Jack.

He shook hands with the Mouse King and returned many thanks for his royal kindness. But all of a sudden, the King, seeing the Gypsy woman, whom he fancied and liked so much, decided to detain the castle until he could persuade her to stay with him. Jack, perceiving his intentions and wanting the Gypsy woman himself for a nurse, instructed the little red men to get going with all possible speed.

So off they went a final time, and it was not long before they reached their journey's end, where Jack's wife came out to meet him with a fine young son.

Now, to make my long story short at last, Jack—having completed all his tasks—decided to make it up to the poor homesick Gypsy woman. He got the loan of one of his father-in-law's largest men-of-war which was lying at anchor, and he sent the three little red men to bring her kinsfolk to her. After a long search they were found and brought back, to the great joy of the Gypsy woman and the delight of Jack's wife's relatives, for in a while they all became very fond of each other. When the Gypsies landed, Jack's people allowed them to camp near a beautiful

*Gypsies have different kinds of whistles, one peculiar to each family, by which they can recognize one another at a distance or in the dark. [Groome's note.]
***Dordi*: a common Gypsy exclamation in the British Isles.

river, and the gentlemen and the ladies used to go and see them every day.

Jack and his wife had many more children, and each one had some of the Gypsy girls for nurses. The little children became almost half Gypsies, for the girls were continually teaching them our language. And the last time I was there, I played my harp for them, before I had to leave again.

One Hundred Cows

Czechoslovakia

This anticlerical tale and the following story were told to Milena Hübschmannová by Laci Tancoš in 1954, at which time he was working as a plumber. The father of eleven children, he was born and still lives in Petrovany, East Slovakia.

There was once a priest who used to give a sermon every week, claiming that anyone who gave him a goose or a cow or a hen would be repaid by God a hundred times over. So the people used to take the priest hens, cows, and geese, and then wait for God to repay them.

A Rom came home from church one day and said to his wife, "Listen here, we've got one cow—I think I'll take her to the priest." (The priest already had ninety-nine cows.)

The woman cried, "Oh, you stupid man, how are we going to feed the children, how are we ever going to look after them?" (They had fifteen children.)

"Don't worry, woman," said the husband. "God will repay us a hundred times over for this cow, just as the priest said."

So the Rom led the cow to the priest. The next day, the Rom's cow was pastured with the priest's cows—now an even hundred. The Rom's cow stood in front, with all the others behind her. In the evening the

Rom's cow ambled back to him, and all those ninety-nine cows followed after her.

The Rom called out to his wife, "Hey, you and the children—go get the ropes, all that we've got in the house, and tie up these cows. God has repaid us a hundred times."

The priest ran after the Rom, shouting, "How dare you steal my cows!"

The Rom replied, "But, Father, didn't you yourself preach in a sermon that whoever gives you anything, God will repay a hundred times over? Well, God has repaid me for giving you my cow."

So what could the priest do? He went home and cried.

And if that Rom hasn't died, he's still living today.

The Romni's Riddle

Czechoslovakia

For a story with a similar message, see the Banjara tale "Husband or Brother?" on pages 19–20.

There was once a Romni whose husband was in prison, and she, poor thing, was left alone with her baby. She was very miserable with her husband away from home, so she went to the city court to try to get her husband set free.

Well, the judge said, "Look here, I'll let your husband go free if you can tell me a riddle I can't solve."

The Romni set out for home, all the while trying hard to think of a riddle that the judge wouldn't be able to solve. All she had with her to eat as she walked from village to village was a small loaf of bread. While passing over a bridge, she paused, took out the bread, and stood eating it and giving her baby the breast. Some breadcrumbs fell into the water and were swallowed by fishes. Not only that, but some birds flying overhead were chirping hungrily. Well, everybody wants to eat, right? So the Romni threw some crumbs to the birds too.

Then the Romni turned around and went back to the court. She said to the judge, "Well, Your Honor, I've brought you a riddle:

> I eat and also he eats of me,
> They eat beneath and over me,
> Tell me then, how can that be?"

The judge thought for a while but couldn't work it out. Then he called in some qualified riddle-solvers, but they couldn't solve it either.

"Well, Romni," said the judge, "explain your riddle, and if it is true, we'll let your husband go—we can't solve it."

"Listen, Your Honor, this is how it goes:

> I stand on a little bridge and eat,
> My baby sucks upon my teat,
> Fishes are eating down below,
> While crumbs to the hungry birds I throw.

Everybody wants to eat, every living thing wants to eat."

Then the judge saw that the Romni was right, and so he let her husband go home.

The Riddle

Turkey

Leon Zafiri, a Turkish Gypsy who was by profession a mower, a musician, and a storyteller, narrated this tale. He repeated many of his stories to Alexandros Paspatis, a Greek doctor who practiced medicine in Istanbul and wrote a classic grammar and dictionary of Romani in 1870. In this work, published in French, he included two of Zafiri's tales in their entirety and fragments from many others. Paspatis reported that Zafiri would tell these stories to other Gypsies during the long winter nights. The second part of this tale is quite similar to the Grimms' "Riddle."

Once there was a rich man who had a son. Both the mother and the father loved their boy very much. He went to school and learned all there was to learn in the world.

One day the boy woke up, took four or five bags of money, and spent all of it here and there. Early the next day he went to his father and asked for more money, and by night he had spent it. Little by little he spent all their money.

Again he awoke early and asked his parents for money.

"My child, there is no more money. Do you want the saucepans? Take them, sell them, and eat."

He sold them and spent the money in a day or two. When he asked for money again, his father replied, "My son, we have no more money. Take our clothes and sell them."

In a day or two he had spent the money. Again he went to his father and demanded money. "My child," his father said, "we have no more. If you want, sell the house."

The boy went and sold the house and in one month had spent all the money.

"Father, I need money."

"My child, we have neither money nor a home. If you want, take us to the slave market and sell us."

The boy sold them. His parents asked him to visit them so they would be able to see him.

It was the king who bought the boy's mother and father. And the boy, with the proceeds from his mother, bought himself clothes; with the money from his father, he bought himself a horse.

After a day or two, when the mother and father realized that their son wasn't coming to see them, they began to weep.

When the king's servants saw them weeping, they went to tell the king that the slaves he had bought were weeping loudly. The king asked that they be brought to him.

"Why are you weeping?"

"We had a son, and we are weeping for him."

The king asked, "Who are you?"

"We weren't always like this. We had a son; he sold our things and then sold even us, and we are weeping for him because he hasn't come to see us."

At that moment the son happened to arrive.

The king then wrote a letter, put it in the boy's hands, and told him where to deliver it. In the letter the king had written, "As soon as you receive this letter, cut the throat of the boy delivering it."

The boy got dressed, put the letter away, mounted his horse, and went on his way.

While crossing a large province, and burning up with thirst, he saw a well. He secured the letter on a string, let it down into the well, then brought it back up and wrung some water into his mouth. Then he decided to see what was in the letter. What did he read? "As soon as you receive this letter, cut the throat of the boy delivering it." The boy was dumbfounded.

At a certain place there lived a princess. Men would go to her and tell her a riddle. If the princess solved it, the man's throat was cut, but if she couldn't solve it, the man would marry her.

The boy got up and went to the king's palace.

"Why have you come, my boy?"

"I want to speak to the king's daughter."

"You will speak to her, and if she solves your riddle, she will have your throat cut. If she can't solve it, you will marry her."

"That's just what I've come for." He sat down in front of the princess.

The princess said, "Tell me your riddle."

The boy said, "I've worn my mother, I've ridden my father, and I've drunk the water of my own death."

The princess looked in her book of riddles, but this one she was unable to solve. She said, "Give me three more days."

"I'll give them to you," said the boy. And he got up and went to an inn to sleep.

The princess realized that she couldn't solve the riddle. She had a tunnel made to the inn where the boy was sleeping. At midnight she woke, went to him, and embraced him. "I am yours and you are mine—tell me the answer to the riddle."

He wouldn't tell her. "Get undressed," he said to the princess.

She undressed. "Tell me," she said.

He explained the riddle.

The princess clapped her hands, and her servants arrived to take her back to the palace. She was wearing the boy's shirt, and he hers.

At daybreak they called the boy to the palace. He mounted his horse and went. People watched him and felt sad that he would be killed.

He came face to face with the king.

"My daughter has solved your riddle," said the king.

"How did she solve it? While I was sleeping last night a bird came to my breast. I caught it, cut it, and cooked it. At the moment I would have eaten it, it flew away."

The king said he was insane and would be killed.

"I'm not insane—I'm the one who solved the riddle for your daughter. She had a tunnel made and came to where I was sleeping. She came into my arms, I had her undress, I embraced her and gave her the answer. She clapped her hands for her servants, who took her away. And if you don't believe me, look: I'm wearing her shirt and she's wearing mine."

The king saw that it was true.

The wedding lasted forty days and forty nights. The boy married the princess and bought back his father and his mother.

Why the Jews and the Gypsies Are Enemies

Bulgaria

This tale, based on the tradition that the Gypsies came from Egypt, was related in the 1960s in Bulgarian by Stefan Demirov, of the Drindari group, who works as a classical musician and conductor in Shumen. Despite the theme of the story, Donald Kenrick, who wrote the tale down, comments, "In fact, sharing a common lot of persecution, there are many links of friendship nowadays between the Gypsies and the Jews, both at an official and a personal level."

In the time of the Gypsy king Pharaoh, the Jewish leader Moses came to him and said that Pharaoh and his people should worship the Jewish god. Pharaoh said that before they would consider being converted, Moses should show by a miracle that his religion was the true one, and a meeting was arranged for the following day. Meanwhile, Pharaoh's engineers set to work and built an installation on the Nile.

When Moses came the next day, Pharaoh asked him to make the waters of the Nile flow in the opposite direction. Moses could not. Then Pharaoh's engineers made the water flow backwards, and Pharaoh said, "You see, our brains can do more than your god."

Then Moses became angry and called upon God to curse Pharaoh and his people. God condemned the Gypsies to wander forever over the face of the earth, and since that day the Gypsies and the Jews have been enemies.

The Three Travelers

England

The following anecdote was sent to me in Romani by Ian Hancock, Gypsy political activist and Professor of Linguistics and English at the University of Texas at Austin, where he teaches courses on Gypsy language and culture and the Gypsy in literature. Hancock says that he heard this story as a young boy in England and that whenever people got together it was repeated and eventually became "more formulaic than amusing."

The story is an example of an in-group poking fun at itself. Whether such stories are to be made available to outsiders is a sensitive issue, particularly when the in-group has, like the Gypsies, been the victim of racism for centuries.

Maybe there were and maybe there weren't three travelers who traveled together a long time on the road. One was Indian, one was a Jew, and the third was a Gypsy.

They stopped one night at a farm. They asked the farmer if they could sleep in his house. The farmer told them he had a small room near a barn but there were only two beds: one of the men would have to sleep in the barn.

"No bother," said the Indian. "I'll sleep in the barn." He went. After a few minutes, back he came. "Brothers, I can't sleep there. You know that we Indians believe the cow is family. It doesn't seem to me a good idea to sleep in that barn."

"Well," said the Jew, "let me go sleep there. Take my place." And he left.

He immediately came back. "I can't sleep there, brothers—there's a pig in the barn, and as you truly know, I'm a Jew. For us, pigs are not kosher. I pray you, one of you change places with me."

"Well," said the Gypsy, "it's nothing for me to sleep in the barn. Take my place here." Then he went.

In a few minutes the two *gaje* in the room heard a knock on the door. When it was opened, the cow and the pig were standing in front of them.

"Listen," said the cow, "now there's a Gypsy in the barn. If you have good hearts, let us sleep here with you. We can't stay in that place with a dirty Gypsy."

The Bird and the Golden Cage

Greece

This tale has elements of two popular and widespread stories: "The Golden Bird" and "The Water of Life." The universal theme of the youngest brother succeeding in his undertaking despite his two older brothers' treachery is found in this and many other Gypsy stories. (See also "Tale of a Foolish Brother and of a Wonderful Bush," pages 55–61.) On the motif of helpful animals, see the introduction to "Jack and His Golden Snuffbox," page 124.

Diamandis Asteriadis, a Thessaloniki shopkeeper, told me the story in the summer of 1985.

Once upon a time there was a king who had three sons. When these sons were of age, their father said to them, "My children, now you're grown. Soon I will die and one of you three will take over the kingdom, the palace, and all the rest. But before I hand over the palace and the kingdom, I have to see who is the most worthy."

The sons then asked, "Papa, what do you want us to do?"

Their father answered, "I've been working for so many years, and now I have a yearning: somewhere on this earth, I've heard, there lives a beautiful bird in a golden cage, and now it's too late for me to go and get it myself. All these years a king and I couldn't get it. Whoever brings me the bird in its cage can have the kingdom."

The two older sons set off, while the youngest stayed behind. After thinking about it, however, he decided to follow his brothers secretly.

After he'd been on his way for about a week, struggling day and night, he found himself at a crossroads. All of a sudden a wolf appeared before him. "Hey," the wolf said. "Stop. Where are you going?"

"Where should I be going?" the youngest prince said. Then he told the wolf of his father's promise. "And if I don't bring him the bird in its cage, he'll disinherit me and I won't get anything."

The wolf said, "Here on this road you're on the way to that bird. But if you want to capture it, you'll have to be very careful: take the bird but not the cage. Afterward you'll get the cage too. Now get on my back," said the wolf, transforming himself into a horse. "I'll take you to the cave where the forty dragons live, and there you'll find the bird."

When they arrived at the mouth of the cave, the wolf said, "I'll wait for you here. It's exactly the hour when all the dragons are asleep, so you can go inside and take the bird. But don't make the mistake of taking the cage as well."

When the prince went in, he saw a cage with a beautiful little bird inside. "Ah," he said, "what a beautiful thing! It was worth all the trouble." He went in, opened the little door, and captured the bird. As he was leaving, he said, "But where could I ever find such a cage? I must take it too," for the cage was even more beautiful than the bird.

Just as he snatched up the cage, bells began ringing, and the next second all forty dragons were right behind him. He ran, jumped on the horse, and galloped away.

As soon as they returned to the crossroads where they had met, the horse changed back into a wolf and went on his way and the prince left for his village, taking the bird and the cage.

On the way back he got tired and stopped to sleep. At the same time, his two brothers were also returning to tell their father that they hadn't found the bird. But when they saw their brother sleeping next to the beautiful bird and the golden cage, they had the evil thought of killing him and taking the bird and cage to get the kingdom for themselves. So they hit him once and killed him. Then they took the bird and the cage and left.

Now, the wolf and the youngest brother had become very close, and at that moment, just by chance, the wolf was passing by. He saw that the boy was dead and understood immediately what had happened. But what could he do?

At last he remembered that somewhere there existed a spring where the water of immortality flowed. But only a certain kind of bird could fetch this water. So he caught a baby bird and said to its mother, "I won't give your child back until you bring me the water of immortality." So the mother bird went and found the spring and brought the water back to the wolf, who immediately used it to bring the prince back to life.

In the meantime, the other brothers were busy celebrating. Since they had brought the bird and cage to their father, he was planning to sign all his wealth over to them. And they had announced the death of the youngest brother (lying, of course, about how he had died).

The wolf once again became a horse. "Come along," he said to the prince. They went to the palace, and as soon as they arrived they saw the celebration. "Now," said the horse, "I'm going to change shape again—this time into a man, and I'll be your witness."

The wolf, being a magical creature, was able to transform both himself and the boy. And so he changed the boy's appearance too. Soon they heard that at midnight the contracts would be signed. Many kings were gathered there. The wolf presented himself as a lawyer and cried out, "Stop! No one is to speak. Everything these two brothers have said is a lie. Your youngest son isn't dead, he's alive. Come here," he said to the king, "I'll show you your youngest son."

The king saw his youngest son (now transformed by the wolf back to his original shape) and couldn't believe his eyes. "Where have you been, my son?"

"Papa, I'm the one who brought you the beautiful bird." And he told his father the whole story. "And now I'm here."

"And how did you get here?"

"You'll see—my witness here will turn himself into a horse."

The lawyer indeed turned into a horse, and the king was convinced. He had the two older sons brought to trial and gave the entire kingdom to his youngest son.

The Gypsy Lawyer

Italy

Good sense prevails in this story told by Bruno Levak (Zlato) to Mirella Karpati, editor of the Italian journal of Gypsy studies, *Lacio Drom*. This version of a widespread tale, published in 1984 in an Italian collection of Zlato's work, has a nearly identical Turkish counterpart, "Nasreddin Khoja as a Witness in Court."

Once there was a very poor priest who always traveled on foot. One day on his way home he became extremely tired, hungry, and too weak to walk any farther. He went into an inn and ordered four boiled eggs. He also had four rolls and half a liter of wine.

Then he said to the innkeeper, "I can't pay—I don't have a cent."

"Okay, no problem. Some other time when you're passing by, you can pay me."

Later on this priest became rich. He married a rich woman (in that place the priests get married, just as we do). Ten years went by, and he had become so rich that he started traveling by horse and carriage.

One day he was passing by that same inn, and—the poor stupid thing—he said, "Right here, I remember, when I was poor I had four eggs, four rolls, and a half-liter of wine. Now, thank God, I've got everything I want and can repay my debt."

So he went in and said to the innkeeper, "Ten years have gone by since I had those four eggs, four rolls, and a half-liter of wine."

"Fine," said the innkeeper. "Let's figure out the bill." Well, he wrote here, he wrote there, and when he was done, that bill wouldn't fit on the wall. It was so large that the priest couldn't pay it with everything he owned. The innkeeper calculated that four hens would have hatched from the four eggs, how many eggs those hens would have laid in ten years, how many hens . . . and so on. The priest would have ended up without anything he had with him: even if he had given up his carriage, it wouldn't have paid that bill.

"I'll get a lawyer," said the innkeeper, "and we'll go to court."

The priest walked home, crying in despair. And who did he find in the street? A poor Gypsy, his mouth full of chewing tobacco and spitting in all directions, who asked, "Why are you crying?"

"A fine thing to ask, my friend!" said the priest. "I'm ruined."

"Ruined? Why?"

"Because I was stupid. Ten years ago I had four eggs, four rolls, and a half-liter of wine on credit. Now my entire fortune isn't enough to repay the innkeeper."

"And *that's* why you're trembling with fear?"

"Yes, he's figured the bill for how many eggs, how many hens in ten years . . . It's endless!"

"Never fear. I'll be your lawyer, and if we win the case all I want is four packs of tobacco and a pipe."

Well! The day of the case arrived, and all the lawyers sided with the innkeeper—they said the priest should pay and maybe even go to prison. But the priest's lawyer wasn't there.

The case was almost closed when in he came, dressed in rags and spitting all over the place. The lawyers and judges began laughing like madmen.

"And this is your lawyer?"

"The very one."

"How come you're late? Where were you?"

"Where was I? Well, my friends, I went home to boil some corn so I could plant it."

"But how can corn grow if it's cooked?"

"And from cooked eggs, how can you get hens?"

The Creation

New Zealand

R. A. W. (Ron) Barnes, the narrator of this tale, had the following to say about his early days: "I started life in a very modest way, followed the Drom [road] until I was about eight years old, then with the great depression in England and there being no casual work available, my family moved to London." After leaving school at fourteen, he got a job in the post office and soon became a postal telecommunications officer. When World War II broke out, he joined the RAF. In 1948 he left England for Australia, and in 1950 he left Australia for New Zealand. In 1987 he closed his health clinic, Opre Roma ("Rise Up, Gypsies"), in Auckland and now teaches health-related workshops around the world.

This story has also been told by Gypsies in Alsace and in Chile.

At the time of the creation God felt that he would like to make human beings in his own image, so he got plenty of flour and water, mixed them into a paste, and shaped little people. He placed them in the heavenly oven to bake, but unfortunately he got involved in something else and forgot about them. When he went to take them out, they had burned—these became the black people.

He then mixed together more flour and water, made the shapes, and placed them in the oven. But he was a bit worried about how long they were baking, so he pulled them out before they were quite cooked. And this is where the white people came from.

So when he tried a third time, he created time and a clock to make sure that the cooking time would be just right—and when he removed the shapes from the oven, they were cooked *just right*, nicely browned. And this is where the Rom came from.

Yannakis the Fearless

Greece

This is a leisurely and chatty version of an episodic farce fairytale extremely popular in Europe, "The Boy Who Wanted to Learn What Fear Is." Katina Makri narrated the tale in the summer of 1985 (see page 35).

The standard ending is that the hero's wife either throws a pailful of cold water and fish on him or drops a fish down his back, though in at least one Italian version the hero dies of fright on seeing his own shadow.

Bruno Bettelheim comments in *The Uses of Enchantment*, "This tale [type] reveals, in fairy-story fashion, that in the last transition needed for achieving mature humanity, repressions must be undone."

Once upon a time there were two orphans, brother and sister, who had no one else in the world. They lived in a village in a large house, and down in the cellar they kept some goats. Every evening the boy, Yannakis, was so tired from cutting wood all day that he'd ask his sister to tie up the goats, but he would always end up doing it himself.

One evening he was especially tired, and again he asked his sister to tether the goats. As soon as she took two or three steps down to the cellar, she cried out, "I'm afraid!"

"*Afraid?* What on earth does that mean?" (He didn't know the meaning of the word, since he had never been afraid of anything.)

Another day the same thing happened, and this time Yannakis said to his sister, "Don't say the words 'I'm afraid' to me ever again, or I don't know what I'll do to you. I'll . . . I'll beat you if you ever say that again."

Well, a week or two went by, and Yannakis was once again tired from his daily routine. He went to lie down but then remembered that he'd forgotten to feed the goats. "Please feed them for me," he asked his sister. It was dark and the girl was scared, so she said, "Yannakis, I'm afraid."

"You're *afraid*!" He took her and beat her and told her, "If you say that once more, you'll never see me again—I'll leave."

But another day came when he asked her to tie up the goats. She started down to the cellar, but after two steps, she said, "I'm afraid."

"You're afraid? Well, tomorrow I'm leaving." When he got up in the morning, he packed his suitcase—actually, in those days they didn't have suitcases, they had bundles. He took his bundle, put it on his shoulder, and went on his way.

After walking for an entire month, he found himself far from home, in a country where every evening at eight the people shut all their doors and windows and locked themselves in.

He had no place to sleep, so he looked around for someone to talk to. "Isn't there anyone here?" he called out. Then he knocked on someone's door, and a voice said, "Go away. At eight o'clock we'll have to lock ourselves in. Otherwise, by morning something horrible will happen for sure. This place is haunted."

Yannakis went to a combination café and grocery store, sat down—the place was still open—and ordered first one ouzo and then another. Then he had something to eat. At exactly eight o'clock the owner said, "Excuse me, I'm locking up."

Yannakis said, "I'm not going anywhere. Lock me in here and go home."

The owner told him no, that he would come to harm, like the others before Yannakis who had tried this—in the morning the villagers had come with priests and a coffin to take them away. But Yannakis said he would stay, and he did. The owner locked him in and left.

Just imagine, thought Yannakis, *they're afraid. What is this thing called fear anyway? It's the same reason I left home, since my sister kept saying she was afraid. Starting at eight in the evening, they're actually afraid enough to lock themselves in.*

The shopkeeper had told him before leaving, "The vegetables are over there, and there's the bread." At least he could eat. So Yannakis started cutting up a tomato and a cucumber and grumbled, "They're afraid! Where are we, anyway? What is this thing called fear?"

As soon as he had sliced everything for his salad, in through the window came a beautiful woman wearing bracelets. When she called his name, he answered, "Get out of here." (Anyone else who had laid eyes on her would have had a heart attack. She was a fairy—and the villagers knew these fairies.)

"Yannakis, come, listen."

He went up to her and said, "Look, woman, get out of here, because once I get hold of you, I won't leave a hair on your head."

She couldn't believe that he wasn't afraid of her.

Remember the sliced tomato and cucumber? Well, suddenly they became whole again. So Yannakis shook the woman by the hair. When he had won the fight, he made her swear, on her mother's milk, never to come back and bother the villagers again. She left him one of her bracelets and disappeared on the spot.

He put the bracelet in his pocket. Then he had to prepare another salad. He said, "That woman upset me—coming in through the window like that . . ." and began cursing. The minute he started to eat his salad, another woman appeared, called his name, and said, "Come near me so I can see you." Again the tomato and cucumber suddenly reassembled.

Yannakis went up to her, grabbed her, and twisted her arm. "What is it you want here? Swear that you won't come back anymore and bother the villagers."

"On my mother's milk," she said. Right away he let go of her, and before disappearing, she left him a ring, which he put in his pocket.

Again he had to slice up the tomato and cucumber for a salad. As soon as he was ready to eat, another woman appeared. (What extraordinarily beautiful women they all were, with long hair.) She called out his name.

"What do you want? To bother me too?"

"What are you eating?" she asked. "May I join you?" She had a baby in her arms. "Don't you feel sorry for my child? Let me keep you company." She wanted to do him some harm.

"Look, get out of here now," he said. "I only feel sorry for the baby, not for you." He grabbed her skirts. "Take an oath not to bother the people of this village."

"On my mother's milk." This one left him a handkerchief, which he put in his pocket.

For the third time now he started cutting up the same tomato and cucumber. When he was done, the sun was rising. All night he'd battled with the fairies, who had sworn that the village would be free of them—the villagers would no longer have to lock themselves in their houses at eight o'clock every night.

Meantime the shopkeeper had gotten a large coffin and a priest, and he was on his way to get Yannakis and give him a proper burial in the cemetery. When Yannakis opened the door of the shop, they were terrified—they thought he was a ghost. "Come in and I'll explain," said Yannakis. "It was nothing. It was three women who were scaring you.

But I've taken care of everything—they won't bother you again. Now you can stay out all night if you want."

They all embraced and kissed him. They gave a big party in the village and stayed around till two or three in the morning, and no one bothered them. "I'll leave tonight," said Yannakis. They all gave him gifts and money for saving the whole village. Yannakis took up his bundle and set out for another country, hoping to find people who weren't afraid.

He kept walking and finally got to an enormous river. To get to the other side, one passenger in the boat had to be sacrificed to whatever it was in the sea, which only then would let the boat pass safely.

Yannakis got on this boat without knowing anything. But when the boat stopped right in the middle of the river, Yannakis noticed that the others were discussing who to throw into the sea. An old man of sixty or seventy said, "Since you're all young, let it eat me."

Yannakis stood up and said, "Tell me what's going on."

"Oh, my son," replied the old man. "In order for us to cross the river, a man must be eaten alive; otherwise, no one will get across."

"No," said Yannakis. "I won't let anyone be pushed into the sea—I'll go myself." So in he jumped with his clothes on.

Just then he saw a mermaid holding on to the boat, waiting for them to throw someone overboard. As soon as Yannakis dove in, he grabbed her by the hair and shook her and said, "Why are you bothering people this way?"

The mermaid was stunned. "Is there really someone brave enough to challenge me?" Then, when she turned and saw him, she wanted to kiss him. But he gave her a slap and got on her back. "Swear that from now on you will let people cross the water freely."

As soon as she had sworn on her mother's milk, he brought her to dry land, holding on to her hair as if it were reins. (The boat had left, since all the passengers thought Yannakis was lost under the sea.) When he got the mermaid onto the sand, she told him, "This is the first time someone has challenged me and won." Then she kissed him and said, "What would you like me to give you? Come see the cave where I live. You must be one of us, since you're not afraid of me."

He said, "I don't want anything."

But she went into her cave and brought out a whole sack of golden things—bracelets and other things she'd found in the sea—and said, "Take whatever you want."

"I don't want anything," he repeated. But he ended up taking one bracelet for his sister, putting it on his wrist to remember the mermaid by. As he started to leave, the mermaid said, "Whenever you want to see me, just come to this cave."

He said, "Right now I wish you'd take me to that city over there."

So she took him there and then went on her way.

Yannakis continued on his journey and eventually knocked on the door of a very rich man and said, "Please, I need somewhere to spend the night."

"I can't think where you could stay, my child—unless . . . the king and his vizier have made a wager, to see if anyone can go at three a.m. and cook halvah on a grave in the cemetery. So far about ninety people have tried and no one has succeeded—they were all found dead in the morning. Whoever can conquer the satanic creature who comes out in the graveyard will get half this country's treasury."

"Why all the fuss?" asked Yannakis.

"Because they're afraid."

"They're *afraid*? What on earth does that mean?" He was fearless, remember. He really didn't know what fear was. "I'll go," Yannakis said.

The rich man took Yannakis to the vizier and said, "I found someone who wants to go and cook halvah."

So the vizier took with him Yannakis, a sack filled with all the ingredients and utensils to make halvah, the saucepan, and matches. They set off for the cemetery at two a.m.

"At two-thirty a.m. you'll make the halvah—the hour when the creature comes out of the grave."

First Yannakis found some firewood—some wooden crosses on the graves—and he broke them up and set fire to them. Then he put the saucepan on the fire and started to cook the halvah.

"When will the halvah be ready?" he wondered aloud. Just as it started to smell good, a foot suddenly came out of a grave, followed by the rest of the corpse, which said, "Give me some halvah too."

"Damn you," said Yannakis, and hit him with the spoon. "Wait till it's ready, and then I'll give you some to eat. It's not ready yet."

The corpse gave him a shove and again asked for some halvah. Yannakis hit him on the leg with the hot spoon. "I'm making it just for you. Wait till it's done—and then I'll throw it at you."

The diabolical corpse kept demanding, and Yannakis kept hitting him with the spoon. The minute the halvah was ready, Yannakis poured it over the corpse. After fighting all night, Yannakis finally defeated him.

At first, when the people saw Yannakis coming back from the cemetery, they were afraid. *What is this thing called fear?* Yannakis wondered once again.

This time his fearlessness made him extremely rich. He took the money they offered him and got as far as the river crossing. As soon as he started to cross in the boat, the mermaid swam up to him and invited him to dinner. He accepted, of course, since he wasn't afraid of anything.

They went to the mermaid's cave, and who did they find there? The fairies he had defeated in the café, the corpse from the cemetery— everyone he had defeated. They sat down at the table, and the first fairy said, lifting her wineglass, "A toast to Yannakis, who defeated me and took my golden bracelet."

Yannakis sat and listened.

The second fairy said, "A toast to Yannakis, who defeated me and took my golden ring."

The third one said, "A toast to Yannakis, who defeated me and took my handkerchief."

Then the mermaid said, "A toast to Yannakis, who defeated me and made me take him onto dry land."

The corpse said, "A toast to Yannakis, who cooked halvah on my grave."

And all these spirits danced with Yannakis—they lifted him high in the air and danced with him till dawn. Then he left, saying, "Now I'm going back home to my sister."

As soon as he finally reached his home, he embraced his sister, kissed her, and gave her all the things he had gathered: all the jewelry and the money. "We're extremely rich," he said, "but I never found out what it feels like to be afraid."

Then he had to defecate. They didn't have a toilet, so he just went behind some trees and pulled down his pants. Just then a stork came up from behind and bit his backside. He went home trembling. "Sister, I'm afraid!" he cried out.

And that's how he learned what fear is. But by the time he did, he had become extremely rich.

And the two of them—Yannakis and his sister—eat and drink, and we're still telling their story.

The Vases of Harmony

France

Pierre Derlon, who once did a stint in a Gypsy circus taking care of the horses, painting posters, and performing as a clown, was told this story by one of the Gypsies he lived and worked with.

The chief of the tribe used to give two vases, one red and one blue, to a newly married couple—or, if no vases were available, two tins would do. One was for the husband, the other for the wife. They were also given a bag of mixed grains, containing corn, barley, lentils, wheat, red beans, and broad beans. Daily the husband and wife each had to choose a single grain to put into his or her vase, according to what kind of day each had spent with the other. For example, a red bean signified a quarrel or anger, corn meant a very good day with much joy. A broad bean showed an exceptional day, really perfect (this was rare), and a lentil meant a day of peace and harmony with no note of discord. The husband and wife continued putting a grain into the vase without showing each other which they put in, until after a certain time they emptied the vases in front of each other. Then the grains were put back in the bag, and the same thing started over again. When both vases were shown to contain only lentils—the sign of harmony between the man and his wife—the young couple planted these lentils, and, after covering them, traced a rough outline of a man and a woman on the earth. They stayed in this place till the lentils started to come up.

The Red King and
the Witch

Rumania

This tale was first published in Rumania in 1878 in a collection by
Dr. Barbu Constantinescu. In 1899 Francis Hindes Groome included it in his collection *Gypsy Folk-Tales* with the claim that it was
probably the most original work in his book. For example, he points
out that the somersault that precedes a transformation in Gypsy
tales has no known parallel in non-Gypsy folklore. But the test of
the three brothers, the quest of the youngest, and his attempt to
escape old age and death make this a universal tale as well as an
original one.

It was the Red King, and he bought ten ducats' worth of food. He
cooked it and he put it in a cupboard. And he locked the cupboard and
from night to night posted people to guard the food.

In the morning, when the king looked, he would find the platters
bare. There was nothing on them. Then he said, "I will give half of my
kingdom to whoever shall be found to guard the cupboard, that the food
may not be missing from it."

The Red King had three sons. The eldest thought to himself, *God!
What, give half the kingdom to a stranger! It would be better for me to watch.
Be it unto me according to God's will.* So he went to his father, saying,
"Father, give the kingdom to a stranger? It would be better for *me* to
keep watch."

And his father said to him, "As God wills, only don't be frightened
by what you might see."

The boy replied, "Be it unto me according to God's will."

And he went and lay down in the palace. And he put his head on
the pillow, and remained with his head on the pillow till just before
dawn, when a warm, sleepy breeze came and lulled him to sleep. Then
his little sister, still an infant at the breast, arose. First she turned a
somersault, then her nails became like an ax and her teeth like a shovel.
She opened the cupboard and ate up everything. Then she became a
child again and returned to her place in the cradle.

At dawn the boy arose and told his father that he had seen nothing. But when his father looked in the cupboard, he found the platters bare—no food, no anything. The king said, "It would take a better man than you, and even he might do nothing."

His middle son then said, "Father, I am going to watch tonight."

"Go, dear son, only play the man."

"Be it unto me according to God's will," replied the second son.

And he went into the palace and put his head on the pillow. And at ten o'clock came a warm breeze, and sleep seized him. Up rose his sister and unwound herself from her swaddling bands and turned a somersault, and her teeth became like a shovel and her nails like an ax. She went to the cupboard and opened it, and ate off the platters what she found. She ate it all, turned a somersault again, then went back to her place in the cradle.

Day broke and the boy arose, and his father asked him what he had seen. When he replied that he had seen nothing, the king said, "It would take a better man than you, and even he might do nought for me if he were as poor a creature as you."

The youngest son arose. "Father, give me also leave to watch the cupboard by night."

"Go, dear boy, only don't be frightened by what you see."

"Be it unto me according to God's will," said the youngest boy.

And he went and took four needles and lay down with his head on the pillow; and he stuck the four needles in four places. When sleep seized him, he rolled his head against a needle and stayed awake until ten o'clock. So when his sister arose from her cradle, he saw her. When she turned a somersault, he was watching her, and her teeth became like a shovel and her nails like an ax. And she went to the cupboard and ate up everything, leaving the platters bare. Then she turned another somersault and became tiny again as she had been and went back to her cradle. And the boy, when he saw that, trembled with fear.

It seemed to him ten years till daybreak. Then he arose and went to his father.

His father asked him, "Did you see anything, Little Peter?"

"What did I see? What did I not see? Give me money and a horse—a horse fit to carry the money—for I'm off to marry."

His father gave him a couple of sacks of ducats, and the boy put them on his horse. First he went and dug a hole at the border of the city. Then he made a chest of stone, put all the money in, and buried it. Last he placed a stone cross above it and departed.

He journeyed eight years before he came to the queen of all the birds that fly. And the queen of the birds asked him, "Where are you going, Little Peter?"

"Where there is neither death nor old age, to get married."

The queen said to him, "Here is neither death nor old age."

Then Little Peter said to her, "How is it that there is neither death nor old age here?"

She replied, "When I whittle away the wood of all this forest, only then will death come and take me, and old age."

Then Little Peter said, "One day death will come, and old age, and take *me*."

So he departed again and journeyed on for another eight years, until he arrived at a palace of copper. And a maiden came forth from that palace and took him and kissed him. She said, "I have waited a long time for you."

She took his horse and put him in the stable, and Peter spent the night there. He woke in the morning and saddled his horse.

Then the maiden began to weep and asked him, "Where are you going, Little Peter?"

"Where there is neither death nor old age."

But the maiden replied, "Here is neither death nor old age."

Then he asked her, "How is it that there is neither death nor old age here?"

"Why, only when these mountains are leveled, and these forests, only then will death come."

"This is no place for me," said the boy. And he went on.

Then what did his horse say to him? "Master, whip me four times, and twice yourself, for you have come to the Plain of Regret. And Regret will seize you and cast you down, horse and all. So spur your horse and escape, don't linger."

They came to a hut. In that hut he saw a boy about ten years old who asked him, "Little Peter, what are you looking for here?"

"I seek the place where there is neither death nor old age."

The boy said, "Here is neither death nor old age. I am the Wind."

Then Little Peter said, "Never, never will I go from here." There he lived a hundred years and grew no older, and when he went out to hunt in the Mountains of Gold and Silver, he could hardly carry home the game.

Then what did the Wind say to him? "Little Peter, go to all the Mountains of Gold and to the Mountains of Silver, but do not ever go to the Plain of Regret or to the Valley of Grief."

Little Peter didn't listen, but went to the Plain of Regret and the Valley of Grief. And Grief cast him down; he wept till his eyes were full.

He returned to the Wind. "I am going home to my father. I will not stay longer."

"Don't go, for your father is dead and you have no more brothers left at home," said the Wind. "A million years have come and gone since then. The spot is not known where your father's palace stood. They have planted melons on it. I know, for it is but an hour since I passed that way."

But the boy left there, and arrived at the maiden's copper palace. Only one stick remained of the entire forest, and she had cut it down and grown old. As Peter knocked at the door, the stick fell, and she died. He buried her and left. Then he came to the queen of the birds in the great forest. Only one branch of her entire forest remained, and that was all but through.

When she saw him, she said, "Little Peter, you are quite young."

Then he said to her, "Do you remember telling me to linger here?"

As she pressed nearer to him and broke through the branch, she too fell and died.

At last he came to where his father's palace had been, and looked around. He was astonished. There was no palace, no anything. "God, you are great!" He recognized only his father's well, and went to it. His sister, the witch, when she saw him, said to him, "I have waited a long time for you, dog." She rushed at him to devour him, but he made the sign of the cross and she perished.

And he left there and came upon an old man with his beard down to his belt. "Old man, where is the palace of the Red King? I am his son."

"What is this?" said the old man. "You tell me that you are his son? My father's father told me of the Red King. His city is no more. Can't you see it has vanished? And yet you tell me that you are the Red King's son?"

"It is not twenty years, old man, since I departed from my father, and do you tell me that you don't know my father?" (It was in fact a million years since he had left his home.) "Follow me if you do not believe me."

And he went to the cross of stone. Only a palm's breadth was above ground, and it took him two days to get at the chest of money.

When he had lifted the chest out and opened it, Death sat in one corner groaning and Old Age groaning in another corner.

Then what did Old Age say? "Lay hold of him, Death."

"Lay hold of him yourself," said Death.

So Old Age laid hold of him in front and Death laid hold of him behind.

The old man took and buried him decently and planted the cross near him. And the old man took the money, and also the horse.

The Wooden Horseshoe and the Three Nails

England

This is one of many tales having to do with the Gypsies' alleged role in the crucifixion. Gypsies are not the only minority group who supposedly made the nails for the cross: both the Falashas (the black Jews of Ethiopia, also metalsmiths) and the Scottish Travelers (also called Tinkers) have been indicted by this legend.

Storyteller Manfri Frederick Wood related this story in his autobiography, *In the Life of a Romany Gypsy*.

There was once an innkeeper who traded in horses, donkeys, and mules. One year the Romans conquered the land and built roads. The horses' hooves suffered a great deal of wear and tear from going over the hard roads instead of the sandy dunes as before. One night the innkeeper's son brooded over the problem, and it occurred to him that it should be possible to fit wooden clogs onto the horses' hooves. So the next day he carved some horseshoes out of cedar—but these were not very durable.

Some weeks after making the first wooden horseshoes the innkeeper's son dreamed of a way of forging iron horseshoes, and within a month the first smithy in the world was built. The innkeeper's son was the first smith and he shoed horses and made nails for the whole world.

One day, when the smith was already very old, a man came to him and ordered twelve large nails; but after having delivered nine of the nails, he found out that these were to be used for nailing Jesus and the two thieves to the cross, so he withheld the other three.

One of the executioners came round to the smithy to get the other three nails, and a search party came with him; but one of the smith's sons had managed to escape with these three nails, and the gentiles never managed to find them. So the crucifixion had to be managed with nine nails only, three for each of the condemned—two through the wrists and one through both feet.

The saying goes that the gentiles' constant search for the three missing nails ever since has led to the persecution of the Gypsies. If these nails are ever found, the persecution will come to an end. But if they are not found soon, the Gorgios [*gaje*] will kill each other off by being too clever by half and only the Gypsies and other wandering people will survive the holocaust.

Anyway, to return to the tale: After the crucifixion the citizens of the town formed themselves into a lynch mob and went to string up the smith and all his friends and relations because they had delivered the nine nails used for the crucifixion. But the smith and all his lot had managed to make a getaway and have been hounded from place to place ever since.

The smith was condemned to eternal life. On bright nights you can see him sitting on the moon with his hammer in his hand, his anvil by his side, and other tools of his trade scattered around him.

One of the smith's sons managed to conceal his identity and marry a princess. Her father, the king of Romania, went blind because of the curse on the smith's family. The smith's son went in search of a magic herb grown by a magician from his tribe. But he was waylaid by the king's three sons, who nailed a red-hot horseshoe on his backside and branded its imprint deep into his skin. However, the smith's son recovered from this torture and procured the magic herb, by which the king was cured of his blindness. But instead of being grateful to the smith's son, he banished him from the country when his daughter, the princess, told him about the mark branded on her husband's backside. However, he did not banish any of the smith's people from the country—partly because they were clever herbal doctors and partly because they forged very good weapons for his army. Only his daughter's husband was banished for making a fool of him and his royal house. So the smith's descendants stayed in Romania for many centuries, and that is why they are to this day known as Romanies and why their way of life is called roaming or roving.

The Fox and the Miller

Bulgaria

This story was told to Kiril Kostov by a twenty-year-old Gypsy from Ihtiman and published in the *Journal of the Gypsy Lore Society* in 1962. Kostov noted that although this Bulgarian Gypsy variant is ultimately derived from a Macedonian-Rumanian version of "Puss in Boots," other motifs are interwoven here, and one feature—that of pretending to wage war—appears to be entirely original.

Although in most West European versions the helpful animal is a cat (as in Perrault's literary version of the late seventeenth century), in Italian, Greek, Russian, and East European versions, the animal is a fox.

Commenting on the apparently amoral nature of this tale type, Bruno Bettelheim in *The Uses of Enchantment* offers a psychological explanation for its continuing popularity: "Morality is not the issue . . . but rather, assurance that one can succeed. Whether one meets life with a belief in the possibility of mastering its difficulties or with the expectation of defeat is also a very important existential problem."

Once upon a time there was a miller named Pirušambi, and there was a fox who came all the time and ate the miller's hens. One day the miller finally caught the fox, who said to him, "Stop! Don't kill me! I'll fix it so you marry the king's daughter." So Pirušambi let her go.

The fox went to the king. "Your Majesty of Majesties, the hen from you, the rooster from us. All right?"

"Why not? Let's see the prospective son-in-law!"

"Wait, I'll bring him to you."

And the fox went straight to Pirušambi. "Pirušambi, let's take a cartful of pumpkins and a cartful of dust to the sea, where we'll throw a pumpkin and a little dust into it and it will roar like a cannon."

The king heard the noise from far away and thought somebody was waging war. Pirušambi and the fox threw all the pumpkins into the sea and then returned home.

The fox went to the king and said, "Your Majesty of Majesties, my son and I have waged a great war. It's a sin and a shame for me to ask you to give some clothes to our son, but he has soiled his own."

"Go and bring your son."

The fox brought Pirušambi and said to him, "The king will offer you coffee, and you will drink half of it. He will give you a cigarette—you'll take two puffs and put it out. He will give you clothes, and you are not to look at them."

Pirušambi went to the king, where he was given a chair to sit on, a cup of coffee, and a cigarette. He lit the cigarette, puffed on it once, twice, and then threw it away. He sipped the coffee once, twice, and put the cup down. He put on the clothes, and the fox said, "Your Majesty of Majesties, I will go first to open the gates—you follow after us."

The fox went not to the mill but to another house. The king set forth with soldiers, carriages, clarinets, and drums to fetch the bride. The king's son-in-law and his young wife were in the carriage, the two of them alone.

The fox in advance caught up with a shepherd with many sheep. "Hey, shepherd, if the king questions you whose are these sheep, you will say, 'These sheep are Pirušambi's.' The king will take out a handful of money and give it to you. If you say nothing, he will cut off your head."

Then the fox caught up with a goatherd. "Well, goatherd, if the king asks, you will say, 'These goats are Pirušambi's.' If you do not speak, he will cut off your head. As soon as you have spoken he will give you a handful of money."

The fox then caught up with a cowherd. "Well, cowherd, if the king asks you whose are these cattle, you will say, 'These cattle are Pirušambi's.' The king will take out a handful of money and give it to you. If you do not speak, he will cut off your head."

The fox caught up with a groom with many horses. "Hey, groom, if the king asks you whose are these horses, you will say, 'These horses are Pirušambi's.' The king will take out a handful of money and give it to you. But he will cut off your head if you do not speak."

The fox went straight to the palace of the winged dragon. "Dragon, the army is coming to kill you."

"Well, where should I hide?"

"In the oven. Faster, sister dragon!"

She threw herself into the oven, the fox put in a little straw and struck a match, and the dragon was burnt up.

In the dragon's palace there were two maids locked up, and the fox helped them get out. The maids at once swept, cleaned, and tidied the place, and straightaway opened the gates. The king went in, came upstairs, and climbed out onto the balcony. Pirušambi got down from the carriage with his wife and went into the palace. Over there the sheep were penned up, the goats were there, the cattle were there, the horses were there—and the king marveled to see how much stock his son-in-law had. "Well, I'm a king too, but I haven't so much stock. He is richer than I am."

The king stayed a day or two.

Pirušambi sat down to eat bread with his wife. The fox pretended to be ill and slept near them. And her rear end went "dj-r-r-r." Pirušambi caught the fox by the leg and threw her out onto the rubbish heap.

The fox got up and went inside to Pirušambi. "Pirušambi, you louse, I brought you here to these riches. Where you came from, you didn't even have a piece of bread. I brought you here so that you could become rich. You have to be grateful to me for bringing you here. If I fall ill now, you must make me a cradle and put a maid at my head to rock me and sing to me."

The Gypsy Smith

England

Another tale of Gypsy superiority. Homi Smith, the storyteller, said: "This is my story . . . told to me by my old mam. Yes, told me by my old mother, it was. And she was told it by her mam, and she was told it by her mam, and so like that ever since our fambly began . . . And that smith what I've been a-telling about, 'e was the first *petulengro*—yes, the very first Smith what started our fambly, long ago."

A very very long time ago there lived a great king. And this great king, he ordered for to be built for 'im a great palace. Everythink there was to be the bestest that could be 'ad, and the men what was got to build it was the cleverest that could be 'ad. And it took a very long time for to build this great palace, 'cause it was so big, and 'cause it 'ad to be so good, but at last there came the day when it was finished.

And the great king, he called together all the men what 'ad worked to build it for 'im, so as there could be a great eatin' and drinkin'—a feast, as the story goes.

Well, they all comes to this great feast, and there was much good food all on gold plates and dishes, and there was much strong drink all in gold cups. And they all sat and ate and drank for a long time. And when they was all full up and couldn't eat nor drink no more, all the men what was there started arguin' who was the bestest one among 'em. First, up spoke the man what 'ad told 'em the right shape, and all that, for to build each little part of the palace. "Without me," he says, "there wouldn't 'ave been no palace, so I reckons as 'ow I must be the bestest man of all."

Then up spoke the man what 'ad laid all the bricks and built the walls. "Without me," he says, "there wouldn't 'ave been no building of the walls. And without walls, there couldn't 'ave been no palace. So I reckon as 'ow I must be the bestest man of all."

Then up spoke the carpenter, what 'ad made all the doors and different things out of wood. "Without me," he says, "there wouldn't 'ave been no doors, nor no furniture. And without all those things, there wouldn't 'ave been no palace."

Then up spoke the man what 'ad put all the glass in the windows. "Without me," he says, "there wouldn't 'ave been no windows. I've fixed glass in a thousand windows, else the wind and the rain would all 'ave blowed in. Without windows, there wouldn't 'ave been no palace."

And after that, one and another all stands up one by one, and tells of the different things what they'd done, and each one says 'ow there wouldn't 'ave been no palace if it 'adn't been for 'im.

And all the time, the great king, 'e just sits, and 'e don't say nothing. Only 'e listens very careful to 'em all. Then at last, they suddenly spies a dark man, standin' apart from all the others, just inside the door.

"Come inside and tell us who you might be," says the great king. So the dark man, 'e steps right inside the great hall. "I am the smith," he says, in a loud voice so as all could 'ear 'im. And then they all sees as 'ow his face is all black from the forge, and he's still got 'is leather apron on, where he 'as come straight from 'is work.

Then one or two of 'em there (them as was dressed up all in fine clothes, and looks down at the *petulengro*—yes, looks down at the smith, they does), they starts a-sayin' to one another, "What right 'as that man in 'ere? He ain't done nothing towards building this 'ere great palace for the great king." So at last, the great king, he turns to the smith and 'e says, "Now answer. What right 'ave you in 'ere? Can you say as 'ow you done anything towards building this 'ere great palace?"

And the smith, 'e smiles, and 'e speaks up and 'e says, "We've heard the windowmaker; we've heard the carpenter; we've heard the bricklayer; and we've heard all the other men what reckons they was the most important men of all. But I says that not one of 'em could 'ave done anythink without their tools. And who was it made their tools?"

And the man stopped and looked all round while they all thought about it. Then he speaks up again: "Yes," he says. "Yes. None of 'em could 'ave done anythink without their tools. And who was it made all their tools? Why, it was me, the *petulengro*, the smith! And now," he says, a-drawin' of hisself up, for 'e was a tall man. "And now," he says, "I'll ask the great king hisself to tell us who he thinks is the most important man of all."

So then the great king, 'e stands up and 'e says, "You 'ave all 'eard what the smith says. And it is a great truth that not one of you could 'ave done any work at all, without the tools what the smith made. Therefore," he says, "therefore, I says as 'ow the smith is the most importantest man of all."

And then the great king 'as a place made for the smith by 'is right 'and. And the smith, 'e sits down there all in 'is workin' clothes, with 'is apron on and 'is face all black from the forge. And the great king give 'im food to eat and drink in 'is gold cup, with 'is own hand.

How It Is in the Gypsy Paradise

Yugoslavia

Inspired by hunger and by feelings of powerlessness, this Bosnian Gypsy fantasy is one of a group of such tales collected by Rade Uhlik and published in the *Journal of the Gypsy Lore Society* in 1944, edited by Frederick George Ackerley. Ackerley commented, "These tales . . . afford . . . an insight into the manner of life, the thoughts and the reactions of the Gypsies of Bosnia to the treatment they receive at the hands of *gaje* [in this case Muslims] and to the miserable conditions of their existence."

In 1975, Carol Miller wrote of American Gypsies: "Middle-aged and older Rom have memories of many days when food was unobtainable. They report that nothing is harder for parents to endure than the sound of children crying from hunger."

The son of holy Alta, the mother of all the Gypsies, said to her, "May you reach old age, little mother, tell me now, how it is in our proud Gypsy paradise?"

The mother of all gathered her thoughts until she was easy in her soul. Then she spoke with a full heart: "In our Gypsy paradise, super-paradise, it's nice, very nice! If you were to know what great joy awaits us Gypsies! The fields are long and large, the horses gallop, there are willows and shade—all the good things that we need. And in the midst are roasted great oxen turning on a spit, and trout are spread out all around them. Into those roasted fat cattle all the golden knives are stuck. 'Come, brothers, up with you, sit and eat as much as your stomach can bear! Carve and swallow as much as you can! Whatever a man wants, he can cut and chew as much as his heart desires. Eat, drink, what you have a mind to!' Oh! holy God, you too must be a Gypsy, when you have given us such riches.

"In that Gypsy paradise of ours all our Gypsy sons meet and boast and drink to each other's health. The sons of the *gaje* are outside shivering with cold and hunger, and beg a morsel of food from our children. Our lucky Gypsy sons laugh, really laugh, at them. They mock them, then eat, and then eat more, but they don't give them one bit of food.

"Our Gypsy paradise is all founded upon trout and cheeses, and above it is covered with eggs. Around it are interwoven sausages and all sorts of meat from the pork-butchers. And just below the ceiling hang dumplings. When it is shaken by the ears all that food will drop down into our mouths. Somewhere on each side there are cheeses and loaves. You can look at a great mountain of cheese and at one of loaves, and each loaf is as big as a house, baked with flour and sixty eggs.

"Our Gypsy paradise is so big that three Gypsy rivers flow through it, their banks all composed of cakes. In one river sweet white milk flows. Another river is full of buttermilk. The third is cream only. The bridges across these three rivers are embellished with dumplings, and the banks strengthened with pork. When a Gypsy crosses these bridges and when they are shaken by the ears and stirred a little by the jaws, he can become as fully satisfied as his soul desires.

"And when our Gypsy horses gallop, the saddles creak and the whip lashes and lashes them. And in our Gypsy souls there is only great laughter and song. 'Oh! Gypsies, eat and drink while we have it. Carve the meat with knives, gnaw the cheese, fill up buckets with milk from the rivers that flow in our great Gypsy heaven and drink.' And indeed all the Gypsies in our super-paradise converse with each other by singing.

"Therefore heed well, Gypsies, what I tell you. In that heavenly country above, you need not fast at all, for there are endless roasted lambs and oxen. Our Gypsy sons will eat and drink, they will never fast, but the Muslims will—they will remain without meat and without milk. Thus the Muslims and their sons up above will weep; not so our Gypsies."

The Gypsy of Tucumán

Argentina

This "true" story illustrates the wisdom of keeping the old traditions alive, in this case the customary series of funeral feasts. In his book *The Gypsies*, Jan Yoors described the mourning customs among the European Lowara he lived with: "This *Pomana*, or feast for the dead, was repeated after nine days, and again after six weeks, after six months and at the anniversary of death. At each *Pomana* certain relatives publicly declared their decision to end their particular period of mourning, which corresponded to their degree of kinship, and renounced the restrictions this imposed on them. Again they would comb their hair, wear jewelry, buy new clothes, dance, sing and get drunk. But black as a sign of mourning was never worn by the Gypsies."

In Tucumán in the north, many Gypsies say that once a Gypsy died in a village there and the other Gypsies didn't perform the burial rites for him, or that he was killed—I don't know the exact truth. But one thing is sure: that his soul was not resting in peace.

Anyway, one time I went there by bus, and when we got to the bridge that we had to cross in order to enter that village where we were going (supposedly the village where his ghost was), the bus stopped. When we Gypsies who were inside tried to get off, we couldn't: we were completely immobilized. Minutes later the bus turned back, and then we got out and tried to cross the bridge on foot, but it was as if there were an invisible barrier that kept us from moving. Then the bus driver explained to us that Gypsies could never enter the village, that there were always accidents, car tires blowing out, or cars skidding into some ditch, or someone injuring themselves somehow. The old people said that's what always happens from not observing the old customs, the *pomana*, and for doing harm to each other. It's the pure truth.

The Three Villages

Greece

"The Three Villages" is a folktale to be told at a wake to console
the survivors, as storyteller Andonios Sotiriou of Ayia Varvara in
Athens makes clear in his closing sentence.

Greek Gypsy wakes last three days and nights, and stories are
always told, as in many other cultures. Czech folklorist Milena
Hübschmannová tells of Gypsy narrators being invited from other
parts of Czechoslovakia to perform at wakes. Some of their tales
are humorous and lascivious, and Hübschmannová adds, "The
mourning participants roar with laughter in between fits of wailing.
'It is natural,' one friend explained to me, 'as life is crying and
laughter, laughter and crying.'"

Once upon a time there was a family with three sons. When his wife
died, the father called his children together and said, "When you are
grown up, you will each receive your share of the inheritance. However,
after you get it, you'll still have to journey to some nearby village to
earn money if you're going to live well."

Some time passed, the old man died, and the three brothers were
left alone. One was thirty years old, one was twenty, and the third was
twelve or thirteen. The oldest son said to his brothers, "Let's go to some
little village to work and earn whatever we can."

They got together and discussed the matter. The oldest one said,
"Up from here are three villages. In the first village you enter, work—
and you can come back whenever you want. The story with the second
little village is: you go and you return quickly. The third village is on a
road—you take that road and you *never* return."

The oldest brother continued, "I'll take the road to the village where
you go and return quickly."

The middle brother said, "I'll go to the village where you can return
whenever you want or stay if you like."

And the third and youngest brother said, "I'll take the third road."

They all started out. The oldest brother went to the second little
village. In his own village he could earn, let's say, a hundred drachmas
a day. In this village he got a hundred twenty—not even a hundred

twenty, more like a hundred ten, so there was no great difference from his own village. He decided he was better off in his own village, and he returned home.

The middle brother left for the first village. In his own village he earned a hundred and twenty drachmas a day, and here a hundred and fifty. So he said, "Not bad. I'll stay a few days." He stayed a few days, got bored, and returned home.

The youngest brother took the road that no one even wanted to go near. But he'd made a decision, and started off.

When he was pretty far along, he heard shouts of "Someone's coming!" and saw people running left and right out of the fields with all their tools to welcome whoever was coming. As soon as he arrived, one of them said, "I'll give him my daughter in marriage." Another: "I'll give him as many lambs and sheep as he wants." Another: "I'll build him a house." Another: "I'll give him all my property." Another: "Whatever he wants."

Right away they offered him a house there. He slept, and from then on stayed in that village. He lives, eats, and drinks like a king there. Well, how could that man return? He just can't . . . Do you understand? Maybe this is how it is with the dead person, who goes and finds a better life and doesn't return.

The Two Children

Czechoslovakia

This revenge fantasy of victory over betrayal and poverty was collected by Rudolph von Sowa and published in the *Journal of the Gypsy Lore Society* in 1891. As in "The Magic Belt" (pages 179–183), the villain is asked to name her own fate.

Somewhere there lived a soldier, the son of a hunter. There was also a shoemaker's daughter. She had a dream that if she should marry the soldier and become pregnant, she would give birth to twins: a boy with a golden star on his chest and a girl with a golden star on her forehead. The soldier did marry the shoemaker's daughter, but she was poor and he was rich, so his parents would not accept her as a daughter-in-law.

The shoemaker's daughter became pregnant before the soldier went off to rejoin the army. After a year she gave birth to twins, exactly as she had dreamed: the boy had a golden star on his chest, and the girl had one on her forehead. But the grandparents threw the twins into adamantine chests, wrote a note for each twin and put those in the chests too, and then let the chests float down the Vah River.

God arranged it that two fishermen saw the chests floating down the river, and they seized both of them and opened them. The children were alive, and the notes were found with them. The fishermen picked the children up and carried them right into the church to baptize them. The boy was called Yanko and the girl Marishka.

So the children lived with the fishermen until their eighth year, when they were already going to school. But the fishermen also had children of their own, and used to beat the foundlings. And Marishka said to Yanko, "Let us go, Yanko, somewhere into the world."

They went into a forest and spent the night there. They made a fire. While Yanko was tending the fire, Marishka fell asleep and a very old man approached him and said, "Come with me. I will give you plenty of money."

He took him to a vault. A stone door was opened, and there was plenty of money. Yanko took two armfuls of money, as much as he could carry—God was with him. He returned to Marishka, who was awake. She had been crying because she didn't know where Yanko was. Yanko said to her, "Don't be afraid, I'm back already. I've brought you plenty of money." God had told him to take as much money as he could—and that the door would always be open for him afterwards.

Yanko and Marishka went into a town. He bought clothes for both of them, and a beautiful house. After buying horses and a small carriage, he took them to the vault and helped himself again, using a shovel to get the money into the carriage. He returned home the possessor of so much money that he didn't know what to do with it.

He arranged for a ball, ordering a band to make music and inviting all the gentry of that country—including his grandparents, as Yanko had planned. Indeed they came; and Yanko recognized his grandmother. And

Yanko said to her, "What does a person deserve who brings to ruin two souls and is still alive?"

The old lady answered, "Such a person deserves only a pyre to be lighted, and to be thrown into the fire."

And that is just what they did: they threw the grandparents into the fire. Yanko remained with Marishka, and all the gentry cried, "Long life to them! Well done!"

Why the Gypsies Don't Have an Alphabet

Greece

Many Greek Gypsy *pourquoi* tales account for the lack of a Romani writing system. The following one was told me in 1985 in Athens by Anastasia Dimou.

In Thessaloniki some Gypsy high school students are working to devise a Romani orthography better suited to their language than the Greek alphabet is.

Once there was a king, and he had the Gypsy alphabet. He wrapped it in some cabbage leaves, since in those days they didn't have bookshelves to put things on, and he fell asleep next to a spring. A donkey came along, drank some water, and ate the cabbage leaves—and that's why we don't have an alphabet.

Why Gypsies Eat Hedgehog

Greece

This tale, which I recorded in Thessaloniki in 1982, tries to explain why the hedgehog seems to be primarily a Gypsy food. Though I've met Greek *gaje* who also enjoy eating hedgehog, the practice is generally looked upon with scorn. Reaction to this scorn is probably what motivated this tale, for it supports a positive interpretation of the custom.

There was once a king, and he summoned everyone to the palace to bring the best meat they had. And they each brought their animals so that the king could see which animal's meat was the best. They all brought different animals, and then a Gypsy went inside with a hedgehog. The hedgehog was cooked, and the king tried it—it was the sweetest-tasting of all those animals. The others wanted to kill the Gypsy, because now they wouldn't be able to sell their animals. They did kill him, and from then on only we, the Gypsies, eat hedgehog.

The Flood

Hungary

This story was originally collected by Dr. Heinrich von Wlislocki in 1886 and offered for comparative purposes by Tihomir Djordjević in a 1934 article on Serbian Gypsy folklore. Many versions of the biblical story of Noah and the flood exist in different cultures; this one comes from Transylvania. Djordjević thought that the fish incident might have been brought by the Gypsies from India.

There was once a time when all people lived together and knew nothing of work, of winter, of illness, or of want. The earth gave its finest fruits, meat grew on many trees, and milk and water flowed in many rivers. People and animals all lived happily together and had no fear of death.

One day an old man came to a peasant and asked him for a night's lodging, and the peasant and his wife gave him hospitality. On leaving the next morning, the old man gave the peasant a little fish in a bowl, saying, "Keep this fish and do not eat it. When I return in a week, I will reward you if you give it back to me."

When the old man had left, the woman looked at the fish and said to her husband, "How would it be if we grilled this fish?" The peasant replied, "I promised the old man to return the fish, and you must swear to keep it until he comes back."

So she swore, "I will not kill the fish but will keep it safe—so help me God."

Two days later, however, the woman thought to herself, *This fish must be very good if the old man thought so much of it he carried it about and wouldn't let it be grilled.*

After thinking it over for a long time, she took it out of the bowl and threw it on the embers. Immediately there was a flash of lightning and she was killed. This was the first death in the whole world.

Then the rains began. The rivers started to overflow their banks and flood the earth. On the ninth day the old man came back to the peasant and said, "You kept your oath and did not kill the fish. Take another wife, collect all your relatives, and build a boat, and you will be saved. Take with you animals and the seeds of trees and plants so that you can spread them afterwards on the earth. All humans and all living things must be drowned—only you will be left."

At this the old man disappeared, and the peasant did as he had been told. Rain fell for a whole year, and nothing could be seen but water and sky. Then the seas dried up and the man came out on dry land with his new wife, his relatives, and the animals. After that they all had to work—plow and sow—in order to live. His life was full of worries and woes, and with them came illness and death, so that people multiplied very slowly. Many, many thousands of years passed before people became as numerous as they were before the flood—and as they are now.

The Gypsy and the Hen

Norway

About two hundred Gypsies live in Norway. In 1979 storyteller Frans Josef told this children's story as part of a TV series called *We Are Gypsies and Norwegians*.

The translator, Kirsten Wang, is a Norwegian anthropologist who works with Presencia Gitana, a Spanish Gypsy association in Madrid. She remarks, "The children go to school like all Norwegian children. The difficulty is that the parents want to take the children out of school when spring comes and they start traveling. This has been solved by sending Gypsy teachers along with them."

Many, many years ago a king and his daughter lived in a house with a garden. One day a witch came into the garden to steal apples, but the princess saw her and cried out, "You old witch! Get out of our garden!"

The witch got very angry and cursed the princess, saying, "You princess, can't you shut up and stop squawking like a hen? I'll make you into a hen until one day a Gypsy boy will come along and catch you— and he will either eat you or marry you." And sure enough, the princess turned into a hen.

One day some Gypsies came along with their carts, and among them there was a very good-looking boy. Many beautiful girls wanted to marry him, but he didn't want any of them. This day the good-looking young Gypsy was looking for hens, because Gypsies like them when they are traveling. The Gypsy saw all the hens the king had in his garden and went away with ten or twelve of them, among them the bewitched princess.

She said to him, "Oh, you nice boy, don't kill me and don't eat me, because I could be your wife."

"You—my wife? When I could marry any one of our beautiful girls, I should marry a hen? What nonsense!"

She replied, "Just do as I tell you."

For some reason the Gypsy believed her, so he went to his mother and said, "We're not going to kill this hen."

"Why not?" asked his mother.

"Because I'm going to marry her."

"What are you saying? Marry a hen?" She thought her son had gone crazy. When his father came home, she said to him, "Do you know what our son wants to do? He wants to marry a hen."

The boy came in and said, "I'm not crazy."

Right away he went to the priest to discuss the wedding. The priest said, "Bring your fiancée and I'll marry you." But when the Gypsy boy came back to the church carrying the hen in a basket he had made, the priest said, "Oh, in Jesus' name, I cannot marry you to a hen!"

"Well," said the boy, "if you won't marry us, I'll have to kill you."

The priest was frightened and said, "All right, all right! I'll marry you." He put the rings on them and said some priestly words, and suddenly the hen changed into the most beautiful princess in the whole country.

The Gypsy boy was so surprised that he dropped the basket on the floor, and it turned into an elegant carriage. He harnessed his horse, lifted his bride into the carriage, and off they went to a big celebration with lots of good food.

Sam Patra
and His Brothers

United States

The October 1, 1927, issue of *The Survey*, a magazine by and for the socially conscious—Jane Addams was a contributing editor—was devoted to the Gypsies. Included were four tales by a fourteen-year-old Gypsy named Steve Demitro, translated from the Romani. Although a photograph of the storyteller is reproduced, there is no information about him except that he was an American Coppersmith (Kalderash) Gypsy. This engaging tale is one of the few published Gypsy stories told by children.

I

Once upon a time there were an old man and an old woman. The old man was a king, and the old woman was a queen. She was about forty-five years old but had never had any babies. But one night she dreamed—and the first dream she had that night was that if she tasted a fish, she would have some babies. So she got up from beside the king and called for her waiter, "Waiter, waiter, go get me a fish."

"What fish?" asked the waiter, and to herself she said, *That old queen is crazy.*

The queen said, "You know the pond . . . that pond has one big fish . . . that one big fish, I want to taste of him . . . I just now dreamed about that fish."

The waiter said, "What about that fish?"

The old queen answered, "I just dreamed about that fish. If I taste it, I will have a son whose name will be Sam Patra."

"Then," said the waiter, "I know what I'll do. If you want the fish, I will put the old fisherman to catch him, and he will surely catch him."

So the waiter went and told the old fisherman. And when she had finished telling him, he said, "I cannot catch any fish in that pond. It is too deep and you cannot see the fish and you need too long a line to reach." But the fisherman tried to reach the fish. Soon he came back and said to the waiter, "I tried my best to catch him, but I cannot."

When the waiter heard that, she looked sorry and went back to the queen.

The queen asked, "Why are you sorry, waiter?"

The waiter's answer was "Why should I not be sorry? The fisherman tried his best to catch the fish, but he couldn't."

As soon as the old queen heard that, she was sorry too, and cried herself back to sleep. This time she dreamed that if she did not eat of the fish, she would die. She woke up frightened and called to the sorry waiter, who had remained by her bed: "Waiter, waiter, wake up, and go get all the fishermen in the town."

The waiter ran out and woke up all the fishermen in the town. They brought all their nets to the pond and soon had the one big fish. They gave it to the waiter, and the waiter gave it to the queen, and the queen got up and gave it to the cook, saying, "Cook, you had better not taste this fish or I will kill you."

The cook said, "All right. I'll cook the fish and I won't taste it." Then she dropped it in the boiling kettle and cooked it.

The waiter came into the kitchen and asked the cook, "Did you put any salt on the fish?"

"No," said the cook. "The queen told me not to taste it, and I cannot season it without tasting."

So the waiter, who knew how the queen liked her food, went and tasted the fish. Right away she grew sick, and she whispered to the cook. But the cook did not understand, and she too tasted the fish and grew sick.

Then the queen shouted from her bedroom, "Why don't you bring me the fish to eat?" The waiter put some in a silver dish and took it to the queen. As soon as she tasted the fish, she also grew sick.

And the queen had a baby, and the waiter and the cook each had a baby at the same time.

The queen's baby was Sam Patra, the cook's son was Sylvius, and the waiter's son was Lazillia. But when they grew older, the three children called themselves brothers because they looked so much alike.

II

When the three boys had grown into men, Sylvius said one day, "Brother Lazillia, let's go for a hunt."

"And with what will we hunt animals?" asked Sam Patra.

Lazillia said, "I will take my bow and arrow," and Sylvius said, "I will take only my sword," and Sam Patra said, "Well, then, I will take my gun with me. Are you ready to go, brothers?" They took their horses and went, leaving the king a note about where they had gone.

When they reached the bridge over the river, they spent the night there because they were afraid to sleep anywhere else.

Soon it was about one o'clock at night, and the giant who rode on horseback in the woods came to the bridge, but the horse shied and did not want to pass. The giant cursed and said, "What is the matter, my horse? You never were scared here before."

The horse seemed to answer, "Giant, you might get killed by Sam Patra."

But the giant cursed again and muttered to himself, "I'll show Sam Patra what I can do with him."

But Sam Patra knew by the steps of the horse that the giant was coming. And as soon as the giant said that, Sam Patra jumped up and said, "Here I am, giant, what kind of fight do you want?"

The giant called back from the darkness, "Do you want to fight with me?"

"Yes, I want to fight. How do you want to fight? Swords are no good, swords are dirty, hammers are dirty, axes are dirty, everything is dirty—God left only wrestling."

The giant answered, "Are you ready to fight by wrestling?"

"Yes," said Sam Patra, "I want to fight."

They threw off their wraps and started to wrestle, and the giant grew angry because Sam Patra was so strong. He shouted loud and grabbed Sam Patra by the toe and threw him into the mud. Sam Patra got hold of the giant's legs and threw him into the mud along the riverbank. Then the giant threw Sam Patra by the hips, but he jumped up and threw the giant from beneath the armpits. The giant got up and threw Sam Patra by the shoulders. Next, Sam Patra got the giant by the neck and held his head in the mud while he reached for the sword. Then he killed him.

The giant's horse now belonged to Sam Patra, so he tied it to the bridge and went to sleep again.

In the morning, when Lazillia and Sylvius awoke, they cried out, "O brother, we had a terrible dream! We dreamed we would meet a two-headed giant." Then they saw the strange horse tied to the bridge and asked, "Whose horse is that?"

"That," said Sam Patra, "was the giant's horse. But now it is mine." But they did not believe him and asked the horse, "Did Sam Patra kill a giant?" The horse just shook its head. So Sam Patra had to show them the giant's head where it was lying in the mud.

Then they were frightened and said, "Now I know we will get killed by the two-headed giant."

Lazillia said, "Let's go back home to the good old king and queen before we get killed."

They all went back home and told the old king, "We have killed a one-headed giant and dreamed that a two-headed giant will follow us. We're afraid to leave the castle."

But the king laughed and said, "I'll put soldiers out to catch the giant and put him in a cage, and then we'll kill him."

But when the two-headed giant heard what had happened to the one-headed giant at the hands of Sam Patra, he got a great sledgehammer and set out to smash in the walls of the castle.

He walked right over the king's soldiers and with one blow made a hole in the castle wall so that he could get in. He went for the king, but Sam Patra snatched up his sword and kept him off.

The giant grabbed the sword and swung it at Sam Patra, just touching the skin of his neck. From behind, Lazillia shot one of the giant's heads with an arrow, and when the giant turned his other head to see what had happened, Sylvius cut off that one with his sword. They all huddled in a corner and watched the giant die. And when he was still, Sam Patra said, "Father King, now each of us has killed a giant. We are exactly alike."

"I am not sure," said Lazillia, "for I want to get married." They all wondered who the girl could be.

When no one was looking, Sam Patra and Sylvius went out the door and over the fields to an old king who they knew had two daughters—the older named Auska, the second Mattilia. Mattilia liked Sylvius, Auska liked Sam Patra. So both sons got married the same day and went back to the castle with their wives on the same day that Lazillia returned with his wife. And they found that the three wives were sisters, but Lazillia's wife had been stolen from her home when she was a baby.

After thirteen years the old king and queen died, and the three brothers ruled the country.

After thirteen more years Sylvius, in a terrible fever, also died. The two brothers who were left looked at each other, and Lazillia said, "Now that our brother is dead, what will we do? Let us kill ourselves."

Sam Patra said, "Why should I kill myself? I am a little bit different from my brothers."

But Lazillia answered, "I am going to kill myself after my brother." Then Lazillia went and shot himself.

Sam Patra felt sad. He said to himself, *My two brothers, born when I was born, and who looked like me and did as I did, are dead. The poor old king and queen are dead. What will I do now? I am not so very different from my brothers.*

That night he gave the kingdom to Auska. Then he took the bow and arrow of his brother Sylvius and shot the arrow straight up into the air. "I will see if it is to be," he said. For three days and nights the arrow did not come down and he did not move. On the fourth day he saw it coming, and he gave a kiss to Auska and said, "Good-bye, wife. And good-bye, wives of my brothers." The arrow struck him right on top of the head and pinned him to the ground.

Gypsy Origins

Spain

This account of Gypsy origins emphasizes the distinctions between Gypsies and non-Gypsies. Traditionally the Gypsies have perceived their "laziness" as an intelligent decision to avoid the rat race. The storyteller is Isabel Fajardo Maya, a Sacro Monte Gitana and the eldest daughter of the famed flamenco performers La Golondrina and Joaquín Fajardo Maya. This tale was originally recorded by Bertha Quintana in 1971. In 1987 the narrator repeated the same tale without any variation.

The Lord, when he was about to go to heaven, first called an assembly of all the peoples of the world in the Great Plaza. He said, "Tomorrow I am going to heaven, and those who want to come here before I go, to them I will assign their position in life. Whoever gets there too late won't get any."

And that way before he left, he assigned everyone a position—a schoolteacher, a doctor, all. And there were two Gypsies who were very lazy, and one said to the other, "Look, cousin, the Lord is leaving today. He is going to heaven, and everyone has already gone to get their destinies. We are going to be late."

And so they started running to the Great Plaza, and when they got there, the Lord was already leaving because they were so lazy. They called to him, "But Father, you have assigned a destiny to everyone in the world. Are you just going to go off and leave the Gypsies here without an assigned place?"

The Lord said, "You get on any way you can."

And so he left us, and so we get on any way we can. This legend is mine, but it is a reality. The Gypsies live or eat by their wits. They have no real assigned place in the world.

The Magic Belt

Greece

This is one of two tales in this collection told by children (the other is the American Gypsy story "Sam Patra and His Brothers," pages 173–178), and here I've retained some of the rambling quality of the original. Several of the themes, including the father wanting to devour his children, are reminiscent of Greek mythology, while others, like the recurrence of the number forty, are common to Turkish folklore.

The narrator is Afroditi Mavraki of Thessaloniki, eleven years old in 1985 when she told this story.

Once upon a time there lived a hunter who would go hunting in the forest every day. One day he didn't shoot anything, and his wife kept wondering what she would feed him. Finally she cut off one of her breasts and cooked it for him.

As soon as her husband came home, she told him to sit down and eat. After he ate he said, "Very good meat. Where did you get it? You should buy this every day."

She answered, "I didn't buy the meat—it's one of my breasts."

"Ah, is human flesh so delicious?"

"Yes."

Then he said, "Wife, if human flesh is so sweet, let's kill our children and eat them." As soon as his wife heard these words, she fainted. When she came to, he said, "Don't worry, you'll get used to the idea."

The next day he didn't go out hunting. They lit a fire under a large cooking pot filled with water. They washed the children, but when the moment came to cut them up, the hunter left the house. He went to the café and sat there drinking a cup of coffee.

In the meantime his wife gave the children a needle and a comb, and she explained to them that their father wanted to kill them and eat them. The children jumped out of the pot. Their mother told them to flee and that if they saw their father approach, they should throw the needle at him and it would become a tall mountain that would take him forty years to cross. And if he caught up with them after those forty years, she said, they should throw the comb, which would become a great sea that would take him another forty years to cross.

The children left, but their father followed them. The moment they threw the needle, it became an enormous mountain.

By the time forty years had gone by, their father had aged and his clothes were in rags. But as soon as he got near them again, they threw the comb, which became a great sea that took him forty years to cross. When he finally got to the other side, he couldn't find his children, who had all gone to a city to find something to eat. The oldest brother said, "Let's get a little water and a little earth and knead them together. And afterwards we'll cook it over a wood fire and eat it."

When God saw them—he was watching them from up above—he came down to earth and pretended to be an old man with a lot of sores and a wooden stick in his hand.

The oldest brother said to him, "Sit and eat with us."

The old man said, "Thank you, children, for I too have nothing to eat."

The youngest sister complained to her brother, "Why did you tell him to come and eat with us? Don't you see he's full of sores and who knows what else? We won't be able to eat, he's too disgusting."

Her brother answered, "He's just an old man. When you get to be his age, we'll see what shape *you're* in."

The old man—who was really God—understood everything. He ate just a little, and then he said, "My children, I need help to wash. Take some water, boil it, put it in a basin, and let your oldest brother bathe me." While the old man was getting bathed, the other children sewed some clothes for him and found him a place to sleep.

The next day, since the basin was large and heavy with water, all the brothers and sisters helped empty it. When they poured out the water, it turned to gold.

The youngest sister said, "Well, who *is* the old man anyway?"

The following day, when the old man was leaving, the oldest brother wanted to give him the gold—the boy wanted to work and earn his own money. But the old man refused to take any gold and went on his way. So the oldest brother, before he went out looking for work, hid the very large treasure in a very small cave. He kept just enough money to buy food until they could all find work.

They did find work at a baker's, where they got both bread and money. Then they built a house, and even after paying for it, they still had some gold coins left.

God came down again to see them and said, "I am God. This"—he took off his belt—"whenever you're hungry, take this belt and strike once, and you'll find a table with enough food for ten years and more. Only when you put the belt back on your arm will the feast be over."

The oldest boy said, "Thank you, God."

"But don't ever give this belt to your little sister," God said, "because she'll take your eyes out, cut you up into little pieces, and throw you down a well."

Well, one day the youngest sister met a very handsome man. After ten or twelve days she told him their whole story, and the man she loved said to her, "Pretend you're sick and put a new package of macaroni in your blouse every day."

Whenever she twisted and turned in her bed, the macaroni would break. She did this every day and finally said to her oldest brother, "Don't you see how sick I am? Give me the belt so I can get well again, and then you can have it back."

"Of course, sister, the belt," he said, but he didn't give it to her. But one day while her brother was sleeping she took the belt and fled to her lover's house. They celebrated for forty days and forty nights.

Another day her brother was on his way to take a swim in the lake. He saw three beautiful women—they were really fairies—swimming there already, and he took their clothes as a prank. When they discovered their clothes were gone, they had to make new ones out of leaves. But the boy gave them their clothes back, and they said, "You'll become our brother because you took our clothes."

The three sisters lived in a nice house, and the oldest brother had a beautiful horse and a dog who were very loyal to him. But eventually the day came that God had warned him about: his youngest sister took his eyes out, cut him up, and threw him down a well. And his brother-in-law-to-be guarded the well so that no one would see her and put her in jail.

One day the dog and the horse were on their way to get a drink of water. One of the fairies gave them some water in a bucket and left. They saw some blood in the bucket and wondered whose it was. "It smells like human flesh," said the dog. "It's our loyal brother's." From then on every day the dog and the horse went round and round the well. One day they gathered up the blood, flesh, veins, everything, in a bucket and took it to the fairies.

The fairies knew how to make people, and they took a little flour and spat on their hands and glued together his veins, his blood, and everything else, and put him back together just as he had been, except that now one of his eyes was a little crooked.

Now the oldest brother took some worthless rings and bracelets and some canteens to put them in. He had cut the tops off the canteens, and he went along selling the jewelry for weeks.

Finally he reached the house of his youngest sister and her husband. They did not recognize him. It was evening, and he said to them, "Oh, if only I could stay here tonight. I have such a long way ahead of me. I'll give you all these jewels—I just want to get one good night's sleep." His sister took several rings and bracelets and chain necklaces and told him he could stay the night.

His brother-in-law didn't want to let him sleep there, but his sister let him stay. After she had hidden the jewelry, she and her husband went to bed. They fell asleep immediately, but her brother didn't close his eyes all night—he was only pretending to be asleep. The minute he saw the belt hanging high on the wall, he said to himself, *Now you'll be at my mercy.*

When he was sure they were asleep, he very quietly moved a big, high table, climbed up on it, and got hold of the belt. As soon as he held it in his hand, he had all God's power—for that's what was in the belt.

"Now you'll wake up, my sister," he said. "You've slept enough. I'm your brother, who you cut into little pieces and threw into the well. I was saved by my horse and my dog. Now get up."

And he asked her, "What do you want, forty horses or forty knives?"

She thought he meant he would give her either forty horses or forty knives, so she said, "I'll take the forty horses."

He got forty horses and tied them one behind the other, and last he tied his sister. And he said to her, "You wanted forty horses, so I've given you forty horses. Now you'll be dragged behind them and I'll light a fire. The horses will run into the fire and you'll go too."

And that's how it was. The girl died in the fire. Her brother married one of the fairies whose clothes he had taken. They had children and he lived like a god, a real god.

St. George and the Gypsies

Russia

Many versions of this tale occur among non-Gypsies in Russia and Poland. A variant among Mexican Gypsies is called "Saint Peter's Saddle," although it is St. George who has a special connection with Gypsies (see "Why the Sea Is Salty," pages 111–113).

One time St. George was riding along when he came upon a Gypsy trailer. A Gypsy was in the riding seat, pulling on the reins.

"Where are you bound for, Gypsy?" asked St. George.

"Where the wind blows," the Gypsy replied. "And you?"

"Jerusalem. To see how the good Lord fares."

"Good fellow," said the Gypsy, "spare us a thought, us Gypsies. Tell the Lord that we wander the land. Let him tell us how to live."

"Very well," replied St. George. "I'll bring you God's word on my return."

"You'll forget us," said the Gypsy, shaking his head.

Gazing at St. George's horse, the Gypsy saw it was a thoroughbred, with a golden harness studded with precious stones, its stirrup of pure gold.

"I'll tell you what, brother," said the Gypsy. "Leave me your harness; then you'll remember Gypsies every time you mount your horse."

"You're a crafty one," said St. George with a grin. "All right, I'll leave you my harness, only remember: I want it back on my return."

"How could you doubt me?" the Gypsy said scornfully.

On that they parted. Off went St. George, on and on until he passed through a village and came upon some peasants felling timber for a house.

He could see that the logs were not long enough to make a wall. The peasants had tied ropes to those logs and were tugging hard from both ends, trying to stretch them. Amazed at this, St. George rode up and asked, "What are you up to, peasants?"

"It's like this, master: the logs are a bit short, so we have to stretch them. But the stubborn devils won't give. Perhaps you can tell us what to do?"

"In your place I would saw more wood, but I'll ask God if you like. I'm on my way to Jerusalem now."

The peasants were delighted.

As St. George rode on, he came upon two wells with women carrying pails on yokes between them: they took water from one well and poured it into the other. As he came into view, the women called him over.

"Hey there, handsome, where are you going?"

"To Jerusalem, to pay my respects to God."

"Oh dear!" they cried. "Ask God to take pity on us. How much longer must we pour water from one well into the other?"

St. George agreed, rode on, and finally came to Jerusalem for an audience with God. He first asked after his health, then ventured to ask about the peasants stretching logs.

"I know all about that," said God. "It's I who made them stupid for being so stingy and sly. They intended to build a house as well as put by logs for winter—that's what they get for being stingy and stupid. You tell those peasants, George, that I forgive them their sins, but they must be kind and wise in the future."

"I saw another marvel," continued St. George. "Women were pouring water from one well into another."

"I know all about that too," said God. "I punished them for watering down the milk they sold in town. But I'll pardon them as long as they mend their ways."

"I'll pass the message on," said the saint.

He was just about to mount his horse when his foot slipped and he all but took a tumble—at once he remembered the Gypsies.

"I almost forgot, God help me. I promised to ask you how Gypsies are to live."

"Tell the Gypsies this," said God. "Let them live by their own laws. Where they pray, where they beg, where they take without leave—that's their affair. Tell them that."

St. George set off on his return. He met the women, told them what God had said, and—slit my throat and hope to die!—they promised never to water the milk down again.

St. George arrived at the village where the peasants were still trying to stretch the logs, and told them of God's word: he forgave them, but no more scrounging! Overjoyed, the peasants set about their task with wiser heads.

On went St. George and eventually came to the Gypsy camp. As he rode in, little Gypsies hopped around him, crying, "St. George is here, St. George is here!" The adults gathered around.

"Well, what does God say of us?" asked the selfsame Gypsy.

"Listen closely: where you pray, where you beg, where you take without leave—that's up to you."

"Thank God he did not forget the Gypsies!" they all cried.

"As for you, Gypsy," said St. George to the man he'd met before, "give back my harness, as you said."

"What harness? Good God, I took no harness from you, on my soul. Oh no, no, no. Let the moon cut me down if I tell a lie. May my children see no happiness if I ever robbed you!"

So the golden harness stayed with the Gypsies. After all, God did say it was up to them where they prayed, where they begged, and where they took without leave.

Languages

Argentina

This version of the Tower of Babel story is told among Honduran and Brazilian Gypsies, as well as Argentinian Gypsies who originally came from Russia.

One day God, before abandoning humankind, announced, "Where I'm going you cannot follow me. Don't try to follow me," and with that he went to live in heaven. But the people didn't pay any attention to him, and they began to build a large mountain (others said it was a tower). They worked and worked without stopping. When they were getting near heaven, God realized that the people had not obeyed him, and then he said, "I am going to mix up your language." And then they weren't able to finish their work, because anyone who asked for a hammer would be handed a nail, and anyone who asked for a saw would get a hammer, and so on and so forth. And that's why we all speak different languages.

A Dead Man Pays Back

Yugoslavia

Here is a variant of the tale type known as the Grateful Dead, where a mysterious stranger returns from the dead to pay a debt of gratitude. The serpent also appears in non-Gypsy Czech, Russian, and Yugoslavian versions of this story. Apparently the narrator, a nail-maker in Aleksinac, also told "The Church of Cheese" (pages 103–104).

A literary version of this tale is "The Traveling Companion" by Hans Christian Andersen.

A certain Gypsy owed another Gypsy five hundred piasters, and while the creditor was away on a trip, the debtor died and so did not pay his debt.

When the creditor came home and learned that the debtor had died without paying his debt, he asked where his grave was, took a rod with him, and began to beat it.

A Gypsy trader passed and asked why he was beating the grave, and he said, "I am beating this man in the grave because he owed me five hundred piasters."

"Don't beat him," said the trader. "Here are five hundred piasters," and he drew out the money and gave it to him.

The creditor went home, but the dead Gypsy rose from his grave, met the trader who had paid his debt, and—without explaining who he was—said to him, "You're a good fellow; let's go into the town and work together, and we'll make a lot of money."

The trader agreed, and they opened a butcher shop in town. The vampire Gypsy always sold the meat, and kept only the liver for himself, because vampires are always particularly fond of liver.

In that town lived a pasha who had a daughter. She had often been married, but every one of her husbands had died the first night.

"Go and woo the pasha's daughter to be your wife," said the vampire to his partner. But the partner—knowing what had always happened to the other husbands—answered that he did not dare, because he was afraid that what had befallen the other suitors would befall him as well.

"Don't be afraid," said the vampire. "I will get her for you, and nothing will happen to you." And he went and wooed her.

When he had won her, he gave these instructions to his partner: "The first evening, do not on any account lie down with her, but stand at the door and tell her that you have forgotten the keys of the shop and must go back for them. Go away and shut the girl in to spend the night alone."

They celebrated the wedding, and in the evening the Gypsy did exactly as the vampire had told him, and remained alive.

The next day the two Gypsies took the girl and led her to the town from which the husband had come. Halfway there, they sat down under an elm tree to rest, to wind up their partnership, and to divide the money they had made from the business.

When they had divided it, the vampire said, "We also earned this maiden between us, so we must divide her too." He tied her to the elm tree and went back twenty paces, then drew out his knife and rushed at the girl, shouting, "Cast out what you have in your heart!" She was so terrified that she vomited a serpent. The vampire cut the serpent into bits and said to his partner, "I have taken my share—now the maiden is yours," and they went on.

When the vampire came to his grave, he said, "This is my home— I go in here. A pleasant journey to you!" The couple began to weep, but he said to them, "I belong to the other world—I only had leave from it for three years to repay the kindness of a man who paid a debt for me."

Then he gave his partner his own share of the money they had made, explained who he was, and vanished.

Frosty

Wales

This story is a Welsh Gypsy version of a popular folktale whose many variants can be found in Gypsy and non-Gypsy collections in Europe, the United States (including Native American versions), Asia, and Africa. In one version from central Africa the heroes are three brothers named Hear-it-however-faint-the-sound, Follow-it-however-great-the-distance, and Put-it-together-however-small-the-pieces. Some modern variants of this story appear to have their origin in the classical literature of India.

"Frosty" is one of the many folktales collected and translated from the Romani by John Sampson (1862–1931), who was known as the Romani Grimm. The narrator was probably Matthew Wood, a member of a prominent family of storytellers and a grandson of Black Ellen, the "Romani Scheherazade" (see page 9). Told in the unadorned style of the Welsh tales collected by Sampson, this tale is essentially the same one found in Grimm as "How Six Men Got On in the World."

An old man was strolling along the road with his hat cocked on one side. His name was Frosty. He had walked half a mile when he met another man. And this man was lying on his belly with his ear to the ground.

"What are you doing here, you fool?" asked Frosty.

"I'm no fool, I'm listening to the Members of Parliament making speeches in London."

"You'll be of use, come with me. You have excellent hearing."

The two walked on down the road. They met another man, with a gun on his shoulder. "What are you doing here?" asked Frosty.

"Don't you see what I'm doing? There is a fly on a rock in America, and I'm going to shoot it."

"You will be of use, come with us."

And the three went on until they met another man. "What are you doing here?" asked Frosty.

"There is a mill far away over yonder, and there is no wind: I am blowing the sails around."

"You will be of use. Will you come with us?"

The man went with them.

They walked along until they met another man, carrying one of his legs under his arm. "Why are you doing that?"

"I've pulled my leg off so I can't run too fast."

"You must certainly come with us."

They went on and soon saw another man, carrying a huge tree upon his shoulder: a great powerful man was he.

At last they came to a town. They heard the talk of the king's court—that he had an old witch who was a swift runner, and that a great reward was offered to whoever could beat her.

"Let's go up to the palace," said Frosty.

They went up to the palace, and Frosty and the king had a parley about the race. "I have a man who will race her," said Frosty. The whole band slept in the palace that night.

They arose early. This was the morning on which Run-well and the witch were to have their race. They began to run.

"Wait a bit, the old witch is beating him," exclaimed Shoot-well to Frosty. So he shot a dart into her knee, and Run-well beat the witch.

The king was enraged at this. *Who are these men?* he said to himself.

The old witch counseled the king: "Tomorrow proclaim that you want the lake in front of the palace to be drained dry."

The six were sleeping in the palace again that night, and Hear-well overheard this talk between the two. He told Frosty what was going to happen.

They arose early. The king came and told them that he wanted the lake drained on the following morning. The day dawned, and out they went, every one of them. Frosty summoned Blow-well. Blow-well blew the lake dry; he blew all the mud and stones out of it and left it bare.

The old king did not know how to deal with them. They had beaten the witch hollow. "I will lodge them in my old iron chamber and kindle a great fire beneath it until it is as hot as an oven, and I will burn them to death."

Night fell. The old king summoned the six men and threw open the door of the chamber. "Would you like to sleep here tonight, Frosty?"

Frosty entered. "Yes, we will sleep here," he answered. "It seems a warm room."

The old king smiled. "Yes, it is a warm room, and it will soon be warmer still."

In went Frosty and his men. "We will sleep snugly here." They sat down and talked a little before settling to sleep. The room grew hotter and hotter. Soon it became too hot to stay there. So Frosty cocked his hat on the other side. The men were chilled to the bone and began to shiver. When they were half dead with cold, Frosty tilted his hat up a very little. Then the room grew cool, and the six lay down and slept.

The old king came in the morning to look for them. He was amazed to find them alive. He called them outside. "Go over there and get your breakfast," he said. When they had finished their meal, he returned and said, "I want a ship built upon that lake. I want to see it before the door tomorrow morning."

Morning dawned, and the ship had been built.

"I want the ship to sail with no water beneath it."

Frosty summoned Blow-well. He blew the ship out of sight, until none could see it.

The king asked Frosty, "How much money do you want to be off?"

"As much as one of my servants can carry."

"You will have it," said the king.

And here comes Strong-man with a huge sack! He opened the mouth of the sack. He half filled it. "That is as much as you can carry," said the king.

Strong-man lifted the sack in his hand. "You call this heavy? Fill it." The old king looked furiously at him. He filled the sack. "I have filled it now. There, take it and be off, and never come here anymore."

They took the gold and departed.

When they had gone, the old king was beside himself with grief at the loss of all his treasure. He sent his soldiers after them. Hear-well heard them coming.

"Wait a moment, I hear an army following us." The men halted and looked behind them.

"Do not fear," said Frosty. The soldiers drew near to them. Frosty cocked his hat on one side. The soldiers were rooted to the spot: they were so frozen they could not stir.

Then old Frosty paid off all his men. He went home alone to his native village and bought a little house for himself. And there he lives to this day, and is flourishing. And the Woods went there and played the fiddle for him.

The Grateful Lions

Estonia

The first episode in this tale is reminiscent of the story of Androcles and the lion, best known through George Bernard Shaw's play. The balance, however, is essentially a dragon-killer story. "The Grateful Lions" was told to Paul Ariste by Edgaris Kozlovskis in 1935, when the storyteller was sixteen. Six years later he and the rest of his family were killed by the Nazis. Ariste published the tale in Tartu in 1973.

There was once a forester who had only one son. One day the boy said, "Father, I am smarter than a king, but still I don't know everything."

His father asked him, "Just what is it you want to do, my son?"

"I want to go out into the world."

"Then go!"

The boy saddled his horse and rode off. After a while he heard screaming in the woods, and he set off in that direction. Lying on the ground was a lion with a splinter in its paw. The boy wanted to shoot it, but the lion shook its head to tell him not to. So the boy got off his horse and removed the splinter. The lion hugged him. When the boy remounted his horse and went on his way, the lion followed him.

Once again the boy heard screams. When he went to look, he saw another lion, which had been trying to jump from one tree to another and now could move neither forward nor backward. So the boy took an ax and chopped down the tree. The lion jumped off and kissed the boy again and again. Now there were three of them.

Then they met a bear who wanted to devour the boy. But the two lions caught the bear and ate him up instead. The boy said to himself, "I can't leave these animals behind. See how clever they are!"

The boy then came to a city where everyone was dressed in black. He went into an inn and asked, "Why is everyone in mourning?" The answer was, "The coachman is going to lead the king's daughter to the devil tonight at midnight."

The boy took a room upstairs in the inn and had dinner with the two lions. He waited for evening, and when the clock struck eleven, he mounted his horse and went down to the sea with the lions. Suddenly he saw the coachman leading the princess to the sea. Both the girl and the coachman saw the boy and thought that he was the devil, so the coachman threw the girl out of his coach and drove away. Then the boy called out, "Don't be afraid of me! Tell me, why did they bring you here?"

The princess answered, "I was being led to the devil."

Sure enough, when the clock struck twelve, a twelve-headed devil came up out of the sea and shouted, "The king has not given me *one*, he has given me *four*. Come, sit on my tongues!"

The boy answered, "I'll tear your tongues out by their roots."

The devil was furious.

The boy said, "Shut up! Come toward me if you dare."

They began to fight. The three of them—the boy and the two lions—fought until all twelve of the devil's heads were gone. The boy tore all their tongues out, and the devil was dead.

The princess put her ring on the boy's finger. As for the lions, she put her golden locket around the neck of the first and her golden watch around the neck of the second.

The coachman, who had seen everything from afar, came for the princess and led her home, threatening, "Take an oath that you will say that it was *I* who rescued you."

"Yes," she replied in fear. "I will say that."

When they returned home and the king saw his daughter, he asked, "Who rescued you?"

She said, "Your coachman rescued me."

And so the coachman was to be made king, and he and the princess were about to be married. Just two hours before they were to be in church, the forester's son suddenly appeared and the girl recognized him.

The boy asked, "Who rescued the king's daughter?"

The coachman explained that he himself had killed the devil.

The boy asked, "Did the devil have no tongues?"

The coachman answered, "He had twelve."

"What happened to the devil's tongues?"

"I tore them out."

"Show them to me."

The coachman produced some wooden tongues. Then the boy said, "My king, am I permitted to speak?"

"You are permitted."

"See here—I have the devil's real tongues!"

Then the two lions came in. When the princess saw them she said, "You see, Father, these two lions and this boy were the ones who really killed the devil. Just look, they have my gifts!"

Her father asked, "How could my coachman say that it was he who brought you safely home?"

She answered, "If I had not taken an oath to be silent, he would have cut off my head."

So the king ordered the coachman to be put into a cask and thrown into the sea, and the forester's son and the princess celebrated their wedding. And they are still living happily today.

The Gypsy and the Giant

Greece

This is one of many Gypsy versions of a very popular tale type reminiscent of the David-and-Goliath story: the small, apparently weak hero outwits the powerful but stupid giant. I collected this tale just before New Year's Day, 1985, in Thessaloniki. The storyteller, Anastasia Makraki, has great enthusiasm and a sense of the comic. So that I wouldn't take the tale strictly as entertainment, however, another woman explained to me that "the giant is the Greek and we are the little Gypsy. And it means that no matter how much power the Greeks have, we're still smarter than they are."

Now that the Greek Gypsies are beginning to fight for equality, perhaps there will be new variations on this tale.

Once upon a time there was a little Gypsy who had six children and a belt with little red threads in it. Well, the Gypsy went off to gather wood, and while he was walking along the road a giant saw him coming— the Gypsy was *very* little—and said to himself, *Aha, here comes my snack.*

Meanwhile, as the Gypsy was going along the road, he met a shepherd. He said to the shepherd, "I'm hungry. Can you spare me some cheese?" The shepherd gave him a little cheese. The little Gypsy hid it in his pocket for his children.

Soon he went off the road and into the giant's cave. When he saw the giant, he started trembling with fear. The giant jumped up and said, "Why are you trembling?"

"I'm afraid of you," he said. "You'll eat me."

"Ah," said the giant, "we'll make a bet to see who is stronger. Grab a stone from over there and see if you can squeeze water out of it. Can you do that?"

So as the Gypsy was bending down to pick up a stone, he took the cheese from his belt and put it over the stone. He squeezed, and out came water. But when the giant tried, he couldn't get any water. He said, "You're stronger than I am. Let's become brothers."

Well, he and the Gypsy went to the giant's mother's house. The giant took her aside and said, "Mother, he's stronger than I am. What should we do?"

"Well, we'll make him your brother," she said. "Both of you go get wood and bring it back so I can do the wash." Then the Gypsy pretended that he was ashamed to go. "Come, I'll carry you on my back," said the giant. "Let's go!"

So off they went to the mountain for wood. The Gypsy reached down to where he had the red threads in his belt. He tied one thread there, one there, and one over there. He told the giant he was going to pick up the whole mountain. (He said this, though, as a trick, because he knew he couldn't lift any wood—that's how short he was.)

The giant said, "What do you think you're doing? I inherited all this land from my father."

The Gypsy said, "I'm ashamed to go to our mother and bring her just small pieces of wood."

"Leave it alone, let me take it." So the giant cut down some large trees and put them on his back, and the Gypsy too.

When the giant got home to his mother, he said, "Oh, Mother, he's very strong. He even wanted to pick up the whole mountain and bring it to you for your washing. Oh, Mama, he's very strong."

"Okay," the giant's mother said. "The two of you take those goatskin sacks and go bring me water." As soon as they started off for water, the Gypsy realized there was no way he could carry the sacks—they were as heavy as a house. The giant said, "What are you doing?"

"Oh, I'm ashamed to bring our mother only one sack of water. I'll bring the whole well so she can wash clothes."

"Don't worry. I'll take them," replied the giant. He took the sacks, dipped them in the well to fill them, put them on his back and the Gypsy too, and went back to his mother. His mother said, "What's going on here?"

"Oh, Mother, he wanted to bring the whole well so you could wash clothes."

"Well, while I finish washing your clothes, you two go catch a rabbit for us to eat," she said.

They set out, and there on the road they found a pear tree. Now, the giant is tall and the Gypsy is short . . . so the giant grabbed the top of the tree. The Gypsy, who couldn't have reached it otherwise, also grabbed the top of the tree, since he was sitting on the giant's back. The giant was eating and eating, and when he was full, he let go of the branch and the Gypsy flew through the air. And when he landed, he caught a rabbit. "What did you do?" asked the giant.

"Brother," the Gypsy said, "I'm embarrassed. I jumped from the tree and caught a rabbit." So the giant picked him up and went to his mother. "Ah, Mother," he said.

"What is it now?" she asked.

"Mother," he said, "he really is stronger than me. He jumped from the tree and caught a rabbit."

"Oh, he'll eat us! We'd better kill him," she whispered.

The giant and his mother decided to kill the Gypsy in the evening. "We'll take the skewers from over there," she said, "and kill him." But the Gypsy overheard all this, and in the evening he got up from his bed and put some large squashes under his quilt. Then he climbed up on the rafters and looked down from there.

"Let him have it!" they kept shouting. But of course they didn't kill him. When they went away, he jumped down on his mattress. He threw the squashes to one side and got himself back into bed. He heard the giant say to his mother, "Oh, Mother, we've killed him." When the Gypsy heard them returning, he called out, "The fleas have been biting me."

"Oh, Mother," said the giant, "he's too strong. Let's give him a sack of gold and take him back to his home in the morning."

When the giant got up in the morning, he said to the Gypsy, "Brother, let's take you home to your children." But the Gypsy said, "I've been traveling for so many years and you're going to give me only one sack of gold? I want *three* sacks of gold."

Well, okay. The giant gathered up three sacks of gold and took him home.

The Gypsy's tent was small, and he had six children. As the giant was walking along, he had to take a deep breath—the children fell down. He let it out—the children stood up. "They're going to eat you tonight," said the little Gypsy to the giant. "They're even smarter than I am. They'll eat you up."

"Why?"

"Oh, they're very mischievous, they're like me. So tonight sleep in the barn, and tomorrow morning leave."

"Okay."

The Gypsy put the giant in the barn. Then he took a little gasoline, sprinkled it all around the barn, and lit it. When he woke up in the morning, he saw that the giant had burned up.

The Gypsy took the gold, built himself a large house, and brought his children inside. And I was passing by there today, and he gave me a piece of pie.

The Young Gypsy Girl and
the Forest Guard

Latvia

Storyteller Anna Katerina Martinkevič, known by the Latvian Gypsies as *phuri Kata* ("Old Kata"), was born in 1900. Unlike many
Gypsies of her generation, she managed to attend some school as
a child. Widowed at the end of the Second World War, she brought
up nine children by herself.

The story was collected in 1963 by Alexander Belugin (known
by the Gypsies as Leksa Manuš), who says he is a "Rom by convic-
tion," and who has written on the grammar of the Latvian Gypsy
dialects. He points out that while most of Kata's stories end badly,
as this one does, they also contain humor and optimism.

The Romani word translated as "forest guard" has the additional
meaning of "evil forest spirit."

There was once an old Gypsy who had many children.

In the past Gypsies led a nomadic life in the forests except in winter,
when they had to find places to settle down. And it was already winter,
and it was cold and raining and snowing.

The Gypsy said to his wife, "We can't live any longer in the forests—
the children are cold. We should go find that peasant we know and ask
him to let us stay with him till spring."

Well, they went to this peasant and asked him, and he said, "You've
always come to me in winter, and you know my house. So come and
live here."

After they had heated the place, they brought their children, ate,
and went to sleep. In the morning the old Gypsy said to his oldest
daughter, "Your mother and I are going to visit some houses. You stay
here and watch your little brothers and sisters until we get back."

The old Gypsy didn't want to say that he was going to steal, but he
had decided with his wife: "Wife, let's go steal a small horse or sheep.
The holidays are coming, and we don't have anything for the children
to eat."

"Okay. Let's go."

So they went, and on a dark night the Gypsy stole a good horse and a sheep.

On the way home they had to pass through some large forests. The night was dark and gloomy, and it was raining. The Gypsies got lost and didn't know how to get out of the forest. They were cold, so they lit a small fire and slaughtered the sheep.

"Wife, cook the sheep. I'm hungry."

"How can I cook it? There's no water, no pot. Cut a little piece of meat, put it on a skewer, cook it, and eat it."

And the Gypsy cooked the meat on the skewer. Just as he was taking the first bite, a forest guard came toward him and said, "What are you doing, Gypsy? Why did you make that fire? Where did you get that meat?"

"I bought it."

"Don't lie. You stole it. Unless you want to be arrested, give me your daughter—then you'll be able to leave the forest free."

And the old Gypsy man said, "Wife, what do you say? Should we give him our daughter?"

The old Gypsy woman said, "What can we do? If we don't give her to him, he'll turn us in and we won't get out of the forest."

And so they told him to take their daughter and went to sleep in the forest, while the forest guard went off in search of the girl.

Now, this daughter had a fiancé she hadn't seen in a long time, for two or three years. Some Gypsies had told the girl that her fiancé had gotten married, but she didn't believe it.

Well, the forest guard got to the house at midnight and knocked on the window. "Wake up, girl, let me in, I'm cold, I've come from far away, you know how much I love you. I found out that your father's not home, and I came to find you."

This woke her up, and immediately she recognized the voice of her fiancé. She let him in and embraced and kissed him. He started to tell her why he had come at night: "Because you know that your father doesn't want me for a son-in-law." Then he said, "Get ready and come with me."

"How can I? How could I leave my little sisters and brothers? You know that my father isn't home. How will they live while waiting for my father's return? My parents have been gone three days, and they could be gone another three. The children would die of hunger and cold."

"No. Your parents will be back tomorrow morning. If you love me, you'll come with me."

So she got dressed, putting on all her skirts—she had a lot of them—and hugged her little brothers and sisters. Then she took her fiancé by the hand.

Outside she saw a gray horse tied to a tree. Her fiancé put her in front of him on the horse. While they were riding, she said, "Before, you seemed like a good man, but now I'm afraid of you. This horse doesn't go on the ground but gallops in the sky, and my feet are bumping into the tops of the pine trees. You don't seem like a man anymore but a devil."

In this way they rode above the forest and then landed in a little wood.

"Well," he said, "your father gave you to me. And now I can do with you what I like. Did you see what we were riding on?"

She looked. It wasn't a gray horse but a white coffin.

Then he said to her, "Now you must sleep in this coffin—it's your fate. I'll leave your bones here, but I'll keep your skin and your heart." He added, "Undress—you have to be totally naked. I can't get at you, because you're wearing your confirmation skirt."

The miserable girl took off her skirts one by one and threw them into the coffin. But she was undressing and dressing at the same time, buttoning and unbuttoning. She wanted the night to end more quickly, and the dawn to come.

"Hurry, hurry," he said to her, "I have no more time."

And while he was talking like this, the girl prayed to God, and the rooster crowed. The devil disappeared, and one moment later the sun came up. But when the girl saw that she was surrounded by graves, fear took hold of her and she dropped dead.

You Will Eat,
But You Will Not Work

Spain

Bertha Quintana, an anthropologist and expert on Spanish Gypsies, points out that Gypsies may work extremely hard but do not like to perceive their lives as revolving around work. "In actuality," Quintana states, "the majority of Sacro Monte Gypsies work throughout their lives engaged in relatively low-paying occupations and trades which require the expenditure of long hours and personal energy."

Reluctance to perceive one's life as work-centered is reflected in this Sacro Monte legend, told to Quintana by Pepe, a *payo* who had married into the Gypsy community thirty years before. His daughter said of him, "My father talks like a Gypsy, and feels like a Gypsy. He has lived among us for many years, more than among his own people. He considers himself a Gypsy, and the same is true of me." These feelings echo those of other *gaje* who have married Gypsies.

Look here, when they crucified Christ, he went carrying the cross to Calvary. He asked for water, and no one would give him water. When he arrived at the top of Calvary, some Gypsies gathered. They got water, and upon approaching Christ, they threw themselves at him and gave him the water. He rested a little and revived. He said, "You, the Gypsies, have my blessing. *You will eat, but you will not work.* And those who follow also will eat, but not work."

That was Christ's blessing to the Gypsies.

The Snake

United States

This psychologically satisfying children's story was told to Allan Cushman by Seattle Rom leader Ephraim Stevens in 1966. It was Stevens who first envisioned the formation of the Seattle Gypsy Alternative School, which opened in 1973 and is at present one of two Gypsy schools in the United States.

This is a children's story. There was a king who had three sons—two were smart and one was dumb. The king sent them all out to get jobs, to see who was smart enough. So the three sons went into the woods; they got all their food together and went looking for jobs. Someplace the road divided into three, and each son took a different road. One son got in trouble with a bear; he went running back home. The second son got in trouble with the farmer's daughter; he went back home. The dumb son—he was really small, tiny—sat under a tree, eating, when a snake came up to him and said, "You're the smartest of them all. All you have to do is get me by the tail and take me home with you, and I'll make you the richest man on earth."

The dumb son wasn't scared. He picked up the snake, wrapped it around his neck, and took it home. Everyone was frightened when he walked into the room with the snake. But the snake said to him, "Take my tail and flash it three times, and that chest will be full of emeralds and diamonds." The dumb son did just that, and sure enough the chest was full of emeralds and diamonds. He gave the chest to his father.

"Look what I brought you, Father." His father the king looked at it and said, "Aha! *You're* the smartest. And I always thought you were the dumbest! You'll get the hand of the princess."

And so they were married, and the little son had all the treasures and all the gold, whatever he wanted, as long as he kept that snake.

The Poor Gypsy and the Devil

Austria

The narrator of this tale, Kalić, was living near Oberwart in the Burgenland when he told this tale to Mozes Heinschink and Paul Meissner in 1976. Kalić worked for a time on road construction in Vienna.

There was once a poor Gypsy who had twelve children. The poor man was very pitiful. He had a fiddle and went to carnivals to play. He had already made his way around the whole village. People gave him bread and money. Now, there was also a miller.

"I should go to this miller," the Gypsy decided.

As soon as he got there, the miller came out with a huge ax and said to the Gypsy, "Don't play for me now. A terrible tragedy has happened."

"What is it? Can I help you?"

"Oh yes," said the miller. "Every night at midnight the Devil comes to the mill."

"I'll join you tonight," said the Gypsy.

By midnight the Gypsy had arrived, bringing a cask of spirits for the Devil. The miller gave him a large loaf of bread and also wine and meat.

When the Devil arrived and saw the fiddle, he asked, "Friend, what is that?"

"Something good. Just wait, you'll see how you'll dance!"

The Gypsy gave the Devil something to drink. When the Devil got drunk, he began to dance—he even went dancing up on the ceiling and wore it out with his horns.

Now the Gypsy got the Devil's hands in a vise, took a big file, and began to file away at them.

The Devil cried, "Oh, stop, my friend, I'm already starting to bleed!"

The Gypsy responded, "I'll work on you until you sign a promise in your own blood that you'll never come to the mill again."

So the Gypsy freed the Devil's hands from the vise, and the Devil signed and went away.

If the Gypsy and the miller haven't died, they're still alive today.

King Edward and the Gypsy

England

This is one of many folktales attempting to explain the origins of
traditional Gypsy life-style. The story was told in Angloromani and
published in England in 1875 in a book on that language.

Other expressions of the same theme can be found in the stories
"The Wooden Horseshoe and the Three Nails" (pages 156–158)
and "You Will Eat, But You Will Not Work" (page 200).

Many, many years ago there was a great king in England. His name
was Edward, and he was a good kind gentleman.

One day he rode, all alone, through a great dark wood. As he was
going under a little tree, a big branch took hold of his hair. The damn
horse ran off and left Edward hanging on the tree.

An old Gypsy man who happened to see this cut down the branch
and let Edward go free again.

The king thanked him and said, "Who are you?"

He answered, "A poor old Gypsy man."

The king said, "I will let you go where you like, and sleep where
you like, in all my kingdom. And all other Gypsies are free to do so
too."

The Gypsy Thief

Hungary

This "true" story was one of many tales narrated by thirty-year-old
Gyula Mágai and collected by Sándor Csenki (1920–1945). Csenki
spent much of his time with the Gypsies in his native village of
Püspökladány in eastern Hungary and could speak Romani fluently
by the age of fourteen.

It's probably a good idea, given the tiresome stereotype of the thieving Gypsy, to point out that thievery, deception, and bluffing are universal folklore themes.

There was once a poor Gypsy who was such an amazing thief that it would be hard to find his equal. One day he was on his way to see a certain peasant who had two beautiful horses, which he had decided to steal at the stroke of midnight.

On the way he met the Devil. (This is a true story—the Gypsy was my mother's father.)

"Where are you heading?" asked the Devil.

"I'm going to Peasant So-and-so, to steal his horses."

"And how are you going to do that?"

"I'll jump over the fence and have a look around. When no one is there, I'll go into the stable, untie the horses, mount one of them, and take the other one too. And where are you going?"

"I'm going to the same peasant, to eat his liver. And the same with his wife and children later."

"And how are you going to do that?"

"I'll turn myself into a fly, slip through the keyhole, and crawl into his nose. He will sneeze blood until it's all gone, and then he will die. But when he sneezes, if someone says 'God bless you,' I can do nothing."

So the Gypsy waited outside till the Devil went into the house and crawled into the peasant's nose. When the peasant sneezed, the poor Gypsy jumped to the window and shouted, "God bless you!" And so it went on until morning, and no harm was done.

The Devil went away, and the poor Gypsy knocked on the peasant's door.

"Good morning," said the Gypsy.

"Good morning to you. What do you want?"

"Listen, I'd like to tell you something."

"Go ahead," said the peasant.

"Here it is. To be frank, I came here yesterday intending to steal your horses."

The peasant was furious.

"Listen to the rest of my story. On the way I met up with the Devil. The Devil asked me where I was going. I told him I was coming here to steal your horses. Then I asked him where he was going. He told me that he too was coming here, to eat your liver and your wife's and children's. I asked him how he would do this. He told me that he would turn into a fly, slip through the keyhole, and crawl into your nose so that when you sneezed, your blood would all flow out unless at each sneeze someone said 'God bless you!' So I have saved your life and that of your wife and your entire family."

"Is this really true?" asked the peasant.

And the Gypsy answered, "Yes."

Whereupon the peasant went into the stable, brought out the horses and their papers, and gave them to the Gypsy.

"You have saved our lives and should have both the horses. Good luck with them."

And this is a true story.

The Bird

Moldavian SSR

"Čirikli" ("The Bird") was collected by L. N. Tcherenkov, the son of a Lithuanian Gypsy mother and a Russian father. The storyteller, twenty-seven-year-old Grigori Cantea, was studying at the agricultural institute of Kishinev in the summer of 1966. Tcherenkov could find no parallel tales in Gypsy literature.

The gentleman's horror at the thought of his daughter marrying the son of a poor Gypsy reflects attitudes that are still very much alive, so the tale's happy ending is all the more satisfying.

Once there was a very poor Gypsy couple who would go from village to village looking for work. And that's how they ended up in one particular village.

One day a very well dressed gentleman came to see the Gypsy at the forge and said to him, "Make me something to put on my boot." The Gypsy quickly made him a copper heelpiece.

The gentleman was pleased and said, "You know, Gypsy, you would be better off living and working here with my people who make picks and shovels and all sorts of other things for me."

The Gypsy accepted and moved to the gentleman's estate.

He worked there until the new year. On New Year's Eve the gentleman gave the Gypsy a little money, a small jug of wine, and cornmeal for polenta. The poor Gypsy went home and asked his wife to prepare some food to accompany the wine. That night she prepared the meal, and they ate, drank, and then went to bed.

The Gypsy got up at midnight as if someone had woken him. An hour later, perhaps more, a bird arrived, beat its wings, and said, "Listen, gentleman! Listen, Gypsy! Tonight both your wives will become pregnant. The Gypsy will have a son and the gentleman a daughter. They will look alike. Their fate is to become man and wife."

Both the Gypsy and the gentleman heard these words. The Gypsy laughed and didn't believe it. But the gentleman couldn't close his eyes all night after hearing what the bird had said. When he awoke in the morning, he called his oldest servant and told him to make sure the Gypsy didn't leave and to give him everything he needed.

The poor Gypsy thought that the gentleman had not heard the prophecy of that night, and he himself forgot it after a while. But the gentleman never forgot those words, and day by day the thought that the Gypsy's son would become his son-in-law tormented him more and more. And day by day he provided more and more for the Gypsy.

And that's how it went until one fine day the Gypsy felt like going on his way. But the gentleman offered to raise his wages so that he'd stay on. The Gypsy, seeing that he was being well paid, remained.

The gentleman couldn't forget the bird's prophecy. He kept counting the days, and finally the night arrived when the children were to be born. The gentleman went and found the two best midwives in the village, then sent one to the Gypsy woman's bedside and the other to his wife's. The babies were born at exactly the same instant. And when the midwives were through, the gentleman ran to see the boy and saw that in fact he looked like his daughter, just as the bird had said.

After two days the gentleman said that it would be a good idea for the little boy and the little girl to sleep in the same cradle. The Gypsy was surprised but told his wife to do what the gentleman said. By this time he had completely forgotten the fateful night.

A month later the Gypsy again told the gentleman that he wished to go on his way. The gentleman replied that he wouldn't let him go unless he left his son behind, and that he would pay as much as he wanted for his son. That's when the Gypsy remembered that night, just as if someone had reminded him of it, and he flatly refused.

But when the gentleman kept insisting and gave him a purse of golden coins, and then another for his wife, the wife couldn't resist anymore. "Let him stay, my husband," she said. "He'll live better here and will become an important man, and we—well, we'll live more comfortably, and we'll have other children."

The Gypsy still didn't want to abandon his child. But when the gentleman gave him four more purses of gold coins, he couldn't resist anymore and abandoned the child. Eyes full of tears, the Gypsy took his tools and left.

When the gentleman, remembering the bird's prophecy, got up the following morning, he ordered his most trusted servant to take the baby deep into the forest the next day and to kill and bury him. The next day, his mind constantly on the prophecy, the gentleman woke the servant and sent him into the forest.

The servant harnessed the best horses. Then he climbed up on the sled—it was winter—and took the road to the forest. On the way, watching the child stretch his little arms and play, he took pity on him. The servant took him into the forest and decided it would be better to just leave him there. *I am only a man*, he thought. *Who knows what could happen to me? And whatever this child's fate may be, it would be a sin to kill him.*

He put the baby on the snow under a tree, turned the horses around, and returned home. After he left, the snow began to fall softly. And when the snow stopped, the sun came out and melted the snow the baby was sitting on.

Nearby, a peasant—neither a poor nor a rich man—who was out gathering firewood came across the baby playing under the tree. He saw how beautiful the child was, and immediately picked him up and embraced him, thinking that God must have sent him the baby because he had no children of his own. He covered the baby with his blanket and took him home in his sled.

The peasant lived in a village far from the criminal gentleman's estate. When he arrived, he called to his wife to come and see what he had brought back from the forest. Then he told her how he had found the little boy. She gave the baby milk. Her joy knew no bounds.

The child grew like asparagus—in one hour he grew as much as other children do in a month. He was lively and clever; he could do anything and had no equal. When he was old enough, they sent him to school.

There was no school in that village nor near the criminal gentleman's estate, but there was one in another village. The boy had just entered the schoolyard when he spotted a girl. This was the gentleman's daughter. The two of them learned more easily than all the other children and finished studying at the same time. From the moment they met, they liked each other so much that they couldn't be apart even for a minute.

Once, while they were arranging where to meet, she said, "Ioniké"— that was the boy's name—"let's get married, because I would die without you." He told her to ask her parents. But she answered that she'd already done so and that they were waiting for him to ask for her hand. He said, "Well, let's go see them!"

When they entered her house so that he could ask permission to marry her, the gentleman recognized him and died of anger on the spot. But his wife, his daughter, and Ioniké all thought that he'd died of joy. The wedding lasted three days and three nights.

Then the servant came and told him the truth—why the gentleman had died and who his real parents were. Ioniké immediately told his wife everything. She and her mother began to laugh and said that in the past they had prayed for the gentleman to die, and that God had decreed the death of a very cruel man.

Then Ioniké's wife and his mother-in-law got someone to bring his real parents, and one night of the wedding party was repeated just for them. Ioniké made the servant owner of all he had. If he has not died, perhaps he is still alive.

I've come from there to tell you the whole story.

The Old Couple and
Their Pig

Greece

This short tale—reminiscent of Greek and Turkish shadow-puppet theater both in its economy and in its slapstick style of aggression—was told to me by Anastasia Dimou, then age twenty-six, in 1983 during one of my stays in Thessaloniki. To give the interested reader an idea of what at least one dialect of Romani looks like, the tale is reproduced in the original Romani on page 223. The same story exists in the Greek non-Gypsy repertoire, though with the ethnicities reversed: there the crafty stranger is a Gypsy and the gullible couple are Greek peasants.

Once there were an old Gypsy man and an old Gypsy woman, and they kept a pig. Whenever the old woman looked at the pig, her heart would melt, thinking how good it would taste. So one day the old woman took the pig and slaughtered it. After washing and cleaning it, she got the old man to help her fetch firewood for cooking their food. As they went, they scattered hay behind them so that they would know the way back.

They brought back the firewood, prepared the pig, cooked it, and put it on the table. After a while it occurred to them that they had no toothpicks to clean their teeth with after eating the meat, so they locked the door tight behind them, hid the key under the mat, and started back into the woods. Once again they took some hay with them and scattered it on the road so that they wouldn't forget the way. As they were going along, they met a Greek, who asked, "Why are you strewing hay about?"

They answered, "We've just slaughtered our pig and cooked it, but we forgot to get wood for toothpicks. That's why we're throwing hay on the road, so we won't forget where our house is, and—oh yes—we put the key under the mat in front of the house. So please don't go there and eat our food."

"Listen, you think *I* would do such things? Are you crazy?" the Greek replied.

Well, while they went to get the wood for toothpicks, naturally the

Greek followed the trail left by the hay. Once he found their house, he took the key, opened the door, ate some of the food right away, and took all the rest home.

When the old people returned, they saw at once that there was no food left, only a couple of bones, and the house was filled with flies. "Where's the pig?" "I don't know." "Maybe the flies ate it."

So they took all the sticks they had brought with them to make toothpicks. A fly on the window—there went the windowpane! One on the door—there went the door! One here, one there. Soon they had destroyed the entire house. Afterward the old woman said, "There's a fly on your foot." There went the old man's foot! "And there's one on your arm," said the old man. There went the old woman's arm!

They kept on like this until they killed each other. And I was there outside the house, but I didn't go in to separate them. That's the only reason they didn't kill me too.

Voso Zachari Tells
His Tale

France

Matéo Maximoff, a noted Gypsy novelist who lives in Paris, introduced this story, part of his "Tales of Terror" collection, as follows:

"At this season, in the month of February, a company of about thirty of us found ourselves sitting around a fire. It was not very cold, but we are accustomed to light fires even in the month of August, when we meet to tell our old stories, strange stories but true. For no Gypsy is allowed to tell a lie before the brothers of his race. If he does they will term him a liar, a stigma which he will always conceal, and he will not be permitted to join in our gatherings. He who tells a story must cite his witnesses, even if it is only a child."

The realism with which Maximoff describes the hero's emotions makes the story's macabre elements—the ghosts and talking corpses—all the more effective.

This evening I will tell you what happened to my cousin Vadia Telaki, and my witness is my brother Diordi: he knows this tale as well as I do myself, for he heard it in my company.

Here, then, is the strange thing that befell Vadia Telaki:

This took place in Poland. My cousin Vadia, with his clan the Telaki and some other clans, were in a village whose name I have forgotten— but perhaps Diordi can bring it to mind?

As far as I remember, it was a Sunday. Vadia had taken his three horses to sell at a big fair in the town. It would take him some time to travel the fifteen kilometers to town. Mounted on one of his horses, he led the other two by a bridle and was followed by his black dog Bolo, as strong and fine a creature as I have ever seen.

By evening Vadia had sold two of his horses at a good profit. He then went to the inn to get a meal, and you may be sure he did not forget Bolo and his remaining horse.

When Vadia set off from the inn, it was already night. He could not see more than two or three yards in front of him. As he was mounting his horse, the innkeeper, who was on the doorstep, asked him, "Are you going far?"

"No, scarcely fifteen kilometers. You see the road? Look! I'm going to another village."

"Are you crossing the bridge?"

"It seems to me there is no other way."

"Then I advise you to spend the night here."

"Why is that?"

"So you know nothing about the bridge?"

"Nothing!"

"For a whole year now a man has disappeared every week on that bridge on this very market day."

Vadia smiled. He thought the only danger he faced was to spend a night at the inn, for the landlord knew he had a large sum of money on him. So he said to him, "Have no fear for me. I have a horse who knows how to gallop, and I will face anyone who may pursue me. If anyone should attack me, Bolo is with me, and I believe there is no man who could win a fight with Bolo. Farewell!"

Half an hour went by. The horse trotted gently on after Bolo. Nothing untoward happened.

The moon rose, and Vadia saw that he had lost his way. He looked all around him. He did not recognize the road, yet he could not have gone astray . . .

Vadia pulled up his horse. He could see clearly now and could distinguish the road before him: on each side of it the fields shone white in the moonlight. He went on very slowly, as if he were afraid of falling somewhere or other. Where was he?

To check his fear, he called, "Bolo." The dog barked but did not run in front of the horse as he usually did. He thought to himself, *Bolo is afraid, but of what? I must go and see.*

He called, "Bolo, Bolo, get him!" The dog barked fiercely and began to explore the right and left sides of the road as if seeking an invisible foe. Vadia sensed that Bolo was not afraid, and he himself felt reassured.

He continued on his way but still could not recognize anything. He realized that he was truly lost, and he thought of turning back and spending the night at the inn. So he turned his horse around. A few minutes passed, then suddenly the horse refused to go forward. Vadia kicked it and lashed it with his whip, but the animal would not budge. Vadia was afraid that it would go mad and throw him, for even in the moonlight nothing now could be clearly distinguished.

And so he dismounted and tethered his horse to a branch of a tree. Vadia was not cowardly. He called his dog to him, and when Bolo barked he made him stop, by petting and gentle words.

Vadia did not stir for nearly a quarter of an hour. He no longer knew where he was. Followed by Bolo, he proceeded for about a hundred yards. There was no sound at all from anyone. He returned to the tree where his horse was waiting for him.

Then Vadia tried once more to return to the town. But the horse balked. It was a great difficulty, for Vadia was obliged to proceed on an unknown road. He had no choice but to go on.

Like all Gypsies, he knew that animals scent danger better than men. If the horse did not want to go back to the town, it meant that danger lay there. And because of all this he was convinced that the innkeeper was a bad man.

The horse proceeded as if he already knew the way. In his Gypsy mind, Vadia felt that an invisible hand was leading him. But whose hand?

Vadia shivered when he thought of it. He was prepared to sell his life dearly: he seized his knife.

Nonetheless, without paying much attention, Vadia reached the river. He was on the right road and felt more relieved. He had to find out, though, which side the bridge was on. Without any hesitation the horse turned right to get to the river.

A few minutes afterwards Vadia saw the longed-for bridge. He smiled and patted his horse. Perhaps it guessed that all was not well with its master and wanted to protect him. Bolo followed behind, and Vadia was surprised that he was calm.

Vadia was about to cross the bridge that the innkeeper had warned him about. Nonetheless he trembled, and was ashamed of himself.

On the planks of the bridge the nails of the horseshoes made a great noise. When Vadia reached the middle, his horse reared, and if he had not been a fine horseman, he would have fallen. But he held on well and calmed the animal.

Then he saw a strange thing in front of him: a man, so tall that his head disappeared into darkness, barred his way. Then this giant seemed to grow smaller until he was no bigger than two normal human beings.

Vadia trembled and turned his horse around. Worse still! Behind him another giant exactly like the first also barred his way. Vadia turned around again, and the first giant had disappeared. But as soon as he tried to go forward, this one was back again. Once more he looked behind him: there was no one there.

Vadia guessed there was only one man, but how did he manage to appear in two places at once? His height enabled him to run very fast, but which way did he disappear? By the bridge? Impossible! By the river? Impossible! One would have heard the water.

What *was* it? Then Vadia shook with fright and murmured, "A ghost." He made the sign of the cross, but in vain: the giant was still there.

A good idea entered his mind. He called out to his dog, "Bolo! Seize him!" The good dog rushed forward and threw himself at the giant. A fierce struggle took place. Vadia spurred on his horse and reached the other side. Behind him the giant and Bolo continued the fight, which the dog could not win.

A short time later Vadia reached the village where he had spent the day. The horse refused to go any farther. He himself was weary. He had to find some spot where he could spend the night.

Vadia saw a little spark of light gleaming in one house. He dismounted and knocked at the door. No one answered. He would have liked to look in at the window, but there were curtains inside. He went back to the door and knocked again, much louder. No one answered. Without paying any heed, he put his hand on the handle. The door opened. Vadia entered, for he thought to himself, *Men are not so devilish as a ghost.*

Ill-fated Vadia! There another thing of horror met his gaze: in a coffin that reposed on two chairs lay a corpse. No one watched over it, there were no flowers, no wreath, but on each side was a tall candle. It was this light that Vadia had seen.

This dead man is like all other dead folk, said poor Vadia to himself. And he gazed without any fear at the corpse.

He was a man of about forty years, dressed like a peasant. He appeared to be asleep. His hands, folded on his breast, held a cross. He must have died that very day, but it was strange that no one watched over him. Could he have no relations? Is it possible, then, for the dead to be left alone?

Vadia removed his hat. Then he took a chair and, despite his surprise and fear, seated himself behind the coffin so that he faced the door. He thought that it was better to be with a dead man who *was* dead than out in the night, followed by a dead man who was alive. How he regretted that he had not passed the night at the inn.

Vadia plucked up a little courage. In the village the church clock struck two. "So late!" said he. "Where have I spent all this time?" What had he done? He no longer remembered.

Only one thing tortured his mind: the giant by the river. Then the neighing of his horse dragged him back from his reverie. The horse was neighing because it was afraid, and it was not afraid without good reason. Vadia no longer had the courage to move. He realized that the ghost was not far off, and he deserted his horse as he had his dog. What else could he do? Doubtless the ghost had already killed Bolo and now would kill his horse, who was stronger than the dog but not so cunning. Then it would be his turn! Who would not have trembled in his place?

Then, as if a thunderbolt had struck him, the door burst violently open, and the dead giant stood in front of it. The door was too narrow for him, but how long could it hold out before giving way?

As Vadia, in terror, remained seated in his chair, there took place the weirdest thing that could be: the dead man in the coffin rose up and then, like a living being, jumped to the ground and prevented the giant from entering.

"What do you want here?" asked the corpse.

"This man is mine."

"No, he belongs to me! He is the only one who watched over me."

"This man is mine," repeated the giant.

Then a fight took place between these two dead men, a fight that Vadia beheld with his eyes starting out of his head. Ah! if the dead giant were to win, how could he, poor mortal, escape from it?

There was still no result to the fight. Who would win? At no moment did the corpse give way to the dead giant. But how could he hold out, when Bolo had been destroyed? Despite his fear, which grew greater every minute, it occurred to Vadia that perhaps all dead men had the same strength.

The fight went on for a long time, one hour, two mortal hours, and every second Vadia trembled within himself. Then, far away, a rooster began to crow, and the two dead men stopped short in their struggle: the day began to dawn. Without having time to return, one to the water beneath the bridge and the other to his coffin, they were caught by a beam of the sun. And they both became like statues.

Vadia had escaped, saved by the unknown dead man in the coffin. Even the dead know who does them a favor: Vadia was the only one to watch over him, although involuntarily.

The two specters kept themselves on their feet, rigid, each supporting the other as if still fighting—they blocked the doorway. Vadia could have climbed out by the window, but in his terror the idea did not even cross his mind. He remained where he was, exhausted, waiting for someone to come and let him out.

It was only half an hour after this when the peasants, going to their work in the morning, saw this weird spectacle. They summoned the priest. He was as terrified as the rest; he had the bells of the church rung. With all the people he went to the place where the dead had appeared.

When Vadia saw all the people, on the spot he uttered a cry like that of a man no longer alive. It was enough to terrify even the bravest, and the priest himself trembled. They had to get the door open, and it was a hard job, even accompanied by prayers. When Vadia climbed out, no one wanted to touch him until the priest had said prayers over him. Then they allowed him to relate how he had spent the night. And despite the presence of the two specters, it seems to me that no one would have believed him if a peasant had not found the corpse of poor Bolo.

The two dead men were burned in the cemetery.

As for Vadia, a peasant who had taken pity on him conducted him home.

I myself would not have believed this story if I had not learned that Vadia, after falling ill for three months, then died at last of fear.

The Rom in the Piano

Czechoslovakia

This delightful story, with its self-assured hero, was told to Milena Hübschmannová in 1967 by Jan Sivák, who was forty years old at the time. He is a scrap metal dealer and the father of six children. Born in East Slovakia, he has lived in Most in northern Bohemia since 1947.

There was once a poor Rom who had seven children, and they were hungry day in and day out—that's the way things were in the old days. His wife went begging and the children had nothing to eat but what she brought home.

One day a beggar came to them and said politely, "God bless your evening, Rom."

"May he also bless your evening, beggar," replied the Rom. "Where are you traveling, where are you wandering?"

"As a poor man from village to village. You know yourself how that is. Wherever God wills, there I spend the night. Listen, Rom, would you be willing to put me up for a night?"

The Rom had no objection. "You are poor and so am I. You can sleep here."

So the beggar slept at the Rom's house for the night. But the Rom's wife made a fuss. "Look here, husband, we have seven children and a single bed, and you bring a beggar here as well!"

"Oh, wife, he is poor, I am poor, and if he can't find lodging with poor people, then he won't find it anywhere. Stop your talk, he'll sleep here."

The next morning the beggar said, "Listen, Rom, after I'm gone shake out the straw I slept on, so that none of my lice will remain in it."

So the wife took the straw and shook it. Then out of the straw—she couldn't believe her eyes—fell real gold pieces, shining ducats. "Husband, husband, just look what happened to our straw!"

The Rom knew at once that the beggar had been none other than God. "So, you see, wife," he said, "now we are rich. And you didn't want to let the poor man spend the night at our house."

The Rom ran after the beggar but couldn't catch up with him. The whole day he sat around without saying a word. Finally his wife asked, "Why are you so deep in thought, husband? You're not even eating, just thinking and thinking."

"Leave me alone. I have such a longing to see the beggar that I am sick from it."

So when evening came, God returned. As before, he was dressed as a beggar, but this time he was carrying an old violin case.

"It's good that you came back!" the Rom rejoiced. "You can't imagine how much I missed you." He led him back into their hut.

"Watch out you don't break my violin!" yelled God.

The Rom fixed God up nicely with his only bed. He ordered his wife, "Wash him and give him food."

"Listen, Rom," said God, "take the violin out of the case, but don't play it till tomorrow after I leave."

The violin—the Rom didn't know this yet—was made in such a way that whoever heard it play absolutely had to dance. But God felt too old to jump around like a fool, so at dawn the next morning he set out on his way.

The Rom couldn't understand why God had given him the violin. Then he thought, *Wait, I want to try it out.* No sooner had he touched the strings than his seven children began to dance. He had to laugh at the way they hopped around so early in the morning. The Rom played on, so beautifully! And soon his wife was dancing too, until she was out of breath.

"Stop playing, husband," she begged. "I can't stand it anymore."

Now that the Rom understood what kind of violin God had given him, he got dressed and went to the village. Soon a baron came by. "Baron," asked the Rom, "do you have a cigarette?"

"I spit on you, you dirty Gypsy."

Just then a king went by. "King, will you give me a cigarette?"

"Never in my life will I take out my golden cigarette case for a stinking Gypsy."

Then an innkeeper came along. For the third time the Rom asked, "Dear innkeeper, give me a cigarette. Everything hurts when I can't smoke."

"Beat it, you miserable Gypsy!"

So the Rom took the violin and set the bow in motion. As he hit the first note, a dance of dances started. My God, how those three danced! The baron, the king, and the innkeeper waltzed and hopped like crazy, yelling again and again, "Stop playing! Stop playing!"

Nearby was a carpenter who had been watching the whole thing. "Listen, Rom," he suggested, "you are a good violin player, I am a good carpenter. I'll build a piano that you can fit into to play your violin. Then I'll go to market and sell the piano. Just wait and see how much money I'll sell you for! I'll live well, and so will you."

Why not? thought the Rom. "Well then, sell me, carpenter, if you want."

So the carpenter built a first-rate piano—I take my hat off to him! It fit the Rom like a glove, and he could play his violin in it comfortably.

The carpenter went to the market and put the piano up for sale. The Rom played his violin inside it, and whoever had legs danced. The king's daughter heard how beautifully the piano played, and she saw the people dancing like fools. Then she said to her father, "Listen, Papa, if you don't buy me this piano, I'll die."

The king tried to talk her out of it. "Do you know," he asked, "how much a piano costs when it plays so beautifully?"

"Whatever it costs, I must have this piano. Otherwise I'll die."

"Of course, I'd rather buy the piano," he said. "How much are you asking for the piano, carpenter?"

"Two bags of ducats."

"God in heaven, that's too much."

"Too much, king? If you looked all over the world, you'd never find such a piano. If you want it, then bring two bags of ducats and it'll be my money and your piano."

The princess pleaded and begged, "Papa, even if the piano cost three bags of ducats, you'd have to buy it for me. Otherwise I'll die on the spot."

"I have only you, my child," said the king. "What else can I do? I'll take the piano."

The king gave the carpenter two bags of ducats and then called his servants to carry the piano into the princess's room, while the Rom remained hidden inside it.

The day wore on. The Rom's stomach began to growl—his hunger was getting worse and worse. But of course he couldn't easily walk out of this coffin of a piano, could he? *Wait*, thought the Rom, and he began to play. Right away the princess had to dance. She danced and danced, and not until she was completely out of breath did the Rom stop playing. The princess threw herself onto the bed and fell asleep immediately.

The Rom opened the lid. *Look, the tables are still set*, he observed. *The guests have eaten, they have drunk, they have celebrated. But what did they leave for me? Dry bread! Is that decent?*

The princess lay in her bed, only half covered. *How beautiful she is*, thought the Rom. He ate what little was left over, drank a sip, and hurry, back into the piano!

The next morning, when the princess had gotten up, he played a little for her and stopped. After a while, he played once more and stopped again. The princess enjoyed the dancing, and both of them felt good. But the Rom kept dreaming that he would sleep in the bed of the king's daughter.

In the evening he again crept out of the piano. *They've eaten*, he thought, *they've drunk. But for me they left nothing. I was better off with my wife, even though I got only roast potatoes.* Still, he felt sorry for the princess, who lay alone in bed, without a lover. What could he do for her? Then he got the idea of tying a silver bow around her foot.

The next morning she was more than a little surprised: never before had she found a silver bow tied around her foot. Where could it have come from? Well, the Rom in the piano played again, and the princess had to dance. Because of this, she forgot to run to her father with the bow.

But you should know that in the meantime the king had written to all the other kingdoms, bragging that nowhere could anyone find such a wonderful piano as his. He even had the letter read on television and printed in the newspapers.

Well, good, the next night came. The Rom did the same as the preceding night, but this time he tied a golden bow around the princess's foot. When the king's daughter woke up early in the morning, she looked and marveled: a golden bow! Yesterday a silver one, today a golden one. She thought, *Tonight I will have to be alert.*

That evening she again danced to her heart's content. When she lay down in bed, she wanted to stay awake, but she was too tired and fell asleep right away.

Can't I give the princess something better than a golden bow? the Rom asked himself. *I have nothing better than myself.* So he lay down next to her in the bed. When the princess woke up and saw the Rom, she thought that he was an evil spirit. Out of terror, she jumped up and shouted, "If you are alive, show yourself; if you are dead, disappear!"

"Have no fear," said the Rom, "I'm alive just like you."

Well, what had to happen happened: the princess took a liking to the Rom. He slept with her in the royal bed, and not until the dawn did she think to ask, "How did you get in here? The door and windows are locked. Who are you?"

"I didn't come from outside," replied the Rom. "I came from inside. I'm the one who plays for you here in the piano. But you're such an ungrateful woman—you leave me nothing to eat and nothing to drink."

When she heard that, the princess laughed joyfully and said, "Listen, my dearest, from today on I'll leave food for you, have no fear."

From then on the princess and the Rom lived like two lovers whose happiness lacks nothing in the world as long as they just have each other.

The other kings, meanwhile, who had read the notices of the piano in the paper came to see it with their own eyes. As soon as the piano began playing, they all danced like fools. Finally the princess said, "Enough of this silliness, let's eat."

The Rom immediately stopped playing and thought, *They will eat, they will drink, and I should sit here in the piano? No, not that again!* The Rom was a stately fellow and decently dressed. He crept out of the piano and mixed among the royal guests.

"Where do you come from?" asked the king, surprised. "Since I've been king here, there has never been such a handsome person among us."

"Oh, I come from far away."

Well and good, they ate and drank. When they were full, the guests asked, "Let's go back to your room, princess, we want to dance again."

They went, but the piano didn't play. Why? The Rom was, after all, not inside.

"Nothing we can do, Father," explained the princess. "A part of the piano is broken. Leave me alone for a while and I'll fix it."

"What, you know about such a complicated thing?"

Oh, if you knew all the things I know! she thought.

The king and his guests left the princess's room. Only the Rom secretly went back. The two lovers quickly kissed and embraced each other a little, and when the Rom was in a good mood, he jumped into the piano. The princess called the guests back in. The Rom played in the piano and everyone danced and waltzed, so that it was a real delight. The foreign kings praised the piano beyond all measure. The only thing that displeased them was that none of them owned such an instrument.

"Do you know what, kings?" They held wicked counsel among themselves. "If he does not willingly hand the piano over to us, we'll declare war on him."

"Look, daughter, what you've done to me!" wailed the king. "Always just piano, piano. Now I, an old man, must go to war because of this piano."

That made the princess feel very bad. Her old father would have to go to war, all because the Rom and she were playing such a nice game? Oh, then she had to confess the truth: "Listen, Papa, that's not a piano that's playing; that's a person who's playing."

"Nonsense—no person can play so well, that's impossible."

"Yes, it *is* possible, dear Father. I'm living with him, so I must know. If you don't believe me, then come and look at him for yourself."

She opened the piano. The king was more than a bit surprised: inside sat the Rom with his violin.

"Girl, I ask you, where did you get this Rom?"

"He was inside the piano when you bought it. Don't ask me idle questions, but instead call in the kings who've challenged you to go to war."

The king asked the other kings to come back to his palace. When they were all gathered together, he said, "Now listen, kings, you're urging me to go to war for no reason. In the piano a completely ordinary person is playing, a Rom. If you don't believe me, have a look at him yourselves."

He opened the piano. They all looked in, and the Rom stepped out with his violin.

"There's no reason to have a war over this," said the Rom. "You certainly have Romani musicians in your lands too. Just give them each two bags of ducats and then you can put them in your pianos."

"That's true!" shouted all the kings, as if with one voice.

"And now we will have a feast," said the princess, inviting her guests to the table.

All the kings dined more happily than ever because they would not have to go to war. But the Rom left the princess and returned to his wife, and if they haven't died, they are still living today.

THE ORIGINAL ROMANI VERSION OF
"THE OLD COUPLE AND THEIR PIG"

Sas te sas yek phuro yek da phuri. Adalen sas yek balo. I phuri dikhelasles ta jalas lako gi leske. Sa phenelas e phureske phurea te činas e bales. O phuro phenelas sikno si o balo. Naklas ebuka vakiti gene i phuri phenel e phureske te činen e bales. O phuro gene phenel lake sikno si o balo. Voida astarel ye gyes sar pašlo o phuro činel e bales. Xalaeles, temizleles, lel e phures jan te anen kašta ya te keren o xabe. Len palapeste pliaves. Čon palapeste ya te prinjanen o drom katar gele. Ande kašta kerde o xabe peklelles lačardeles. Sona die pes gogi sosa ka temizlerun pe danda ta ka xan o mas. Phanden šukar o udar garaen o kilito talo pato len palapeste gene pliava. Čon gene po drom ya te na bristen o kher. Sar jan arakhel len po drom yek gajo. Phenel lenge soske čon i pliava? Čindam phenen adala yek balo kerdamles xabe ama bristardam te astaras amenge kile ya te ikalas e masa andar amare danda kana ka xas o mas. Onutsin čas i pliava po drom te na bristas o kher o kilito da thodamles talo pato kai si anglo udar. Te na jas ta te xas o xabe. Ašun šukar. Me kerav gasae bukia? Dile sanus? E, gele von te len kašta vovda gelas pale pliave arakhlas o kher lel o kilito putrel o udar xal ebuka othe okovada leles khere. Aven von den andre dikhen ninai o xabe sade e dui kokala. O kher pherdilo makia. Mo kai phurea o mas? In janav, phenel. Galiba phenes xaleles e makia. Ta kai len e kile kai ande! Yek mak po jamo, pat o jam, ak yek mak, po udar, pat, gelo o udar, yek kate yek kote, phagle čorde o kher. Sona phenel i phuri yek mak pi ki čang pat geli e phures ki čang ak yek mak po ko vas phenel o phuro gelas e phurako vas. Mudardepes. Meda semas avral ama in gelem te kurtarumlen ya te na mudaren manda.

NOTES

BIBLIOGRAPHY

PERMISSIONS ACKNOWLEDGMENTS

INDEXES

NOTES

Complete references to works cited here only by author's last name are in the Bibliography (pages 239–243). Unless otherwise noted, the stories have been translated by me.

INTRODUCTION

2 Estimate of world Gypsy population: Acton, p. 17.

3 "The Gypsies, moving about in their nomadic groups . . .": Liégeois, p. 104.

3–4 "The Little Gypsy": Sara Nomberg-Przytyk, *Auschwitz: True Tales from a Grotesque Land* (Chapel Hill: University of North Carolina Press, 1985), 83–84.

5 On the sterilization of Gypsy women in Czechoslovakia: Liégeois, p. 113.

5 *New York Times* article from Rome, 18 November 1987, p. A3.

6 Syrian folktale: "Women's Wiles," in Inea Bushnaq, *Arab Folktales* (New York: Pantheon, 1986), 318–322.

6 "I'll make you dance, all right": from Linda Dégh, ed., Judit Halász, trans., *Folktales of Hungary* (Chicago: University of Chicago Press, 1965), 267.

9 Quote from Yates about Black Ellen: Sampson, pp. vii–viii.

9 Quote about the Coppersmith Gypsies: Walter Starkie, *Don Gypsy: Adventures with a Fiddle in Southern Spain and Barbary* (New York: Dutton, 1937), 115–116.

11 "Certain aspects of Gypsy life . . .": Liégeois, p. 178.

11 The relevant quote from Hearn's essay "A Glance at Gypsy Literature" can be found in Edward Larocque Tinker, *Lafcadio Hearn's American Days* (New York: Dodd, Mead, 1925), 117.

12 "The body itself is usually given . . .": Acton, p. 36.

12–13 "One day I read somewhere . . .": Liégeois, p. 185.

STORIES

15–17 "How the Gypsy Went to Heaven"

Told by Najma Ayashah, New York City, 1986. Recorded in English by Diane Tong. This story has many Gypsy parallels. A Welsh one with the same incidents and motivation, "The Old Smith," can be found in Yates, pp. 31–36. For a Russian Gypsy variant see "Death and the Gypsy" in Druts and Gessler, pp. 68–69. The African-American version can be found in Virginia Hamilton, *The People Could Fly: American Black Folktales* (New York: Knopf, 1985), 126–132.

17–19 "The Mouse's Wedding"

Told by Najma Ayashah, New York City, 1986. Recorded in English by Diane Tong.

19–20 "Husband or Brother?"

Told by Najma Ayashah, New York City, 1986. Recorded in English by Diane Tong.

20–21 "The Faithful Mongoose"

Told by Najma Ayashah, New York City, 1987. Recorded in English by Diane Tong.

21–22 "The Gypsy Boatman"

Told by Najma Ayashah, New York City, 1987. Recorded in English by Diane Tong.

22–25 "Vana"

Name of storyteller unknown. D. C. Marriner, "A Ghost Story from Yugoslavia," *Journal of the Gypsy Lore Society* 40 (1961):127–130. Thompson, p. 256.

25–29 "The Enchanted Frog"

Told by Catherine Philippo, Toronto, 1982. Recorded in Romani and translated into French by Chantal Hilaire.

29–34 "The Mosquito"

Storyteller unknown. Jan Yoors, "A Lowari Tale: Collected and Translated, with Notes and an Introduction," *Journal of the Gypsy Lore Society* 25 (1946):3–21.

34–35 "Why Gypsies Are Scattered About the Earth"

Storyteller unknown. Druts and Gessler, p. 139. The following Bulgarian variation on this tale is found in Kenrick and Puxon, p. 13: "We used to have a great king, a Gypsy. He was our prince. He was our king. The Gypsies used to live all together at that time in one place, in one beautiful country. The name of that country was Sind. There was much happiness, much joy there. The name of our chief was Mar Amengo Dep. He had two brothers. The name of one was Romano, the name of the other was Singan. That was good, but then there was a big war there. The Moslems caused the war. They made ashes and dust of the Gypsy country. All the Gypsies fled together from their own land. They began to wander as poor men in other countries, in other lands. At that time the three brothers took their followers and moved off, marching along many roads. Some went to Arabia, some went to Byzantium, some went to Armenia."

Kenrick remarks, "Since I printed this tale in the first chapter of *Destiny of Europe's Gypsies*, I have learnt that Ali Čaušev spent some time with Chaman Lal during the latter's visit to Bulgaria and I now feel that the tradition of Ali Čaušev's own family has become mixed with historical information received from Chaman Lal to create a new tale" (*Lacio Drom*, Supp. to 6 [1985]:75).

Chaman Lal's tale can be found in his book *Gipsies: Forgotten Children of India* (New Delhi: Publications Division, Ministry of Information and Broadcasting, Government of India, 1962), 7.

35–41 "The Tailor's Clever Daughter"
Told by Katina Makri, Thessaloniki, 1985. Recorded in Greek by Diane Tong. A variant from Palermo, "Catherine the Wise," is in Italo Calvino, *Italian Folktales*, trans. George Martin (New York and London: Harcourt Brace Jovanovich, 1980), 540–546. In that story the children's names are Naples, Genoa, and Venice.

41–43 "A Deceiving Sleep"
Told by Hulda Baltzar, Jyväskylä, Finland, 1987. Recorded and translated into English by Yrjö Qvarnberg.

43–45 "The Silly Man Who Sold His Beard"
Told by Johan Dimitri Taikon. Jagendorf and Tillhagen, pp. 17–20. For a description of Taikon's life and aspirations, see Esty, pp. 62–77. See Max Lüthi, *The Fairytale as Art Form and Portrait of Man*, trans. Jon Erickson (Bloomington: Indiana University Press, 1984), for examples throughout of Taikon's narrative skill. The language book (which also includes more of Taikon's folktales) is Gjerdman and Ljungberg. For a description of Miloš's funeral, see Esty, pp. 62–63.

45–47 "The Gypsies' Fiddle"
Told by Johan Dimitri Taikon. Jagendorf and Tillhagen, pp. 102–106. The quote from Taikon is on p. 102.

48–49 "Jorška Who Came Back from the Dead"
Told by Johan Dimitri Taikon. C-H. Tillhagen, "Tales of the Living and the Dead," *Journal of the Gypsy Lore Society* 31 (1952):103–115.

49–50 "The Bride and the Egg Yolk"
Recorded by Carol Miller. Seattle, 1967.

50–53 "The Jealous Husband"
Storyteller unknown. Groome, pp. 121–123.

54–55 "The Toad's Revenge"
Storyteller unknown. Pégon, p. 124.

55–61 "Tale of a Foolish Brother and of a Wonderful Bush"
Told by John Čoron. Recorded by Isidore Kopernicki. Groome, pp. 155–161.

61–62 "The Dream"
Told by Bruno Levak (Zlato). Recorded by Mirella Karpati. Levak and Karpati, p. 73. Three other Gypsy variants of this tale are: the Slovenian "How the Gypsy Outwitted the Priest," *Journal of the Gypsy Lore Society* 1 (1907):66–68; no. 5 in Ješina, p. 226, where there are three Gypsy boys and a piece of bread; and "Xoxavno Peter," *Lacio Drom* 15 (1979):2–13.

63–65 "The Golden Girl"
Told by Mihály Jakab, Gyöngyös, Hungary, 1985. Recorded in Romani and translated into English by Judit Szegő. See Zita Réger, "Language Groups Among the Gypsies in Hungary and Some Aspects of Their Oral Culture," in *The Less Widely Taught Languages of Europe* (Dublin: IRAAL, 1988).

65–68 "The Gypsy Woman and the Cave"
Told by Lazaros Harisiadis, New York City, 1987. Recorded in Greek by Diane Tong.

68–71 "Forty Scatterbrained Gypsies"
Told by Lazaros Harisiadis, New York City, 1987. Recorded in Greek by Diane Tong.

71–75 "Yerasimos"
Told by Lazaros Harisiadis, New York City, 1987. Recorded in Greek by Diane Tong.

76–77 "Phara-un, God of the Gypsies"
Told in English by Diana Mafa. Frances R. Vandercook, "Phara-un, God of the Gypsies: A Tale Recorded from a Russian Gypsy," *Journal of the Gypsy Lore Society*, 18 (1939):109–112.

77–80 "The Sixty-One Skills"
Told in Portuguese by Mena. Serra, pp. 126–129. Translated into English by Maria Clark.

81–82 "How the Devil Helped God Create the World"
Storyteller unknown. Vladislav Kornel, ed., "Gypsy Anecdotes from Hungary," *Journal of the Gypsy Lore Society* 2 (1890):67–68.

83–84 "A Dish of Laban"
Storyteller unknown. Hampden, pp. 111–112.

84–86 "A Wicked Fox"
Storyteller unknown. Hampden, pp. 105–109. On the fox's nickname see Inea Bushnaq, *Arab Folktales*, p. 215.

87–102 "Alifi and Dalifi"
Told by Persa Bimbo, New York City, 1947. Recorded in English by Rena Gropper.

102–103 "How the Gypsies Became Musicians"
Storyteller unknown: the only attribution is "From a Vlach Gypsy in Ripanj." Fanny Foster, "Jugoslav Gypsy Folk Tales," *The Slavonic Review* 14 (1936):290. Translated from Tihomir Djordjević, *Ciganske Narodne Pripovetke* (Gypsy Folk Stories).

103–104 "The Church of Cheese"
Storyteller unknown. Fanny Foster, "Jugoslav Gypsy Folk Tales," p. 290. Translated from Tihomir Djordjević, *Ciganske Narodne Pripovetke*. For a very similar version, also from Yugoslavia, see "The Church of Cheese" in Yates, pp. 96–97.

    The Argentinian version, sent to me by Lolo Vitróvič, who says it is current among the Terkaroni Gypsies, goes as follows: "Do you know why we Gypsies don't have institutions and other things like that? I'll tell you why: It's because one day God got together with the Christians, the Jews, and the Gypsies, then he up and gave to the Christians a stone church, to the Jews a wax church, and to the Gypsies a church of cheese. The Gypsies, as always, were very hungry because they hadn't eaten in several days, so then they decided to eat the church. And since that time our world isn't very solid and is without representation, as opposed to the *gaje*, who have more solidity and material things because their church was and is of stone."

104–110 "The Robber and the Housekeeper"
Told by "Noah Lock and Others." Yates, pp. 139–145. T. W. Thompson was an early member of the Gypsy Lore Society. In the T. W. Thompson Notebooks at Leeds University, "some of these tales are only summarized, but they provide most valuable evidence of the survival in English oral tradition of some international tale types not otherwise known in [England]," Katharine M. Briggs and Ruth L. Tongue, eds., *Folktales of England* (Chicago: University of Chicago Press, 1965), xxx. A Polish Gypsy version, "The Brigands and the Miller's Daughter," is found in Groome, pp. 168–175.

111–113 "Why the Sea Is Salty"
Set down in Greek by Yannis Vrisakis, Athens, 1987. Information on St. George's Day in Acton, p. 26.

114 "Death and the Old Gypsy Woman"
Ješina, pp. 227–228. Original in Romani.

114–117 "Napolina"
Storyteller unknown. "Napolina: A South German Gypsy Tale recorded by E. Wittich," *Journal of the Gypsy Lore Society* 9 (1930):170–178.

118–120 "The Magic Whistle"
Storyteller unknown. George A. Agogino and David W. Pickett, "The Magic Whistle: A Folktale of Gypsy Cunning," *Journal of the Gypsy Lore Society* 40 (1961):106–109. On the answer "No," see Thompson, p. 157.

120–122 "Bread"
Told by Fatma Zanbakli Heinschink. Recorded in Romani and translated into English by Mozes Heinschink, Vienna, 1987. An American Machvanka commented to Carol Miller after hearing this story, "Well, I can understand that, even if it's Turkish . . . You notice how we always put the bread on the table first at *slavi* [feasts], at Easter, and the candle goes in it for *pomana* [death feast]. That's for you to always have bread. Our people say that bread is the face of God. That shows you how you should take care of it."

122–123 "The Enchanted House"
Told by María Jiménez Salazar. Antonio Gómez Alfaro, "Some Stories of Spells, Ghosts, Treasures," *Lacio Drom*, Supp. to 6 (1985):48–52. Translated into English by the Study Team of Presencia Gitana.

123–132 "Jack and His Golden Snuffbox"
Told by John Roberts. Groome, pp. 209–218. Groome comments on p. lxxvii that the feature "of the big cake and curse, or the little cake and blessing, is found, to the best of my knowledge, in no folk-tale outside the British Isles." See Bettelheim, pp. 76–78.

132–133 "One Hundred Cows"
Told by Laci Tancoš, Petrovany, East Slovakia, 1954. Recorded in Romani by Milena Hübschmannová and translated into English by Hübschmannová and Donald Kenrick.

133–134 "The Romni's Riddle"
Told by Laci Tancoš, Petrovany, East Slovakia, 1954. Recorded in Romani by Milena Hübschmannová and translated into English by Hübschmannová and Donald Kenrick.

134–137 "The Riddle"

Told by Leon Zafiri in Romani and published in Romani and French by
Paspatis, pp. 594–601. A description of Zafiri appears on pp. 34–35.

137–138 "Why the Jews and the Gypsies Are Enemies"

Told by Stefan Demirov and translated from Bulgarian into English by
Donald Kenrick, "Three Gypsy Tales from the Balkans," *Folklore* 78
(1967):60. Kenrick's comment is from his article "The Oral Tradition Among
the Romanies in Bulgaria (some notes)" in *Lacio Drom*, Supp. to 6 (1985):71–
76.

138–139 "The Three Travelers"

Set down in Romani by Ian Hancock, Austin, 1987. For more on the issue
of publishing in-group data, see Alan Dundes's introductory remarks to
Langston Hughes, "Jokes Negroes Tell on Themselves," in Dundes, ed.,
Mother Wit from the Laughing Barrel (New York and London: Garland,
1981), 637.

139–142 "The Bird and the Golden Cage"

Told by Diamandis Asteriadis, Thessaloniki, 1985. Recorded in Greek by
Diane Tong.

142–143 "The Gypsy Lawyer"

Told by Bruno Levak (Zlato). Recorded by Mirella Karpati. Levak and
Karpati, pp. 74–75. This tale is quite widespread, the protagonist not always
being a Gypsy, of course. The Turkish version, "Nasreddin Khoja as a
Witness in Court," is found in Warren S. Walker and Ahmet E. Uysal, *Tales
Alive in Turkey* (Cambridge: Harvard University Press, 1966), 236–237. In
Russian folklore there is a similar story whose protagonists are Tsar David
and Tsar Solomon: W. W. Strickland, *Panslavonic Folk-Lore* (New York:
B. Westermann, 1930), 436–437.

144 "The Creation"

Set down in English by narrator R. A. W. (Ron) Barnes, Auckland, New
Zealand, 1987. The Manouche version from Alsace and a reference to the
Chilean version can be found in Aparna Rao, "Some Mānuš Conceptions
and Attitudes," in Rehfisch, p. 145.

In contrast, there is a Finnish (non-Gypsy) legend which attributes the
Gypsies' color to an accident: "When God was creating man, he happened
to drop one on the embers in the fireplace. It became black and that was
the origin of Gypsies": David M. Andersen, "Finnish Folk-Accounts for the
Origins of the Gypsies," *Journal of the Gypsy Lore Society* 1 (1976):75.

There is also a version where the carefully made people are the whites:
Veronika Görög-Karady, "The Image of Gypsies in Hungarian Oral Literature," *New York Folklore* 11 (1985):150–151.

145–150 "Yannakis the Fearless"
Told by Katina Makri, Thessaloniki, 1985. Recorded in Greek by Diane
Tong. The Italian version is in Italo Calvino, *Italian Folktales* pp. 3–4.
Bettelheim discusses the sexuality in the more usual version of this folktale
on pp. 280–282.

151 "The Vases of Harmony"
Storyteller unknown. Daphne Maurice, "Pierre Derlon: A Friend of the
Gypsies," *Journal of the Gypsy Lore Society* 51 (1972):92–96.

152–156 "The Red King and the Witch"
Storyteller unknown. Groome, pp. 58–62. Groome's comment on p. lxvi:
"Indeed, 'The Red King and the Witch' to me appears as good as anything
in the whole field of folklore . . ."

156–158 "The Wooden Horseshoe and the Three Nails"
Told by Manfri Frederick Wood. In Wood, pp. 74–75.

"One of the most striking legends tells of the Crucifixion. The ancestors
of the Gypsies, it says, forged the nails used to crucify Christ; three of these
were used, but the fourth, a red-hot piece of iron, has followed them and
their descendants everywhere: they are unable to cool it or to escape it"
(Liégeois, p. 18).

On the Falashas' alleged role in the crucifixion, see Louis Rapoport,
Redemption Song: The Story of Operation Moses (New York and San Diego:
Harcourt Brace Jovanovich, 1986), 33.

158–160 "The Fox and the Miller"
Storyteller unknown. Collected and edited by Kiril Kostov, "The Vixen and
Pirušambi," *Journal of the Gypsy Lore Society* 41 (1962):31–38. Bettelheim,
p. 10.

161–163 "The Gypsy Smith"
Told by Homi Smith. Webb, pp. 139–141.

163–164 "How It Is in the Gypsy Paradise"
Storyteller unknown. Frederick George Ackerley, "Five Tales from Bosnia,"
Journal of the Gypsy Lore Society 23 (1944):97–106. Miller quote in Rehfisch,
p. 49.

165 "The Gypsy of Tucumán"
Told by Teresa and Rosa Ivanovič, 1983 or 1984. Recorded by Lolo Vitróvič.
Yoors, p. 235.

166–167 "The Three Villages"
Told by Andonios Sotiriou, Athens, 1985. Recorded in Greek by Diane
Tong. Milena Hübschmannová's comments can be found in her article "Oral
Folklore of Slovak Roms," *Lacio Drom*, Supp. to 6 (1985):61–70.

167–169 "The Two Children"
Storyteller unknown. Collected by Rudolph von Sowa, "Three Slovak Gypsy Tales," *Journal of the Gypsy Lore Society* 3 (1891):81–85 ("The Two Children," pp. 82–84). Originally published in the collector's *Die Mundart der slovakischen Zigeuner* (Göttingen: Vandenhoeck & Ruprecht, 1887), 165.

169 "Why the Gypsies Don't Have an Alphabet"
Told by Anastasia Dimou, Athens, 1985. Recorded in Greek by Diane Tong. Also in D. Tong, "Aspects of Narrative Tradition in a Greek Gypsy Community," *Lacio Drom*, Supp. to 6 (1985):83–90.

170 "Why Gypsies Eat Hedgehog"
Storyteller unknown. Thessaloniki, 1982. Recorded in Greek by Diane Tong. Also in the paper mentioned in the previous note, p. 86.

170–171 "The Flood"
Storyteller unknown. Tihomir R. Gjorgjević [Djordjević], "Two Bible Stories in the Tradition of Serbian Gypsies," *Journal of the Gypsy Lore Society* 13 (1934):34–35. From Heinrich von Wlislocki, *Märchen und Sagen der Transilvanischen Zigeuner* (Berlin: Nicola Verlag, 1886), 4–5.

172–173 "The Gypsy and the Hen"
Told by Frans Josef, Norway, 1979, for Norwegian television. Translated into English by Kirsten Wang.

173–178 "Sam Patra and His Brothers"
"Folk Tales Told by Steve Demitro," *The Survey* 59 (October 1, 1927): 19, 58–59. For an Irish folktale that has many of the same motifs, see "Children of the Salmon" in Eileen O'Faolain, *Children of the Salmon and Other Irish Folktales* (Boston: Little, Brown, 1965), 287–298.

178–179 "Gypsy Origins"
Told by Isabel Fajardo Maya. Quintana and Floyd, p. 84.

179–183 "The Magic Belt"
Told by Afroditi Mavraki, Thessaloniki, 1985. Recorded in Greek by Diane Tong.
   "Offering a choice of types of execution is common in Turkish folktales. The unlucky person is often given the choice between forty swords and forty horses. Knowing that the swords can mean only death but thinking that the horse may provide a means of escape, the victim invariably chooses the horses. He chooses the worse death, however, for he then has forty ropes attached to his body, each rope tied to one horse. When the horses are whipped, they run off wildly, and the victim is torn into small parts" (Warren S. Walker and Ahmet E. Uysal, *Tales Alive in Turkey*, p. 268).
   The trick of using macaroni to simulate broken ribs is paralleled, for

example, in the Palestinian tale "Seven Magic Hairs," this time with dry, toasted bread (Inea Bushnaq, *Arab Folktales*, p. 116).

183–185 "St. George and the Gypsies"
Storyteller unknown. Druts and Gessler, pp. 25–27. For the Mexican Gypsy variant, see D. W. Pickett and Rafael Gonzales, "A Mexican Gypsy Legend," *Journal of the Gypsy Lore Society* 43 (1964):3–11.

185–186 "Languages"
Told by Teresa and Rosa Ivanovič, 1983 or 1984. Recorded by Lolo Vitróvič. Frédéric Max collected a tale in Honduras from Pochela Miklos of Tegucigalpa which combines this tale with the one about the nails of the cross.

186–188 "A Dead Man Pays Back"
Storyteller unknown. Fanny Foster, "Jugoslav Gypsy Folk Tales," pp. 288–289. Translated from Tihomir Djordjević, *Ciganske Narodne Pripovetke*. For a very similar variant, also from Yugoslavia, see Yates, pp. 94–96.

188–191 "Frosty"
Probably told by Matthew Wood. Sampson, pp. 55–57. "The Story of Fiovatsi," a Swedish Gypsy variant told by Taikon, is in Gjerdman and Ljungberg, pp. 174–186.

191–193 "The Grateful Lions"
Told by Edgaris Kozlovskis to Paul Ariste, 1935. Mode and Hübschmannová, Vol. IV, pp. 490–492. Translated from the German by Dana McDaniel.

193–196 "The Gypsy and the Giant"
Told by Anastasia Makraki, Thessaloniki, 1984. Recorded in Romani by Diane Tong. A Swedish Gypsy version of Taikon's is "The Gypsy and the Snake," Jagendorf and Tillhagen, pp. 24–34. A Rumanian Gypsy version, "The Deluded Dragon," is in Groome, pp. 80–82. There are countless Gypsy and non-Gypsy versions of this story.

197–199 "The Young Gypsy Girl and the Forest Guard"
Katia Martinkevič, "Čhaj te Vešéskīru," *Etudes Tsiganes* 22 (1976):1–8. Text in Romani and French.

200 "You Will Eat, But You Will Not Work"
Told by Pepe. Quintana and Floyd, pp. 99–100. Compare the following non-Gypsy tale from North Bosnia, "The Origin of Man": "In the beginning there was not anything but God, and God slept and dreamt. Ages and ages his dream lasted. But it was destined that he should awake. Starting from sleep, he gazed around him, and every glance transformed itself into a star. God wondered, and prepared to journey forth, to inspect what he had created with his two eyes. He journeys and journeys, but nowhere is either

end or limit. Journeying, he at last reaches even our world; but now he was tired; the perspiration poured from his brows. On the earth falls a drop of sweat, and lo! you have the first man. Divine was his birth, but he was not formed for happiness; from sweat was he born; already from the beginning it was destined that he should toil and sweat" (W. W. Strickland, *Panslavonic Folk-Lore*, p. 308).

201 "The Snake"
Told by Ephraim Stevens, Seattle, 1966. Recorded in English by Allan Cushman and sent to me by Carol Miller. For more information on the school in Seattle, see Leita Kaldi, "Alternative Education for the Rom," *Explorations in Ethnic Studies* 6 (January 1983):21–27.

202 "The Poor Gypsy and the Devil"
Told by Kalić. Translated from Romani into German by Mozes Heinschink and Paul Meissner, "Der arme Zigeuner und der Teufel," *Mitteilungen zur Zigeuner-Kunde* 2 (1976):6–10.

203 "King Edward and the Gypsy"
Storyteller unknown. B. C. Smart, M. D., & H. T. Crofton, *The Dialect of the English Gypsies* (London: Asher and Co., 1875), 215–216.

203–205 "The Gypsy Thief"
Told by Gyula Mágai. Sándor Csenki, *Ilona Tausendschön: Zigeunermärchen und -schwänke aus Ungarn,* trans. into German by József Vekerdi (Kassel: Erich Röth-Verlag, 1980), 158–160.

205–208 "The Bird"
Told by Grigori Cantea. L. N. Tcherenkov, "Čirikli (L'Oiseau)," *Etudes Tsiganes* 13 (1967):1–11. Text in Romani and French.

209–210 "The Old Couple and Their Pig"
Told by Anastasia Dimou, Thessaloniki, 1983. Recorded in Romani by Diane Tong.

210–216 "Voso Zachari Tells His Tale"
Matéo Maximoff, "Paramiča Darane: Tales of Terror," *Journal of the Gypsy Lore Society* 28 (1949):82–97. Text in Romani with English translation by Dora Yates.

216–222 "The Rom in the Piano"
Told by Jan Sivák. Milena Hübschmannová, *Janitschek im Räuberschloss: Märchen Slowakischer Rom,* trans. Erika and Reimar Gilsenbach (Berlin: Der Kinderbuchverlag, 1983), 69–78. Translated from the German by Dana McDaniel.

BIBLIOGRAPHY

This bibliography includes suggested reading on the Gypsies, the books and journals from which tales in this anthology were taken, and references found in shortened form in the Notes. Readers wanting more information on bibliographic matters can write to me in care of the publisher.

Acton, Thomas. *Gypsies*. London: Macdonald Phoebus, 1981; Westwood, NJ: Silver Burdett, 1983. A children's book in the publishers' Surviving Peoples series. Provides a highly informative and thought-provoking overview of the culture, history, and struggles of the many different groups of Gypsies. Illustrated with photographs and original art.

Bettelheim, Bruno. *The Uses of Enchantment: The Meaning and Importance of Fairy Tales*. New York: Vintage Books, 1977.

Cohn, Werner. *The Gypsies*. Reading, Mass.: Addison-Wesley, 1973. A short, personal book which explains the methods and objectives of anthropological fieldwork. Illustrated with the author's photographs of Gypsies in Canada, the United States, and Europe.

Cotten, Rena M. [Gropper]. "Gypsy Folktales." *Journal of American Folklore* 67 (1954), 61–66. Describes and discusses four types of narrative employed by American Gypsies and offers several suggestions for future research, all of which remain valid.

Druts, Yefim, and Alexei Gessler. *Russian Gypsy Tales*. Trans. James Riordan. Edinburgh: Canongate, 1986.

Esty, Katharine. *The Gypsies: Wanderers in Time*. New York: Meredith Press, 1969. A potpourri of information about Gypsies and scholars of Gypsy lore, much of it a popularization of material found in scholarly articles in the *Journal of the Gypsy Lore Society*.

Etudes Tsiganes: French journal of Gypsy studies, which began publication in 1955. Published by L'Association des Etudes Tsiganes in Paris, a nongovernmental organization connected with UNESCO.

Gjerdman, Olof, and Erik Ljungberg. *The Language of the Swedish Coppersmith Gipsy Johan Dimitri Taikon.* Copenhagen: Munksgaard, 1963. Contains a complete and detailed grammar of Taikon's speech, the meticulously transcribed texts of eight folktales, and a 3,600-word dictionary with a corresponding English wordlist. Gjerdman's preface describes the long collaboration of Taikon and Ljungberg that resulted in this classic work on Romani.

Groome, Francis Hindes. *Gypsy Folk-Tales.* London: Hurst & Blackett, Ltd, 1899. Classic collection of Gypsy folktales with a long introductory essay on the history, language, and folktales of the Gypsies. Notes throughout focus on comparative folklore.

Gropper, Rena C. *Gypsies in the City: Culture Patterns and Survival.* Princeton: The Darwin Press, 1975. Written by an anthropologist who has done fieldwork with the Gypsies since 1947, this account of Gypsies in New York City is full of intimate information not available elsewhere and has a refreshingly dynamic approach to anthropology. Annotated bibliography.

Hampden, John. *The Gypsy Fiddle and Other Tales Told by the Gypsies.* New York: World, 1969. A collection of Gypsy folktales taken from Groome, from the *Journal of the Gypsy Lore Society*, and from Sampson's *XXI Welsh Gypsy Folk Tales*, retold for children. The introduction by writer and artist Jan Yoors, who lived with the Gypsies for many years, is an interesting addition to the stories.

Hancock, Ian F. "The Gypsies: Le Rom And'o Texas." In *The Folklore of Texan Cultures.* Ed. Francis Abernethy. Austin: Encino Press, 1974, pp. 344–354. An ethnographic and folkloric overview of Gypsies in general and Texan Gypsies in particular, with regard to occupations, taboos, social occasions, food, sports, religious beliefs, language, attitudes toward women, and the legal system.

———. "The Origin and Function of the Gypsy Image in Children's Literature." *The Lion and the Unicorn* 11 (1987):47–59. A succinct analysis of the reasons for the stereotyped portrayal of Gypsies in American and British fiction for children and young adults, with examples from the literature as well as some historical background on the Gypsies.

———. *The Pariah Syndrome: An Account of Gypsy Slavery and Persecution.* Ann Arbor: Karoma, 1987. An illuminating and important account by a Gypsy of his people's oppression, concentrating primarily on slavery in Eastern Europe and on the Holocaust. Bibliography.

Jagendorf, M. A., and C. H. Tillhagen. *The Gypsies' Fiddle and Other Gypsy Tales.* New York: Vanguard, 1956. A collection of Taikon's stories (see Gjerdman and Ljungberg, above).

Ješina, P. Josef. *Romani Čib.* Leipzig: Von List & Francke, 1886.

Journal of the Gypsy Lore Society. British journal of Gypsy studies. Old Series 1888–1892; New Series 1907–1916; Third Series 1922–1974; Fourth Series 1974 to date.

Kenrick, Donald, and Gratton Puxon. *The Destiny of Europe's Gypsies.* New York: Basic Books, 1972. A significant study focusing on the atrocities suffered by the Gypsies in Nazi-occupied Europe and in the concentration camps. The book includes previously unpublished testimony from survivors as well as a history of the persecution of the Gypsies before and after the Holocaust—what amounts to an unremitting series of human rights violations down through the centuries. Bibliography.

Lacio Drom: Italian journal of Gypsy studies, which began publication in 1964.

Levak, Bruno, and Mirella Karpati. *Rom sim: La tradizione dei Rom Kalderaša.* Rome: Edizione Lacio Drom, 1984.

Liégeois, Jean-Pierre. *Gypsies: An Illustrated History.* Trans. Tony Berrett. London: Al Saqi Books, 1985. An excellent and insightful history of the Gypsies, illustrated with black-and-white photographs. Although Liégeois conveys the difficulty of writing about a group with great cultural and linguistic diversity, he manages to trace thoroughly and sensitively both the fear and hatred engendered by the Gypsies ("everywhere seen as ideologically disruptive") as well as the flexibility and adaptability that have always marked Gypsy culture. Bibliography.

Mode, Heinz, and Milena Hübschmannová, eds. *Zigeunermärchen aus aller Welt.* Leipzig: Insel-Verlag, 1983–1985. A four-volume anthology of Gypsy folktales, many of them from Hübschmannová's large collection of Czech stories. Good source notes with comparative folklore information.

Paspatis, Alexandre G. *Etudes sur les Tchinghianés ou Bohémiens de l'Empire Ottoman.* Constantinople: Antoine Koroméla, 1870. Grammar and dictionary of Ottoman Empire Romani, based on the author's collection of folktales, unfortunately lost except for six tales published in this work. Fragments from the lost folktales appear as examples in the dictionary.

Pégon, Lucien. *Contes et récits du pays qui n'existe pas.* Lyon: CRIN, 1982.

Quintana, Bertha B., and Lois Gray Floyd. *¡Qué Gitano!: Gypsies of Southern Spain.* New York: Holt, Rinehart and Winston, 1972. Reprinted Prospect Heights, Illinois: Waveland Press, 1986. By an anthropologist and a psychologist, this thought-provoking interdisciplinary study uses both direct observation and interviews to examine many aspects of the life and culture of the Gypsies of Granada's Sacro Monte. Included is the Gypsies' severe critique of American culture based on observations during their stay in New York in 1964–1965 when performing at the Spanish Pavilion of the World's Fair.

Rehfisch, Farnham, ed. *Gypsies, Tinkers and other Travellers.* London: Academic Press, 1975. Multidisciplinary collection of articles, many of them on the Gypsies. See especially the articles by Willy Guy, "Ways of Looking at Roms: The Case of Czechoslovakia," pp. 201–229; William Kornblum, "Boyash Gypsies: Shantytown Ethnicity," pp. 123–138; and Carol Miller, "American Rom and the Ideology of Defilement," pp. 41–54.

Sampson, John, ed. *Gypsy Folk Tales.* London: Robinson, 1984. A reprint of Sampson, ed., *XXI Welsh Gypsy Folk Tales.* London: Gregynog Press, 1933.

Serra, Maria João Pavão. *Filhos da Estrada e do Vento: Contos e Fotografías de Ciganos Portugueses.* Lisbon: Assírio & Alvim, 1986. A collection of Portuguese Gypsy folktales, with photographs of people from the community.

Thompson, Stith. *The Folktale.* New York: Holt, Rinehart and Winston, 1946. Reprinted Berkeley/Los Angeles: University of California Press, 1977.

Tong, Diane. "Language Use and Attitudes Among the Gypsies of Thessaloniki." *Anthropological Linguistics* 25 (1983):375–385.

———. "Romani as Symbol: Sociolinguistic Strategies of the Gypsies of Thessaloniki." *Papers* from the Fourth and Fifth Annual Meetings, Gypsy Lore Society, North American Chapter (1985), 179–187.
Both articles by Tong deal with the various adaptations Greek Gypsies make to a racist environment and show how these choices are mirrored in language use and attitudes.

Tyrnauer, Gabrielle. "The Fate of the Gypsies during the Holocaust." Washington: U.S. Holocaust Memorial Council Special Report, 1985. Prepared but not released for distribution.

UNESCO Courier, October 1984 ("The Gypsies"). A collection of historical and cultural articles about Gypsies around the world, some of them by Gypsies.

Webb, G. E. C. *Gypsies: The Secret People.* Westport, Conn.: Greenwood Press, 1974.

Wood, Manfri Frederick. *In the Life of a Romany Gypsy.* London: Routledge & Kegan Paul, 1979. Informative, nostalgic, and entertaining autobiography of an English Gypsy. Includes detailed descriptions of Romani occupations, values, and belief system.

Yates, Dora E., ed. *A Book of Gypsy Folk-Tales.* London: Phoenix House, 1948. A collection of stories, many of which were published in the *Journal of the*

Gypsy Lore Society between 1899 (the year of publication of Groome's *Gypsy Folk-Tales*) and 1948.

Yoors, Jan. *The Gypsies*. New York: Simon and Schuster, 1967; Touchstone, 1983. Reprinted Prospect Heights, Illinois: Waveland, 1987. Probably the best-known popular work about Gypsies, a lyrical, macho celebration of life on the road with a group of Lowara horse traders. By a Belgian non-Gypsy who was adopted by the Rom at the age of twelve and lived with the group for many years, this book has served as the inspiration for many sensationalistic novels about Gypsies. Yoors would not have been pleased by the ethnocentric copy on the back cover of the Touchstone paperback: "At the age of twelve, Jan Yoors ran away from his cultured Belgian family to join a wandering band . . ."

PERMISSIONS ACKNOWLEDGMENTS

Every effort has been made to secure all necessary permissions for the selections included in this volume. The author would appreciate any additional information concerning sources.

"The Magic Whistle" from *Journal of the Gypsy Lore Society*, vol. 40, 1961. Used by permission of George A. Agogino and David Pickett.

"The Sixty-One Skills" from *Filhos da Estrada e do Vento: Contos e Fotografias de Ciganos Portugueses* by Maria João Pavão Serra. Copyright © 1986 by Assírio & Alvim. Used by permission of Assírio & Alvim.

"Why Gypsies Are Scattered About the Earth" and "St. George and the Gypsies" from *Russian Gypsy Tales* by Yefim Druts and Alexei Gessler. Copyright © 1986 by Yefim Druts and Alexei Gessler. Used by permission of Canongate Publishing Limited.

"The Gypsy Smith" from *Gypsies: The Secret People* by G. E. C. Webb. Copyright © 1960 by Herbert Jenkins Ltd. Used by permission of Century Hutchinson Publishing Group Ltd.

"The Gypsy Thief" from *Ilona Tausendschön: Zigeunermärchen und -schwänke aus Ungarn* by Sándor Csenki. Copyright © 1980 by the estate of Sándor Csenki. Used by permission of Erich Röth-Verlag.

"The Young Gypsy Girl and the Forest Guard" from *Etudes Tsiganes*, vol. 22, 1976. "The Bird" from *Etudes Tsiganes*, vol. 13, 1967. Used by permission of the editors of *Etudes Tsiganes*.

"Why the Jews and the Gypsies Are Enemies" from *Folklore*, vol. 78, 1967. Used by permission of the Folklore Society.

"Napolina" from *Journal of the Gypsy Lore Society*, vol. 9, 1930. Used by permission of Joachim S. Hohmann.

"Gypsy Origins" and "You Will Eat, But You Will Not Work" from *¡Qué Gitano!: Gypsies of Southern Spain* by Bertha B. Quintana and Lois Gray Floyd. Copyright © 1972 by Holt, Rinehart and Winston, Inc. Reprinted by permission of the publisher.

"The Rom in the Piano" from *Romské Pohádky* by Milena Hübschmannová. Copyright © 1973 by Milena Hübschmannová. Used by permission of Milena Hübschmannová.

"The Grateful Lions" from *Zigeunermärchen aus aller Welt* edited by Heinz Mode and Milena Hübschmannová. Copyright © 1985 by Insel-Verlag Anton Kippenberg. Used by permission of Insel-Verlag Anton Kippenberg.

"The Dream" and "The Gypsy Lawyer" from *Rom sim: La tradizione dei Rom Kalderaša* by Bruno Levak and Mirella Karpati. Copyright © 1984 by Edizione Lacio Drom. "The Enchanted House" from *Lacio Drom*, vol. 6, 1985. Used by permission of Mirella Karpati.

"The Fox and the Miller" from *Journal of the Gypsy Lore Society*, vol. 41, 1962. Used by permission of Kiril Kostov.

"The Vases of Harmony" from *Journal of the Gypsy Lore Society*, vol. 51, 1972. Used by permission of Daphne R. Maurice.

"Voso Zachari Tells His Tale" from *Journal of the Gypsy Lore Society*, vol. 28, 1949. Used by permission of Matéo Maximoff.

"The Poor Gypsy and the Devil" from *Mitteilungen zur Zigeuner-Kunde*, vol. 2, 1976. Used by permission of Paul Meissner and Mozes Heinschink.

Excerpt from *New York Times* article by Roberto Suro, 11/18/87. Copyright © 1987 by The New York Times Company. Reprinted by permission.

"The Toad's Revenge" from *Contes et récits du pays qui n'existe pas* by Lucien Pégon. Copyright © 1982 by Lucien Pégon. Used by permission of Lucien Pégon.

"The Wooden Horseshoe and the Three Nails" from *In the Life of a Romany Gypsy* by Manfri Frederick Wood. Copyright © 1973 by Manfri Frederick Wood. Used by permission of Routledge & Kegan Paul.

"The Church of Cheese," "A Dead Man Pays Back," and "How the Gypsies Became Musicians" from *The Slavonic Review*, vol. 14, 1936. Used by permission of the *Slavonic and East European Review*.

"Jorška Who Came Back from the Dead" from *Journal of the Gypsy Lore Society*, vol. 31, 1952. Used by permission of Carl-Herman Tillhagen.

"The Little Gypsy" from *Auschwitz: True Tales from a Grotesque Land* by Sara Nomberg-Przytyk, translated by Roslyn Hirsch, edited by Eli Pfefferkorn and David H. Hirsch. © 1985 The University of North Carolina Press. Used by permission of The University of North Carolina Press.

"The Silly Man Who Sold His Beard" and "The Gypsies' Fiddle" from *The Gypsies' Fiddle and Other Gypsy Tales* by M. A. Jagendorf and C. H. Tillhagen. Copyright © 1956 by M. A. Jagendorf and C. H. Tillhagen. Used by permission of Vanguard Press.

"A Dish of Laban" and "A Wicked Fox" from *The Gypsy Fiddle and Other Tales Told by the Gypsies* by John Hampden. Copyright © 1969 by John Hampden. Used by permission of A. P. Watt Limited on behalf of The Executors of the Estate of John Hampden.

"The Robber and the Housekeeper" From *A Book of Gypsy Folk-Tales* by Dora E. Yates. Used by permission of the author's estate.

"The Mosquito" from *Journal of the Gypsy Lore Society*, vol. 25, 1946. Used by permission of Marianne Yoors.

INDEXES

TITLES